WHAT WE ARE BECOMING

WHAT WE ARE BECOMING

Developments in
Undergraduate Writing Majors

Edited by

GREG A. GIBERSON
THOMAS A. MORIARTY

UTAH STATE UNIVERSITY PRESS
Logan, Utah
2010

Manufactured in the United States of America
Cover design by Barbara Yale-Read

ISBN: 978-0-87421-763-6 (paper)
ISBN: 978-0-87421-764-3 (e-book)

Library of Congress Cataloging-in-Publication Data

What are we becoming? : developments in undergraduate writing majors / edited by Greg A. Giberson, Thomas A. Moriarty.
    p. cm.
   Includes index.
    ISBN 978-0-87421-763-6 (pbk.) – ISBN 978-0-87421-764-3 (e-book)
    1. English language–Rhetoric–Study and teaching (Higher)–United States. 2. Report writing–Study and teaching (Higher)–United States. 3. Creative writing (Higher education)–United States. 4. Writing centers–United States. 5. English philology–Study and teaching (Higher)–United States. I. Giberson, Greg. II. Moriarty, Thomas A.

   PE1405.U6W46 2010
   808'.0420711–dc22

2009047229

CONTENTS

SECTION 2: CURRICULA, LOCATION, AND DIRECTIONS OF WRITING MAJORS

FOREWORD

Janice M. Lauer

This collection of essays addresses one of the key needs in the field of rhetoric and composition today. As the field developed in the sixties and seventies, its energy focused largely on the initiation of graduate programs, especially doctoral programs. One reason was the need to claim a place for the field as a scholarly discipline in addition to its teaching mission. As these programs grew and matured, they struggled to varying degrees with acclimating to their host English departments or starting separate departments. Rhetoric and composition faculty in each program were frequently few in number at the beginning and were heavily burdened with courses, mentoring, and dissertation directing, often far exceeding the loads of their literary colleagues. This factor left little time to initiate undergraduate majors in many institutions.

Now more attention and energy have turned to the development of undergraduate majors in rhetoric and composition. This is not to say that during the last thirty years there have been no such majors or even undergraduate courses in the field. But their visibility and character have not reached the same level of national attention as the graduate programs, especially the doctoral programs. For example, since the 1960s and 1970s, undergraduate courses in composition theory, as well as undergraduate survey courses in the history of rhetoric, have been taught in the whole range of higher education. During the last decade, faculty—often graduates of doctoral rhetoric and composition programs—have been working to start undergraduate majors in their departments, both at large and smaller universities and at liberal arts colleges, including places like the University of Wisconsin at La Crosse, University of Texas at El Paso, Salisbury University, York University, Oakland University, Southwest Missouri State University, and the University of South Florida.

Recently at the Conference on College Composition and Communication (CCCC) attention has been given to the undergraduate major: its nature, its difficulties in getting approval in English departments, and its need for dedicated faculty. At a workshop at the 2008 CCCC, aspects of undergraduate majors were discussed by some of the contributors to this volume as well as others, speaking of the importance of shaping programs in response to local conditions, creating relations with policy makers and funding agencies, linking with professional organizations, and networking among these programs.

Clearly one impact of such undergraduate majors on graduate programs is that students will enter them having read historical primary texts and central rhetoric and composition theory texts and research. Even now, doctoral programs continue to admit some students with little background in rhetoric and composition, requiring these programs to help these students fill their gaps before specializing. Also, rhetoric and composition undergraduate majors will make visible to other English majors the alternatives within English studies and will provide those tutoring in writing centers with a disciplinary background for their efforts. Further, undergraduate majors will offer rhetoric and composition doctoral graduates a wide variety of upper-level courses to teach beyond first-year writing.

This rich volume addresses a wide range of matters surrounding undergraduate programs, including complex issues such as the competition for majors within departments, the future relationship between these majors among teachers and students, the job market for undergraduates, varying focuses and curricula of such majors, and the formation of them in departments separate from English. Other related matters discussed here include the importance of flexibility, arguments for a rhetorical core for this major, the relationship between rhetoric and composition majors and disciplinary integrity and with civic discourse, and the role of multiliteracies in the major. Consequently, this collection makes a vital contribution to the field and is an indispensable resource for building undergraduate majors.

INTRODUCTION
Forging Connections Among Undergraduate Writing Majors

Greg A. Giberson
Thomas A. Moriarty

When we first discussed this book back in 2005, we had just revamped the undergraduate track in writing in the English department at Salisbury University (SU) in Maryland. After the revision of the program was complete, we continued to discuss the particular program we had developed, the courses we had chosen for the core, and the possible changes that might be made in the future as the program grew. We talked about how lucky we were that we had such a supportive (or uninterested) department, given that there was very little discussion in full department meetings about the changes we were proposing and the fact that we virtually eliminated literature as a requirement for the major. (In the past, writing students were required to take several literature courses.)

We also talked about how our particular location on the eastern shore of Maryland and the student body that came with that location impacted the goals for our program and the curriculum, how our own different specialties in the field of rhetoric and composition shaped what we had done, and on and on. After a while, it became clear that we should put our experience and discussion to some good use, and we decided to put out a call for proposals. This book is the result of that decision.

After reading through several dozen proposals and finally settling on the ones appearing in this volume, we realized we had stumbled across an important—and complex—topic for those of us in rhetoric and composition and English studies in general, and working in writing programs in particular. We quickly realized that all of the issues we discussed about our program at SU, as well as others we hadn't thought of, were not simply micro, local issues that spoke to our location and position in the English department at Salisbury University on the eastern shore of Maryland.

Indeed, the issues we faced and the choices we made in dealing with them are being made all over the country. And just as our location and unique circumstances impacted the program we developed, so do the locations and circumstances of each individual department developing a program, as this volume demonstrates. In other words, the unique, local circumstances faced by our colleagues developing and participating in individual programs and the decisions they make in regards to those local circumstances have important implications for the broader discipline.

These programs can and should be understood as micro-manifestations of the discipline itself. When we write proposals, make curricular decisions, construct arguments for those outside of our field about what a local program should consist of and why, we are constructing concrete representations of the current state of our field that resonate beyond our local circumstances. We put in place the requirements for students who, upon graduation, become the practical embodiment of the programs we develop and the discipline those programs represent. As the number of programs and graduates continues to grow, the importance of understanding what it means for our discipline to be moving toward a ubiquitous major is extremely important.

The growth of undergraduate majors in writing and rhetoric is unmistakable. They are appearing at big research universities, small liberal arts colleges, and every kind of campus in between, from independent writing programs to those housed in traditional English departments. According to the Conference on College Composition and Communication's (CCCC) Committee on the Major in Rhetoric and Composition, there are, as of this writing, sixty-eight institutions with writing majors or tracks, and "the number of writing majors is increasing rapidly."

In addition to a rapid growth in programs, there has been a small, but steady, scholarly discussion of the topic. The first calls for developing full-fledged undergraduate majors in writing and rhetoric appeared in the late 1990s and early 2000s. David Fleming, writing in the pages of *College English* in 1998, for example, called for the development of undergraduate majors as a way for rhetoric to fully secure its place in the modern university. The Alliance of Rhetoric Societies echoed this call five years later, in 2003, and suggested that such majors could play an important, if not vital, role in civic education in the new century. By 2007, Brian Jackson, writing in the pages of *Rhetoric Society Quarterly*, claimed that there was a "growing consensus in the field" that the focus of undergraduate education in rhetoric should be on civic rhetoric. But others, writing in a special issue of *Composition Studies* the same year, disagreed, arguing that undergraduate majors should focus on more practical concerns.

Our field has not come to a consensus on the shape, content, or focus of our majors. But as we develop, refine, and nurture these programs, one thing has become clear: it is important for us to think about them in ways that go beyond our particular circumstances, to theorize them in ways that secure their place on our campuses, and in our discipline, for years to come. And this book is an effort to do just that.

In Section 1, "Disciplinary and Interdisciplinary Issues for Writing Majors," we focus on the many unique challenges posed by the different institutional structures within which writing specialists seek to develop and implement writing majors. From writing programs in large English departments in research-intensive universities to stand-alone programs that have never been affiliated with an English department, the challenges the discipline faces for establishing a broadly accepted undergraduate major become clear in these chapters, as do the challenges for creating majors with any sort of inter-institutional consistency.

In the first chapter, "A Major in Flexibility," Rebecca de Wind Mattingly and Patricia Harkin provide a compelling argument for the development of post-disciplinary undergraduate degrees in rhetoric and composition at research-intensive institutions. They argue that multiple stakeholders stand to benefit from the development of such programs, including students, faculty, universities, and outside institutions. According to de Wind Mattingly and Harkin, students stand to benefit as increased capital investment, and the increased awareness across campus of the importance of writing that goes along with it, leads to more varied writing experiences becoming available to students of differing writing abilities. Much like students, faculty will benefit from increased university exposure and legitimacy, including additional resources, while universities themselves will benefit from the multidisciplinary and socially useful nature of rhetoric and composition, which supports the mission of the university. Finally, tertiary institutions, such as potential employers, will benefit from the unique skills graduates from these programs will possess, including the ability to communicate effectively through writing and strong problem-solving and critical-thinking skills. The chapter ends with a narrative that explores de Wind Mattingly's successful attempt to create a hybrid course that embodies the qualities of the undergraduate major described in the chapter and the negotiations with the various stakeholders needed to ultimately win approval and implementation for the course.

In "Redefining the Undergraduate English Writing Major," Randy Brooks, Peiling Zhao, and Carmella Braniger discuss the challenges faced when developing undergraduate majors in writing at small, comprehensive universities by focusing on the hurdles they faced initiating a major at Millikin University. The primary challenges unique to smaller institutions are twofold. First, there is the problematic nature of modeling undergraduate majors on established graduate programs, as the goals for such programs are dramatically different. And second, there is a lack of scholarly attention paid to the development of undergraduate majors, especially new program models that bridge the rhetoric-poetic split that "hinders the healthy growth of English departments." Brooks, Zhao, and Braniger outline Millikin's English writing major and explain how their courses work to connect theory and practice to alleviate the challenges posed by the unique circumstances of the small, comprehensive university.

In chapter 3, Lisa Langstraat, Mike Palmquist, and Kate Kiefer explore the personal and material consequences of program development through research on victim advocates. While they do not equate the trauma of crime victims to the "injustice of departmental hostilities," they do claim that disciplinary and professional conflicts that often arise in departments developing writing programs can cause distress resulting in "significant personal and material consequences." The authors argue that the development of undergraduate degrees presents an ideal opportunity to "restory" the history and professional identity of rhetoric and composition to deal with the narrative of victimization and marginalization so common in our disciplinary histories. They follow this with a narrative of the development of an undergraduate degree program at Colorado State University that explores the many challenges they encountered, and continue to encounter, as they utilize the metaphor of restorying injustice to heal the wounds "from the moments when we've experienced . . . disorder, disempowerment, and disconnection" from the material, disciplinary, and professional structures of their department and university.

Wallis Andersen's "Outside the English Department" chronicles the history of Oakland University's (OU) writing program and the institutional hurdles it has overcome while working to establish an undergraduate major. OU's writing program is rather unique as it has never been affiliated with an English department. This history explores how a first-year writing program without a departmental home overcame an institutional history of marginalization to develop a unique and impressive undergraduate major. While Andersen discusses the many challenges the OU writing faculty faced, she also shows how that unaffiliated history provided a unique situation where the undergraduate degree could be developed from the ground up, without having to worry about departmental politics and turf wars that too often lead to compromises that weaken the intellectual and academic composition of new writing majors developed in English departments (see chapter 5, for example).

Chapter 5 offers an analysis of what can go right with a writing major as well as what can go wrong. Kelly Lowe and William Macauley explore their experience developing a major in the English department of a "somewhat selective, liberal arts school," where, though one might assume it would be easy to develop such a major, the authors found that the price they eventually paid for it was far too high. As a cautionary tale, this chapter explores the historical marginalization of rhetoric and composition within English departments by considering the practical realities writing faculty must face when vying for resources within a "strong English Department." Lowe and Macauley end the chapter with a thorough discussion of the lessons they learned from their experience and provide readers with specific suggestions for building a viable writing major within an already strong English department; they emphasize the importance of creating an institutional need for the major and an understanding of what it is and why it is integral to the mission of the university.

In the sixth chapter, "The Writing Major as Shared Commitment," Rodney Dick argues that, at least at smaller institutions with combined departments, it is often necessary to find a " 'middle ground' of English studies rooted in a shared commitment to literature *and* writing, rhetoric *and* theory, producing *and* consuming texts." While offering a history of the writing major at Mount Union College, Dick explores the evolution of the requirements and expectations and how changes in the program offer a history of shared compromise that eventually led to a viable writing major built upon the interests of all stakeholders. While the major's current form might not be a perfect representation of the discipline of rhetoric and composition, it does appear to be a realistic and acceptable version of it given the more than common circumstances within which it was created. Read together, chapters 5 and 6 show the important role that personal perspective plays in institutional and professional politics.

In "Dancing with Our Siblings: The Unlikely Case for a Rhetoric Major," David Beard discusses the place of rhetoric in the undergraduate writing major and argues that while rhetoric is part of the core of our discipline, it is also one of our greatest liabilities. Beard argues that we should be aware and wary of the history of rhetoric in the twentieth century, given the way that rhetoric in the university has fragmented during the last century and now many different departments claim ownership of it. Given that rhetoric is spread throughout the university, a major in rhetoric, Beard contends, will be an incomplete major. Because of its fragmentation, Beard questions whether it is in the best interest of all stakeholders to continue to pursue and grow the undergraduate major, claiming that "the historical moment for rhetoric to manifest itself fully in a major . . . is lost." As a part of his discussion, Beard describes two different (and seemingly failed) rhetoric majors that were developed and eventually dismantled at the University of Minnesota. While his position is at odds with most of the other chapters in this book, Beard does agree that the undergraduate major has the potential to fundamentally change the field of rhetoric and composition and should be developed cautiously and deliberately, taking into consideration the micro and macro implications for all stakeholders.

Much like chapters 5 and 6 are interconnected, chapters 7 and 8 provide readers with two perspectives on historically connected programs. In the final chapter of the second section, Lori Baker and Teresa Henning analyze their department's professional writing and communication major and its roots in one of the rhetoric majors discussed in the previous chapter. After defining rhetoric as "the use of language for a purpose in a specific communication situation, and as such, we acknowledge that texts are designed to bring about material effects in the world," Baker and Henning explore the implicit consequences for program development of such a definition. Through a thorough discussion of their curriculum, they demonstrate how their operational definition of rhetoric allowed them to resist "impoverished definitions of writing" while providing a sense of disciplinary integrity.

Section 2, "Curricula, Location, and Directions of Writing Majors," looks at curriculum and program development—the content and focus of individual classes and courses of study—as well as the impact of these decisions on the programs themselves, the students who graduate from them, and the discipline as a whole. The first six chapters in this section argue that programs should be attentive and responsive to a variety of disciplinary influences and concerns, such as classical rhetoric, civic rhetoric, textual production, creative nonfiction, process-based program assessment, and program identity formation. The final chapter of this section offers a heuristic for mapping the many different majors discussed and proposed throughout the book.

In the first chapter of section 2, Dominic Delli Carpini and Michael Zerbe argue that the growing number of undergraduate degrees in rhetoric and writing "provides a catalyst for examining how we deliver writing instruction at all levels." Delli Carpini and Zerbe focus on the five canons of rhetoric and consider the reasons style and memory have so often been ignored in favor of invention, arrangement, and delivery. These three canons have been emphasized because of institutional pressures on "the practical and under-resourced delivery of first-year writing," they argue, pressures that have historically defined what the authors aptly refer to as "the first generation of composition studies." Through a general discussion of their undergraduate major and an in-depth look at their Advanced Composition course, the authors explain how they have designed a curriculum to include, and indeed emphasize, style and memory as integral to an undergraduate writing major built on a foundation of rhetoric. Finally, they offer a compelling argument for the inclusion of the progymnasmata, exercises in rhetorical style, in the advanced composition curriculum.

Thomas A. Moriarty and Greg Giberson argue in chapter 10, "Civic Rhetoric and the Undergraduate Major in Writing and Rhetoric," that in order for our new programs to thrive, they must be rooted in civic rhetoric. Moriarty and Giberson argue that as we develop our writing majors, we must resist the temptation to ground them in practical concerns. "The history of our field suggests that our programs grow and prosper along the lines drawn by our guiding focus," they write, and a focus solely on practical concerns will weaken our programs in the long run. A focus on civic rhetoric, however, will secure our place in the academy because such majors will prepare students for their public lives, an important sphere of human activity long neglected by other majors on campus.

In chapter 11, "Composing Multiliteracies and Image," Joddy Murray argues that undergraduate degree programs must take into account how the emerging "creative economy" necessitates a valuing of many literacies. Focusing specifically on multimodal composition, he argues that as society continues to value technological innovation and technological literacies (specifically the rhetorical use of images), so must undergraduate programs be designed to produce hyper-literate graduates. To accomplish this, "new undergraduate majors must develop the necessary scaffolding and preparation required to become multiliterate and accustomed to multimodal textual production technologies." However, familiarization with technology alone does not necessarily make one literate. He argues that it is just as, if not more, important for students to understand the centrality of the image in textual production and how new technologies are changing our understanding of how texts are created, how they function, and the processes through which they are produced. Undergraduate majors designed with this in mind have the potential to produce graduates prepared to develop the kind of innovation demanded by the creative economy.

In chapter 12, "Not Just Another Pretty Classroom Genre," Celest Martin makes the case for the inclusion of creative nonfiction (CN) as a form of professional writing in the undergraduate writing major. Acknowledging that the inclusion of creative nonfiction as a part of the discipline has been an issue in the past, Martin argues for its more recent establishment within composition studies. She suggests that the study of CN provides students the opportunity to practice a craft with professional and business applications, the experience of writing and reading in personal and literary genres that are craft- and audience-oriented, and the skills to become freelance or staff writers for various types of publications that value CN writing.

"The Writing Arts Major" explores the development of a ten-year-old, award-winning undergraduate degree in writing arts at Rowan University. Jennifer Courtney, Deb Martin, and Diane Penrod argue that for the undergraduate writing major to remain strong not only at their institution but at any institution, it is necessary for those working in undergraduate degree programs to keep the notion of revision in the forefront of their programmatic thinking because institutional, departmental, and disciplinary changes threaten to make static programs irrelevant. Through a discussion of their institutional and department history, as well as the development and continued revision of their undergraduate major, the authors provide a glimpse into the various revisions they have made and anticipate making to keep their degree program viable and relevant for students. Notably, in their discussion of the various mechanisms they use to provide direction for their revisions, the authors describe their inclusion of current students in the program, as well as former graduates, arguing that they can provide the realistic and practical assessments of the program that, perhaps, faculty cannot.

In "What Exactly is This Major?," a second chapter from colleagues at Rowan University, Sanford Tweedie, Jennifer Courtney, and William Wolff explore the practical and theoretical development of an introductory course in Rowan's major in writing arts. Recognizing that individual undergraduate writing degrees are developed "based on local exigencies," they argue that the inclusion of an introductory course that provides students with an introduction to the discipline itself can provide a more coherent vision of it "in both national and local terms." The authors observe that there are very few, if any, undergraduate majors that currently require an introductory course for "non-specialized writing within a disciplinary context," and that most courses that are introductory in nature tend to be genre-specific, such as professional writing or creative writing. The introductory course at Rowan is designed to "provide an introduction to the goals, objectives and curricular content of the major" as well as "introduce students to potential careers based on the major," all the while exposing "students to some of the characteristics foundational to all writing." As a part of the discussion of the actual course, the authors provide an analysis of the development and revisioning of the course per the process discussed in the previous chapter, building on the argument that degree programs, as well as individual courses, must be open to revision to be and remain successful.

In the book's final chapter, "Toward a Description of Undergraduate Writing Majors," Lee Campbell and Debra Jacobs suggest that while some sense of consistency between undergraduate and graduate degrees in rhetoric and composition is desirable, it is important to celebrate the fact that "the field has not suffered a forfeiture of its crucial multidimensionality," which so many chapters in this volume amply demonstrated. Campbell and Jacobs offer a heuristic for mapping undergraduate majors to provide some direction to those developing or revising undergraduate majors—not to discipline and standardize programs but to help mitigate the difficult work of program design. By exploring how courses might fit within a matrix consisting of two continua (general to specific and liberal to technical), the heuristic offers a way of thinking through program design while allowing for the localized nature of program development. While acknowledging that their map is one of many possible configurations, their work demonstrates the possibility and importance of a more systematic discussion of course and program design for the continued growth and development of undergraduate degree programs.

MAKING SENSE OUT OF MULTIPLICITY

The contributors to this volume do not speak with one voice—far from it. But their varied experiences and the programs they have developed and imagined represent the state of the art in program design and implementation. And though they sometimes disagree, they do share some basic notions about undergraduate majors in writing and rhetoric. First, they all agree that undergraduate majors should be more than a collection of old service courses, stitched together and called a major. They should include specialized courses that draw upon our vast disciplinary knowledge. Second, they recognize the potential for these new majors to change the very nature of our writing programs and, more broadly, our discipline—from pushing us into new alliances to broadening the focus of graduate education in rhetoric and composition. And finally, they see the potential for these majors to attract many new students to our programs, students who will clamor for new and innovative course offerings and whose numbers will change the power dynamics in our departments and on our campuses.

These are boom times for writing programs, and we hope the following chapters inspire you, challenge you, and, most importantly, empower you to develop innovative undergraduate majors that will enrich your students and invigorate our discipline for many years to come.

REFERENCES

Fleming, David. 1998. Rhetoric as a course of study. *College English* 61.2: 169–91.

National Council of Teachers of English Committee on the Major in Rhetoric and Composition. Writing majors at a glance. Conference on College Composition and Communication. http://www.ncte.org/cccc/committees/majorrhetcomp (accessed July 1, 2009).

Jackson, Brian. 2007. Cultivating paideweyan pedagogy: Rhetoric education in English and communication studies. *Rhetoric Society Quarterly* 37.2:181–201.

SECTION 1

Disciplinary and Interdisciplinary Issues for Writing Majors

1

A MAJOR IN FLEXIBILITY

Rebecca de Wind Mattingly
Patricia Harkin

In this essay our argument will be that a post-disciplinary major in rhetoric and composition is a particularly good idea for research-intensive universities in the current technological and fiscal states of affairs. We shall describe the benefits such a major would potentially offer to contemporary students, to the faculty members who teach them, to tertiary institutions (especially state-sponsored ones) in general, and even to multinational capital. We shall also necessarily describe the institutional impedimenta that such an innovation is likely to encounter. Finally, we describe a course that might serve as the entry to such a major at research-intensive universities.

We begin by emphasizing that our argument is for rhetoric and composition as a *major*—not as a discipline. Historical and theoretical arguments about disciplinary status for rhetoric have already been made by many scholars and critics from many points of view (Lauer, Mailloux, Harkin, North, Sosnoski), and it is not our intention to rehearse them here. Our concern is institutional: As Steven Mailloux observes in *Disciplinary Identities: Rhetorical Paths of English, Speech, and Composition,* "academic disciplines are hierarchically organized, institutionally supported, self-perpetuating networks of practices for knowledge production and transmission. . . . That is, disciplines are, fundamentally, the transformation of practical wisdom into accredited techniques" (2006, 5). In one sense, of course, the network of practices that such scholars as Sharon Crowley, Victor Vitanza, Susan Miller, Richard Lanham, Susan Jarratt, Michael Leff, and Chaim Perelman have called "rhetoric" has existed since the fifth century BCE. The transmission of those practices, however, has occurred in such diverse institutional venues as departments of English, speech, communication, journalism, media studies, classics, political science, schools of business, and online instruction in winning friends and influencing people. In most research-intensive universities, no single institutional venue has been the locus in which the practical wisdom known as rhetoric is transformed into *accredited techniques.*[1]

Techniques become "accredited" through institutions such as departments, curricula, and majors. In most research-intensive universities, it is not currently possible for an undergraduate to earn a baccalaureate degree in rhetoric and composition in a department *of that name.* One can be an English major with a writing emphasis or a communication major who concentrates on composing and analyzing "speeches." One can be a literature major with an affection for "rhetoric" as Paul de Man used the term in the 1970s and '80s. One can get an MA or PhD in rhetoric and composition. And one can get an undergraduate degree in journalism or writing for the media.

Our argument is that rhetoric and composition should have an institutional space—a tenured and tenurable faculty, adequate office space, a budget, a copy machine, and at least one administrative assistant. In that way, (and perhaps only in that way) within the university's own symbolic system of value, rhetoric and composition can be understood not only as a service but also as an institutionally constituted area of inquiry.

Because its networks of practices are not available to undergraduates as a single major *under that name,* rhetoric (and composition) lacks the status that comes in the academy from a unique budget and the other aforementioned perquisites. That prestige, or lack of it, is noticed and felt on the pulses of undergraduate students. It is also felt by faculty members in all departments. In the departments of English and communication, however, the lack of status has important implications. It is, we think, the overwhelming tendency among English faculty in research-oriented universities to think of writing as a service and rhetoric as an attempt to graft a research agenda onto this service. In departments of communication oriented toward social science, on the other hand, writing is often ignored (or minimized) and rhetoric regarded as a remnant of the bad old days before new media studies. Administrators notice that the emphasis on writing is more often than not lip service. And so they relegate rhetoric to the back burners of their development agendas, as something different from—and less than—a "real" major.

---

1. Notable exceptions include Berkeley.

We believe that a major in rhetoric and composition would change attitudes toward writing and rhetoric on the part of students and faculty by demonstrating (with cash) that the university believes writing and rhetoric are important enough to support. It would provide research-oriented universities with data for arguments that they are addressing the crises in literacy that are decried by media and government at regular intervals (as well as with an opportunity actually to address the problems underlying those calls of "crisis"). It would also provide corporate capital with employees who are aware that differing situations call for differing approaches and appeals.

STUDENTS

First, focusing on rhetoric and composition is a good idea for students who are thought of as "problem writers," especially, to offer only one example, when their "problems" occur (or are seen) as a consequence of technology. Students who successfully navigate text messages, e-mails, blog entries, online forums, and the like, tend, in more formal, traditional situations such as the environment of work, to produce writing that audiences (in those spheres) judge as underdeveloped, lacking in transitions, and often orthographically and syntactically "incorrect." Hence, the authors of these messages are characterized as underprepared.

The reasons for this characterization are obvious: e-mail, texts, and the like are typically produced without extensive revision, for a specific recipient (frequently unnamed and not noted by the author beyond pressing the "reply" button) who can be presumed to know what the author is talking about, based on previous, recent-in-memory communications the two have shared. Successful examples of these kinds of written exchanges rely on brevity, so no time is wasted reestablishing the context for the utterance or expressing the niceties of polite address. Dates and times are provided by the device or program used to compose the message, so the author is relieved of the burden of noting those crucial tools for reconstructing text conversations. In short, these technologies of writing de-emphasize the articulation of context and quite thoroughly excise conscious acknowledgement of the audience from the written artifact itself.

The authors of these kinds of computer-enabled utterances develop skills that serve them admirably so long as they remain in the technological sphere, communicating with like-minded acquaintances who are well-acculturated in the digital domain. The writers' difficulties arise when they are thrust into formal letter or memo writing, proposal or report construction, sales-pitch-drafting, or other, more professional, writing scenes. More critically for our purposes, technology-sphere writing habits become problematic when students are expected to enter disciplinary discussions in their first-year classes. In these situations, audiences may sometimes require elaborate articulations of context (such as the "literature review" of a social science research report), while on other occasions they require writers to assume that the sender and receiver are both already in the discourse. Professional writing sometimes requires direct attention to the intended recipients of the message while at other times demands rhetoric general enough for Perelman and Olbrechts-Tyteca's (1969) universal audience. Writers from the technological sphere have minimal practice in providing such audience analysis. Frustrated readers interpret the lack of these crucial aspects of the writing in formal, traditional genres as a lack of skill or capability, and they punish the writer accordingly with their inattention or disapprobation.

It's an obvious statement, but one that the ease, speed, and copiousness of computer-enabled writing seems frequently to mask: Students who don't get enough exercise in paying attention to context and audience in their native forms of computer-enabled writing are more likely to fail to meet the needs of context- and address-sensitive audiences in the types of writing situations encountered in college and the workplace. Margaret Gonzales (2007) asserts that, "[Students'] written literacy skills may be defined by their use of instant messaging and text messaging, where abbreviated and context-free is the norm. . . . A writing major would help them learn that written communication comes in many forms, and those forms are determined by context, audience, and purpose for writing. Communicating with your boss in writing is not going to be the same as communicating with your friend."

What a rhetoric and composition major can do is introduce students to a broad range of situations that call for what Bill Hart-Davidson characterizes as "solving problems by writing."[2] These situations require conscious attention to audience and context in ways technology-sphere natives may not otherwise encounter. For the students who have been labeled as underperformers in formal, traditional writing situations, the classes they would take as rhetoric and composition majors could help

---

2. Hart-Davidson's Web site: www.msu.edu/~hartdav2/.

them leverage their native competencies in concise, reactive composition to address the concerns their teachers and employers have about their writing skills in more formal and professional spheres.

A rhetoric and composition major is also a good idea for contemporary students who are thought of as good writers. "Good" student writers often earn that acclaim because they are facile with traditional elements of "correctness." Such students need to expand their sense of writing beyond the simple correctness that characterizes many secondary and even college English programs. For these students, a rhetoric and composition major would provide an opportunity to understand rhetoric as a multidisciplinary field of study into questions about "what happens when human beings make texts," rather than merely as a "service" to other departments in the university and to the students in general.

A major in rhetoric and composition is a good idea for the many, many students who attend four-year colleges or universities for the same reasons students attend community colleges and technical institutions and for the same reasons they participate in online programs: to gain certification in skills they understand themselves to need to secure employment.

For example, in a 1999 survey of reasons University of Colorado students chose to attend college, that university found that, "When just the *most important reason* [for attending college] is considered, by far, the two most often cited reasons to attend college are to gain skills or knowledge for a job, graduate school, or later in life and needing a degree to get a good job or go to graduate school; together, two-thirds (66 [percent]) of students mentioned one of these two reasons as most important" (Office of Planning, Budget, and Analysis, University of Colorado at Boulder 2001; emphasis in original). An informal survey we conducted of a dozen or so colleagues and friends gave similar results: When asked how important certain considerations were to them when they started going to college, three-quarters of them said the "requirements for a career you preferred" and "interest in making more money by qualifying for a better job" were somewhat or very important to them. In contrast, less than a third of them cited "Interest in making a lasting contribution to the world of knowledge" as similarly important to them.

In acknowledging the importance students place on getting job skills out of their college and university experiences, we bring to light another reason an undergraduate major in rhetoric and composition would be a good idea: students specifically stipulate that they want practical, wage-earning proficiency in real-world abilities like composing employee reviews, documenting processes, charting progress, crafting effective proposals, writing press releases, developing advertising campaigns, and so forth. Providing a rhetoric and composition major would allow schools to offer a system of classes in writing that would prepare students to meet those kinds of writing challenges appropriately and effectively *because students would understand theories of persuasion and argument.* Students would likely be receptive to selecting such a major because of their hopes of gaining authority or higher salaries in work situations through impressing employers with their competence.

Although all of the skills we have just enumerated are already available to students as courses and parts of courses in English, communication, business administration, and so forth, they are, in most research universities, not available *as an undergraduate major.* The message that students inevitably receive is that these skills are not important enough to constitute a major. A rhetoric and composition major can introduce students to the notion that writing is not simply a tool through which content is transmitted (unchanged) from sender to receiver but rather an area of study—a topic about which research is being conducted. A major (as against a required course) in rhetoric and composition would attract students who like to write and who want to learn about writing's processes. Too often, in required first-year writing courses, teachers are inclined to skip the theoretical accounts of writing in favor of offering instruction in specific assignments—whether those assignments are part of a project of fostering community literacy, "inventing the university," or finding and expressing a self. As described by the editors of this volume, a rhetoric and composition major would include courses in, for example, journalism and media writing, professional writing forms, aesthetic forms such as poetry, fiction, creative nonfiction, and so forth. Our point is that the major would attract persons who are interested in those forms and the differences among them. The very fact of there being a rhetoric and composition major would increase the prestige of writing courses, whether they were required or not. Further, this rising tide would be likely to lift all boats. Even students who "don't do well in English" would, we think, be inclined to notice that people who do like to write are employable. At the moment, in our research university, students tend to think that there are no jobs for English majors.

It does not seem to us that such a major would inevitably pander to consumerism. Rather, we think it appropriate for a course of study to prepare students for situations they are likely to encounter in the world. There is a difference, however, between instruction in specific forms (the memo, the proposal, the sales pitch, and so forth) and instruction in attention to context and audience (even if/when those forms are the examples).

Much current, curricular thinking holds that students arrive at the university with assumptions about writing that are no longer valid at the college level. These assumptions include, for example:

- That language is merely an instrument for pointing to knowledge that has already been made or discovered.

- That manipulating words and sentences has little effect on the knowledge to which these words and sentences point.

- That the manipulation of these words and sentences is governed by rules that students learn in English classes. The knowledge itself, however, resides in other departments.

By contrast, a rhetoric and composition major would demonstrate to students that language is an instrument through which knowledge is made discursively.

FACULTY

Additionally, a rhetoric and composition major is a good idea for research-university faculty because it represents an institutional way of interrogating tacit assumptions about language that lurk beneath many faculty complaints about student writing. Like students, faculty in sciences and social sciences often (in our view) carry an unexamined, positivistic view of language.

Faculty complaints about student writing reveal the assumption that language is a pellucid medium through which stable knowledge is communicated. The complaints that we've heard, oddly enough, seem to limit themselves to matters of form and correctness—that students can't spell and punctuate or that they fail to format disciplinary forms correctly. By contrast, when problems of audience, context, and development become apparent, faculty tend to regard them as disciplinary problems with the topic in question rather than as writing problems. Such complaints reveal, we think, the tacit assumption that language becomes disciplinary after it has first been "ordinary." It is, in the complainers' view, the job of departments of English to give instruction in "ordinary language" so that students will be ready to learn discipline-specific lexicons and genres. Such a perspective, we think, works to constrain thought, not expand it.

A department having rhetoric as its institutional focus would be uniquely positioned to address issues such as these. Whereas departments of English tend to focus on the interpretation of texts and departments of communication tend to look at the ways in which texts function in the world, a department of rhetoric and composition could uniquely look at the production and reception of texts of all kinds, attend to their ambiguity, and address problems of their dissemination.

UNIVERSITIES

A rhetoric and composition major, then, would change the conditions of work not only for students who elect that major, but also for the entire university culture. A major in rhetoric and composition is a good idea for universities themselves. Universities are frequently seen as being tasked with reacting to and meeting the needs of several disparate audiences: students, of course, but also parents, faculty members, administrators, state and federal officials, and the corporations and industries that hire their graduates and offer much-needed monies back to the universities to continue their educational work.

We should pause here and emphasize that we are not characterizing universities as the necessary puppets of their constituents, particularly of the industries that hire and sometimes direct the educational experiences of university students. We make our assertions here instead on the grounds that capital is a requirement for the successful day-to-day running of universities, and corporations can be a source of capital. We are interested in this argument in the ways that necessity can be turned to the advantage of students and the universities who serve them.

A rhetoric and composition department will therefore benefit universities themselves because its institutional focus would be multidisciplinary, socially useful, and lucrative.

More and more often, "vision statements" seem to acknowledge that the problems the world presents resist solution within single disciplinary paradigms. The proliferations of multidisciplinary programs—peace studies, neurobiology, urban studies, disability studies, gender studies, and the like—suggest that narrow paradigmatic thinking has proved unequal to the task of addressing the social and scientific problems that confront us. Statements with titles like "Vision 2010: The Challenge of the Future" that land on our desks and enter our in-boxes consistently emphasize the importance of collaboration among departments, units, and even colleges to keep the university viable against the threat of for-profit institutions, declining state funding, and rising costs. Within this milieu, it seems appropriate to constitute writing as an institutional object and to look carefully at the multiple ways in which it has been and can be defined, described, explained, and analyzed. Post-disciplinary programs save money, draw students, and impress the public. A post-disciplinary major in rhetoric and writing would accomplish these goals with ease. The faculty, in most cases, is already in place; the demand is there; the research inquiry has already been deemed a vital national priority in such initiatives as the No Child Left Behind legislation.

The relations with corporate culture that such a major would encourage are a selling point for prospective students. Our experience has been that corporations that ask us to prepare persons with "good communication skills" know *exactly* what they are asking for. They do not, in general, ask us to send them a worker who knows a particular corporate genre but rather a person who knows that as situations change, discourse must change to meet that challenge. The corporate representatives with whom we have spoken consistently stress that good engineering skills, for example, are no longer enough. The engineer must be able to explain her conception to multiple audiences, argue its usefulness and profitability, describe the procedures for its production, and chat amiably with prospective customers.

Our experience has also suggested that, in spite of good intentions, writing-intensive courses in majors tend not to "improve" writing behaviors generally but rather to enhance skills in the genres native to that major—the lab report, the term paper, computer documentation, and so forth. In our view, discipline-specific writing assignments in Writing Across the Curriculum (WAC) and Writing in the Disciplines (WID) programs in research-oriented universities often fail to achieve their avowed purpose precisely because research faculty have little experience and less interest in the teaching of writing and are disinclined to remedy that situation. Prompts prepared by these faculty members often tend either to ignore the rhetorical situation completely or to stipulate it more stringently than is necessary or useful. In our work developing assessment procedures for graduating seniors, for instance, we have encountered faculty-prepared writing prompts that ask simply, "What is [discipline] 'x'?" Offering no context, this prompt gives the student too little information about the rhetorical situation. The student writer has no idea to whom she is writing, nor does she have a sense of how her writing is likely to be used.

On the other hand, other prompts function basically as knowledge-tests in which the situation is firmly established and the writer's task is constrained. The student writer is faced with a dizzying array of answers his writing must provide, yet he is again left in the dark as to how his writing relates to any context outside of the paper he will hand to his teacher. Once again, we think a rhetoric and composition major with departmental status would go some distance toward helping faculty members with this problem.

Now is the time for such an endeavor. With all the words people regularly produce in their native genres, paying attention to what happens when writers make texts is an appropriate task for researchers at universities. Unfortunately, these inquiries, when they do occur, take place within specific disciplines. So researchers in psychology attend to the ways in which writing might be thought of as problem-solving behavior but eschew questions of self-expression. Philosophers of the Derridean persuasion might see writing as the manifestation of presence but evince little concern for the ways in which the "inscriptions" they study may or may not be successfully communicated to audiences. Members of departments of communications tend to assert that the medium is the message and then study the medium.

MULTINATIONAL CAPITAL

A rhetoric and composition major is a good idea for multinational capital. Corporations require workers with the ability to solve problems by writing rather than merely to follow stipulated formats. Many corporations actively seek alliances with schools. In return for their scholarship monies, however, they want "input" into curricular matters. In our experience, this "input" is not limited to formulaic matters. Indeed, many such corporations specifically say that they will take responsibility for teaching practice in the workplace so long as potential employees have a sense of the theory of rhetoric.

Students find the idea of working with/for a prominent business as an intern highly palatable—they see it as a chance to get "in" with a good company and as a good use of their academic sentence before they graduate and would have to compete with other candidates for these jobs (our jailhouse imagery is intended: many students tell us they feel they are putting in time in college just so they can become productive members of society when they are released). Students like the idea of having easy access to businesses that use their skills. Schools that have program or internship relationships with corporations in place are thus more attractive to prospective students. Corporations with those relationships in place have easy access to qualified (in some cases, pre-trained) new workers when students graduate. It is therefore anomalous that so few research-intensive universities offer undergraduate majors in rhetoric and composition that take advantage of this synergistic potential.

WHY IS THIS?

We see several reasons why rhetoric and composition majors are not already part of the research-university system as it is commonly experienced by students in North America. Although research-intensive universities are now beginning to reward research into writing, they do so as part of an effort to improve a service, to perform what the Morrill Act requires of them, that is, to serve the interests of the state that supports them. And, as anyone who has ever waited in line at the Secretary of State's office can attest, those who exist merely to serve the interests of the state are rarely those who are passionate about and committed to the service they are providing.

But for most research-intensive universities, research into what prevents writers from making coherent paragraphs is not considered as important as research into scientific inquiries. Therefore, research on writers is less likely to be funded internally. And since internal funding is usually a precondition for external funding, writing research goes down the tubes. Science is sexy: headlines on the discovery of a new star, a tinier physical particle, or the gene for a physical affliction sound much more current, much more important, and much more worth the time of a university than do the kinds of modest statements compositionists and speech theorists make about the developments in their fields, such as: students write better when they are asked to write in response to a real-world exigency rather than to a fake "prompt"; and, speakers are using more indirect locutions in their criticisms of government policies than did their counterparts thirty years ago. We are still the grandchildren of the Age of Reason and the Enlightenment: if an inquiry doesn't touch on fastidious science, it doesn't seem worthwhile.

ONE EXPERIENCE—A FIRST-PERSON JOURNEY INTO
INSTITUTIONAL INTERSTICES

We set out in this essay to make a case for granting institutional status to an undergraduate major in rhetoric and composition. We turn now to possibilities, to the ways in which the material realities of the university can be negotiated in order to produce a class like one which would be part of such a program. Such a project would require a change in the belief system that characterizes research-intensive universities. Sharon Crowley has recently written that

> [w]hat is necessary [to change entrenched belief] is for rhetors to be heard, for attention to be paid. Story is, perhaps, the most efficient means of garnering attention. I use the term here in its ancient rhetorical sense, where it refers to some exemplary narrative, historical or fictional, that makes a point by illustration or comparison (Aristotle, *Rhetoric,* II, 20). Aristotle says that examples are effective because they serve as witnesses. (2006, 197–98).

We therefore end our essay with a "witness" narrative that we hope you will find persuasive. We shift here to the first-person singular as one of us describes her actual experiences crafting and implementing a class that blended approaches to speechmaking and writing in a single, hybrid course that centered on the successful production of argument for first-year students. We suggest that such a hybrid course would be a realizable step forward for large, research-intensive universities interested in the advantages of an undergraduate major in rhetoric and composition but not yet ready to commit the resources required by a full-blown department of that ilk. We offer this story as an exploration of the institutional impedimenta to such a course, the forms that it can take, and the impacts it might have on the students who take it. We add a few thoughts on the lessons it offers to teachers, administrators, and university leaders guiding their students and their institutions toward improved undergraduate rhetoric and composition opportunities.

~ ~ ~

When I first started pursuing my idea for a hybrid speech and writing first-year class, I met several blank stares—both in the department of English, where I was housed as a graduate student, and in the head offices of the department of communication, where I was at the time taking a course in the teaching of first-year speech. I had been teaching first-year writing in the department of English for several years and knew my students were not really getting what they wanted or needed despite the department's much-touted composition-program structure that allowed me to teach writing based on a centralized inquiry. In those classes, whenever I offered my students opportunities to share orally the investigations they were conducting for their papers, they jumped at the chance. In many cases, they did a better job of explaining themselves orally than they did presenting their arguments in their actual papers. Surprising numbers of them wrote warmly in class evaluations about their little speeches and the experiences they had preparing for and giving them. But it was not a straightforward process for me to turn my instincts about what students needed into an institutionally approved course for my students to take. There were obstacles, some expected and some surprising. I'll point out a few of them as I explain how my course came to be, what it looked like, and how students reacted to it.

When I took the graduate course in teaching first-year speech, I was struck by the similarities between the central messages of first-year speech and those of first-year writing—they seemed to have a significant overlap in their course content. There were similarities in the instruction of thesis-based argument development, ethical use of researched sources, and awareness of audience requirements, among others. But despite the number of years I had spent in graduate school, I had never run across any formal, institutionally approved information that would have directed me to think the first-year classes could be related in any substantial way for contemporary students. A smattering of information I'd received on the history of ancient rhetoric had indicated that speeches used to be considered the primary mode of argument presentation but that the whole history of the teaching of writing since Aristotle had been directed toward removing the taint of orality from writing in pursuit of "true" clarity. So my first obstacle was one of imagination, of knowing what was possible in and with other disciplines. If I hadn't inserted myself into both the first-year-writing and first-year-speech programs (a move not prohibited but certainly not encouraged by the chilly chasm of silence between the two departments at our university), I wouldn't have had a clue that students' first-year experiences in the two programs could be so similar.

Despite the absence of thorough rhetorical history I'd encountered in my graduate English courses, the facts of the similarities between the two first-year classes spurred me to imagine what a productive resonance between speech and writing could mean for students. I theorized that students might be able to apply the lessons learned from developing well-done written or spoken presentations to the ones with which they struggled. I designed a first-year course that would give students equal chances to give and pay attention to spoken and written presentations of argument. I used the concept of argument as a stable bridge between the institutional formations of English composition and public speaking. The professor running the speech-teaching-training course accepted my hybrid syllabus as a credit-earning, grade-bearing, final project. But she gently pointed out that if I were to be invited to teach first-year speech, I would be expected to follow the communication department's guidelines for a regular speech class. In other words, my syllabus was great as a theoretical exercise, but the real format for teaching first-year students to speak would remain in the hands of the department. The obstacle of institutional(ized) authority, of doing things the way they had long been done, was a stumbling block in my path.

My interest had been piqued, however, so I began testing the waters in the department of English to see what the response to offering my hybrid class would be. My inquiries into the possibility of creating a new class, complete with new course number, were met with resounding silence, with one pitying suggestion from a senior professor that navigating the shoals of the university's course-creation committees was challenging enough for a junior professor and certainly a stretch too far for a graduate student to consider taking herself. The institutional expectations for the limited contributions graduate students should make to the organization of the department provided another stumbling block.

However, I was lucky to have worked previously for two years as an associate director of the first-year writing program, so I took my ideas there. I expended no little cultural capital in pitching my idea to my former program-administrator colleagues, who did eventually support my efforts to go forth with teaching speech inside a writing class as long as I promised to require "substantial writing" in support of the speeches. I met their constraint by introducing a requirement for speech portfolios of preparatory written materials, works-cited sheets, speech-delivery note cards, written peer reviews, and long post-speech reflections. But even so, my course was viewed with some suspicion by my fellow teachers of first-year writing, and I was told that my "nonstandard" syllabus had to receive special treatment from the directorship of the first-year writing program in order not to be flagged as nonconforming and therefore troublesome to the department. Reworking my hybrid syllabus to meet the text-production requirements of a first-year writing class introduced another small obstacle to my process of effecting change in the university.

In the end, though, I received all the permissions I needed to proceed with a special, hybrid section of the regular first-semester, first-year writing course. The class I designed presented students with opportunities to give both speeches and papers. To make sure all the students had equivalent learning opportunities, students had to complete both spoken and written arguments early in the semester and to choose each option at least once again on their own, but they were given the choice of precisely which assignments to respond to in spoken form and which to answer with written presentations. They were thus able to take ownership of the decision to offer a speech or a paper in a way that highlighted the impact the required argument of the assignment had on their choice. They were able to match the mode of presentation to the rhetorical situation described in the assignments and to see that choice as yet another in the many choices they exercised as rhetors in response to real-world opportunities to present effective arguments.

Perhaps a few more details about how the hybrid class worked would be in order here. Throughout the semester, students read chapters on analyzing everyday conversations, both public and private, as arguments. They established early on a definition of argument that included all kinds of persuasive utterances and which did not limit "argument" to mere squabbling or quarreling.

Students read case studies on an issue like language discrimination in the workplace, then they were presented with a situation like one which in the real world would naturally call for the construction of some kind of thesis-based argument in response. They were instructed to communicate to a specific audience, in a specific genre, for a specific purpose. For example, after becoming familiar with conversations about language discrimination in the scholarly and popular press, they were asked to imagine themselves working in a restaurant where jobs were apparently assigned based on workers' status as native speakers of English. They were asked to advocate for change in those hiring practices with restaurant officials. They decided whether to respond in text (with a written argument) or in speech (with a spoken argument) based on what they thought would work best for that argument, that audience, and themselves.

My hybrid course was created around the central idea that all thesis-based college argument, regardless of the class it's assigned in or the people it's given to, is based on the same central tenets of logical organization, careful analysis, and appropriate, ethical use of evidence; the final form that argument takes as it's related to its audience is much less vital to its success than is the careful construction of the underlying logical idea. In a liberal arts-university context, this kind of flexible understanding of argument seems very useful to students who are asked time and time again to communicate ideas to very different audiences, in different situations, and for different purposes. In the workplace, it seems even more useful, as new projects arise for new audiences and workers must navigate a complex matrix of generic expectations from their bosses, colleagues and clients. But convincing my students that learning to think in such flexible ways was worth the additional work required in the classroom was tough. Some students asked around and reported to me that they were being asked to do "more work than other people" in other first-year writing courses. So that was another obstacle: the reluctance of students to undertake what is admittedly a bigger, more time-consuming task in the hybrid course than that with which they would be faced in a typical first-year writing classroom.

What my students took away from having participated in my class started, of course, with the understanding and practice of giving speeches and papers. But it was interesting to me that they talked a great deal in their cumulative reflections about metadiscourse lessons they were happy to have learned about the different impacts speeches and papers had on their audiences. For instance, they embraced the passionate expression of emotion as an indicator of authenticity and authority in their own and their colleagues' arguments. When they gave spoken presentations, they definitely placed a high premium on lively engagement with an audience. But when they wanted a message to have long-lasting impact, they switched to written arguments, finding in written expressions the best chance to be thorough, descriptive, and far-reaching. Many students commented that they felt grateful for having had a chance to practice giving speeches in their first-year writing class because they felt they had been deficient in their ability to stand before people and speak. Few of them made any reference to being glad they had been given the chance to write papers in their first-year writing class. But, then again, they probably came into the course fully expecting to write copiously, so making speeches may have seemed more remarkable to them.

One of the primary things I learned from developing and teaching my hybrid course is that the distinctions we make as academics between the institutional formations of English composition and public speech are actually irrelevant to giving students good, sound experience in the skill of communicating thesis-based arguments of the types given credence in college and the workplaces beyond college. Based on my students' experiences as described in their reflections on the class, I claim that whichever of the body's senses an audience member uses to take in a student's argument doesn't fundamentally matter as long as the argument itself is sound and well-constructed (although I acknowledge, of course, that other situational realities have an impact on whether a speech or a piece of writing will be received as the best possible response).

But what of the future of my hybrid course? Some students definitely reacted positively to the course, even asking whether my class would be open to their friends and younger siblings in coming semesters. But I had to inform them that it would not be. After I graduated, no one would be around to teach it. The first-year writing program was willing to let an established old colleague take some chances in the classroom but wasn't any more ready to adopt the hybrid model as its own than had been the folks in the department of communication. So, with my departure, the hybrid first-year course at my university would die. And that marks the final obstacle to implementing a hybrid course that I'll mention: the short times most people have to spend in any one department, at any one school, to get a program established before other responsibilities call them away from the project.

LESSONS LEARNED

We take from this class-implementation experience three main lessons to apply to our larger argument: students do hunger for and respond well to being given the chance to see writing and speechmaking as a field of study worth theorizing; departmental obstacles to strange, new classes can be overcome by specific individuals with the drive and personal connections to implement them; and without an institutional structure like a department, a new class is unlikely to last in the curriculum beyond the tenure of a single graduate student or professor.

And thus we are brought to a discussion of how research-intensive universities can go about introducing the benefits of an undergraduate major in rhetoric and composition to their students. As we've explained, there are a lot of advantages to such a program when it is given institutional status as a department, but there can be a number of obstacles to developing its courses in large, research-intensive universities. What we modestly propose, then, is that teaching a course similar to the hybrid speech and writing course we talked about can be a first step toward achieving departmental status for a major in rhetoric and composition. By focusing on the real-world exigencies that call alternately for speeches and writing, for formal and informal responses, and for arguments that center on the issues most important to their intended audiences, university innovators can initiate fully institutionalized departments of rhetoric and composition. The key, though, is to get into the classroom and get teaching.

Creating room to teach such a course requires making arguments like the ones we've shared in this essay to students, faculty, university administrators, and funding-ready corporations. It requires wresting space for offices, copy machines, and administrative assistants from overcrowded campus buildings. It requires the drive and passion of a person or persons in affiliated disciplines to spearhead the campaign to transform the idea of such a course into an accredited technique for offering it to students. It requires awareness of and willingness to overcome obstacles at each point as the course develops. And lastly, we argue, it requires a departmental structure that allows it to last beyond just one person or just one term.

As we said, we believe now is the time for such an endeavor. Now is the time to begin working our way out of the constraints into which we have been written. Our suggestion is that institutional change might be effected by beginning with teaching—not with research—by inventing a course that serves student and corporate interests and that leverages the existing skills of university professors to produce something more and better than what students would learn on the job or at a vocational school.

REFERENCES

Crowley, Sharon. 1998. *Composition in the university: Historical and polemical essays.* Pittsburgh, PA: University of Pittsburgh Press.

———. 1990. *The methodical memory: Invention in current traditional rhetoric.* Carbondale: Southern Illinois University Press.

———. 2006. *Toward a civil discourse: Rhetoric and fundamentalism.* Pittsburgh, PA: University of Pittsburgh Press.

Gonzales, Margaret. Instant-message interview. July 5, 2007.

Harkin, Patricia. 1991. The post-disciplinary politics of lore. In *Contending with words: Composition and rhetoric in a post-modern age,* ed. Patricia Harkin and John Schilb, 124–38. New York: Modern Language Association.

Hart-Davidson, Bill. Advanced technical writing course objectives. *Bill Hart-Davidson.* http://www.msu.edu/~hartdav2/atw/atwsyllabus.html (accessed July 30, 2007).

Jarratt, Susan. 1991. *Rereading the sophists: Classical rhetoric refigured.* Carbondale: Southern Illinois University Press.

Lanham, Richard A. 1983. *Literacy and the survival of humanism.* New Haven, CT: Yale University Press.

Lauer, Janice M. 2004. *Invention in rhetoric and composition.* West Lafayette, IN: Parlor Press.

Leff, Michael. 2000. Rhetorical disciplines and rhetorical disciplinarity: A response to Mailloux. *Rhetoric Society Quarterly* 30:83–93.

Mailloux, Steven. 2006. *Disciplinary identities: Rhetorical paths of English, speech, and composition.* New York: Modern Language Association.

Miller, Susan. 1989. *Rescuing the subject: A critical introduction to rhetoric and the writer.* Carbondale: Southern Illinois University Press.

North, Stephen. 1987. *The making of knowledge in composition: Portrait of an emerging field.* Portsmouth, NH: Boynton/Cook.

Office of Planning, Budget, and Analysis, University of Colorado at Boulder. Why students attend college, why pick CU-Boulder. 2001. *University of Colorado at Boulder.* http://www. colorado.edu/pba/surveys/ug/99/college.htm (accessed July 12, 2007).

Perelman, Chaim, and L. Olbrechts-Tyteca. 1969. *The new rhetoric: A treatise on argumentation.* Trans. John Wilkinson and Purcell Weaver. Notre Dame, IN: University of Notre Dame Press.

Sosnoski, James J. 1994. *Token professionals and master critics: A critique of orthodoxy in literary studies.* Albany: SUNY Press.

Vitanza, Victor J. 1997. *Negation, subjectivity and the history of rhetoric.* Albany: SUNY Press.

2

REDEFINING THE UNDERGRADUATE ENGLISH WRITING MAJOR
An Integrated Approach at a Small Comprehensive University

Randy Brooks
Peiling Zhao
Carmella Braniger

The steady growth of undergraduate majors in rhetoric and composition in the last two decades has prompted discussions about the challenging development of these majors. In this chapter we will discuss the development of an undergraduate writing major with an integrated model at a small comprehensive university. This model provides us with a means of addressing some of the challenges faced by any English department in developing an effective undergraduate writing major. The first challenge is the difficulty of modeling an undergraduate writing program on graduate programs in rhetoric and composition. A second challenge we address deals with the place of undergraduate writing programs within liberal arts and professional schools of higher education. Within our own discipline of English studies, the undergraduate writing major must also address historical challenges in bridging the splits between theory and practice as well as between rhetoric and poetic. We also discuss the challenge that first-year writing programs often do not value how the integration of rhetorical theories and practices can benefit all students, not just writing majors. English departments trying to implement an integration model may have to address the challenge of traditional roles of English faculty that reinscribe the split between reception and production of text. Finally, the development of a new integrated undergraduate writing major presents potential challenges to curricular design of rhetoric and composition graduate programs.

INTRODUCTION: THE DIFFICULTIES IN MODELING AFTER GRADUATE PROGRAMS IN RHETORIC AND COMPOSITION

It is important, first of all, to examine the way undergraduate composition programs have taken cues from graduate programs. The current status of the undergraduate writing major is "an amorphous and still-developing construction" with diversity in "missions, purposes, and course requirements" (Carpini 2007, 15). Inarguably, the development of undergraduate comp/rhetoric programs owes to the steady growth of graduate programs in this field. Comp/rhetoric today is no longer "the stepchild of the English Department" (Kinneavy 1971). Several comprehensive surveys on doctoral programs in comp/rhetoric over the last four decades attest not only to the field's growing legitimacy but also to its "growth, consolidation, and diversification" (Brown, Jackson, and Enos 2000, 240). In 2004, Brown et al. found such programs to be thriving, with increasing numbers of students, while the overall number of English majors declined. The growing legitimacy and increasing vitality of the surveyed graduate comp/rhetoric programs has created more supportive guidance for establishing and redefining undergraduate writing programs in general.

While drawing upon the vitality and legitimacy of graduate programs in comp/rhetoric, undergraduate programs have difficulties in modeling after such programs. One challenge involves the assumption that undergraduate students, lacking the maturity of graduate students or the practice of teaching, do not need the theoretical foundation that underpins graduate programs in comp/rhetoric. This assumption derives partly from a failure to understand the transformative power of rhetorical theories, along with writing process theories. Such theories have not only challenged the core curriculum of English studies but have also redefined important principles such as knowledge, language, text, reading, and writing. While this redefining power has been recognized in scholarly journals and professional conferences, many still believe that these theories should remain within the purview of graduate studies. Undergraduate writing programs designed with these assumptions tend to focus only on creative writing or professional writing skills.

The integration of comp/rhetorical theories faces widespread resistance at the undergraduate level, but it is widely acknowledged that continued growth in this field persists as a professional development opportunity for graduate students. As Brown and others conclude, rhetoric and composition "is now well positioned to assume an even more pivotal role in the academic instructions that prepare our students and the professional environments that employ them" (2000, 11). In contrast to the low demand for English graduate students in general, PhDs in comp/rhetoric are under-produced, according to Gail Stygall (2000, 382); this is due largely to initiatives and programs that prepare graduate students in this field for a too-broad spectrum of teaching, research, publishing, and administrative roles. These roles rely heavily on general expertise in multiple areas such as general writing programs and writing center administration, business, professional, and technical communication, and, most of all, rhetorical and composition theories and pedagogies. So, while advocating professionalism for graduate comp/rhetoric programs, many are unsure how to effectively implement professional courses such as business and professional writing, Web publishing and editing, and teaching writing in undergraduate curriculum for the sake of promoting future employment.

In spite of these resistant attitudes, surveys suggest that comp/rhetoric has irrevocably changed undergraduate English curriculum. Between 1976 and 1986, undergraduate comp/rhetoric courses became more widespread across institutions, which offered more variety in specialized writing courses, similar to graduate writing courses, such as composition theory, rhetorical theory, business, technical, and professional writing, and teaching writing (Werner et al. 1988). According to a MLA survey of undergraduate English programs during the 1991–1992 academic year, about 53 percent to 77 percent of course offerings were devoted to writing courses, and 14 percent to 38 percent to literature courses (Huber 1996). A review of online catalogs demonstrates the growth of undergraduate comp/rhetoric programs, named and configured differently across institutions.

Undergraduate writing majors have always been bookended: an overemphasis on first-year writing programs on the one end and graduate programs in comp/rhetoric on the other, according to Stygall (2000). This overemphasis creates two challenges for undergraduate writing major programs. First, undergraduate comp/rhetoric programs cannot easily follow the models for doctoral and master's programs in rhetoric and composition. Neither the Great Books model (like that of Harvard or Yale) nor the Expertise model (like that of most research I and II schools) fits. The Great Books model "discourages programmatic diversity" (Young and Steinberg 2000, 392), and the Expertise model merely *introduces* undergraduate writing majors to theory. More importantly, though, models for comp/rhetoric programs have inherited the entrenched rhetoric-poetic split, among other splits, which greatly hinders the healthy growth of English departments, including their faculty and majors. As comp/rhetoric professors and literature professors fight their theoretical battles, the overall strength of a department weakens or drains completely, and the students' holistic development is oftentimes sacrificed by the faculty's perpetuation of such a split.

A second challenge involves recent scholarly and institutional overemphasis on first-year writing instruction, while positively promoting to the public the importance of writing and the importance of teaching writing, has constructed a negative notion that "writing instruction is exclusively skill-based and that it is to be administered to those with 'substandard' writing skills" (Howard 2007, 1). Such an emphasis creates an institutional rationale for separating rhetorical theories and strategies from writing skills. The result is that it physically separates first-year students into two groups: those who need more practice in writing skills and those who can be exempted by placement exams or other standard tests.

To configure an undergraduate comp/rhetoric program, one must develop a more desirable model to cope with all of these challenges. During the 1980s, some graduate comp/rhetoric programs, like that of the University of South California, Texas Woman's University, and the University of Pittsburgh, attempted to connect rhetoric and poetics (Chapman and Tate 1987). As Chapman and Tate warn in their survey, such an integration in many cases can be only cosmetic, because a genuine integration must ask literature, rhetoric, and composition faculty to reexamine their own fields in relation to English studies as a whole and to redirect their attention toward the holistic intellectual growth and professional preparation of their students. Drawing upon socio-epistemic theory, we believe that genuine integration happens when we position undergraduate writing major students as both consumers (interpreters and critics) and producers of text and when we encourage them to use writing to engage, challenge, resist, and revise their own realities, as well as those of their communities and professions.

In this chapter, the example of a small comprehensive university outlines how rhetorical and writing theories have been actively integrated into our undergraduate writing major curriculum—journalism, professional writing, academic writing, literary writing, book design, computer-aided publishing, and the teaching of writing. Instead of expecting students merely to practice or prepare for future development, the integrated approach emphasizes the public use of writing, reading, editing, and English teaching abilities in near-professional performances. At Millikin University, the point is that writing is a profession, and with an integrated curriculum, students can gain entry into the profession as undergraduate students. However, the integrated model, though developed at a small comprehensive university, can provide theoretical and strategic framework for developing undergraduate writing majors at a variety of institutions.

Developing a Model of Integration for an Undergraduate Writing Program

The English department at Millikin University, a small comprehensive private university in Decatur, Illinois, has developed an integrated model of an undergraduate English writing major over the last fifteen years. The department emphasizes public student performance as writers, readers, and publishers. Through a combination of rhetorical theory and practice, English writing majors gain rhetorical strategies and demonstrate production capabilities necessary for professional employment or admission to graduate studies.

With Millikin's institutional emphasis on the integration of theory and practice, the English department seeks to create a holistic model encouraging students and faculty to embrace reading, writing, publishing, teaching, and professional technologies in English studies. Simply put, our model of "doing English" celebrates opportunities: to read a variety of texts, to create new texts for a variety of audiences and purposes, to publish original works, and to understand the role of rhetorical and writing theories for personal, professional, and community literacy.

RESISTING THE PROFESSIONAL SCHOOL AND LIBERAL ARTS SPLIT

"What do you do with an English major?" The answer we often hear is that English studies provide students with general critical and analytical thinking skills that will be useful only in other professions. Other disciplines can claim an immediate application of disciplinary knowledge and professional skills. If we accept this assumption, we do not believe that students need real-world experiences to practice their reading, writing, and publishing abilities. At Millikin, English faculty have resisted the idea that the humanities are a "preliminary" area for students to develop general skills. Instead we embrace the idea that English writing majors can engage in professional activities related to reading, writing and publishing.

How can English faculty bridge this supposed gap between general liberal arts skills and vocational preparation? At Millikin, we celebrate writing as a profession. We declare the several contemporary professional writing career avenues available in journalism, editing, publishing, entertainment, literary arts, business, industry, and nonprofit sectors. Professional writing is not limited to technical or business writing. Creative writing, for example, is understood as a possible area of professional writing. No matter what the professional context, Millikin faculty encourage students to take writing performances seriously and to publish finished work.

Professional Writing Courses Developed

In the late 1980s and early 1990s, the English department created several new advanced professional writing courses, and we established a professional writing internship program. Eventually, we offered several variations of advanced professional writing courses such as report writing, grant writing, public relations writing, and newsletter writing to give English students and others more specific learning opportunities. This effort proved quite valuable to students in search of work after graduation.

In the late 1980s, Deborah Bosley (now associate professor of English and director of University Writing Programs at the University of North Carolina at Charlotte) developed Millikin's professional writing internship program. She sought professional writing internship sites throughout the central Illinois community, providing English students with the opportunity to immediately employ their writing and analytical skills in a wide range of workplaces. The writing, editing, and publishing internships provided students with access to networks of professionals, leading to professional employment. The internship experiences also led to an awareness of needed improvements in curriculum. Reviewing the professional writing internship reports from both students and site supervisors, Millikin English faculty decided to offer more courses in editing and publishing, especially using current technologies for designing newsletters, magazines, brochures, Web sites, and related materials. The professional writing internship program continues to be a strong element of our English writing major, communicating the professional nature of writing.

The Publishing Requirement

In addition to developing traditional analytical reading, writing, and thinking skills, Millikin English writing majors need competency with the technology necessary to publish in the contemporary professional workplace. As editors and publishers, they need to create rhetorically effective texts in all possible media including print media, Web media, and new forms of interactive hypertext media. When writing is professional, when it makes a difference in the "real" world, when it reaches a public, it does so because it has been presented or published.

As the English faculty took up the question of how to prepare students for professional success, we borrowed valuable curriculum design strategies from programs in the fine arts, natural sciences, and professional schools. We saw the importance of hands-on workshops, laboratory experiences, studios for practice, and deliberate instruction on the use of the tools used by professionals in the discipline. We needed a computer-publishing classroom and lab for English writing majors. Grants in 1991 and 1996 allowed us to both develop instruction for computer-aided publishing and to create a media arts center, which helped the English department develop instruction in Web publishing.

But effective curriculum development is more difficult than acquiring a publishing lab. We needed to truly integrate publishing instruction into our curriculum in ways that made it clear to the students that the computer technology is merely the current professional tool of the trade. Students needed to know how to use the current technology, but the long-term goal was to learn how to get engaging writing out to the public—the rhetorical act of publishing—regardless of changes in the technology.

For our writing majors, every publication is a rhetorical act, a public performance. English faculty seek ways for majors to encounter writing, editing, and publishing experiences in the real world. As writing students encounter venues for publishing, they learn lessons that come only from public performance—they learn that hard work and discipline can result in public recognition of a quality performance. And, as the students' record of successful publicity grows into a strong portfolio of accomplishments, they also learn that public performance pays well, in the form of professional internships, or jobs in writing, editing, or publishing.

How do English faculty and students reach a public in English studies? We present research and analysis on campus and at conferences—we collaborate with our students and invite them to participate. We host readings of poetry and literary texts. We publish our students' work in a variety of print and Web media. For English studies, such means of performance are types of publication. And as much as Millikin English students remain shy, hesitant, and apologetic, they also get the point: professional writing works because it reaches people who value it.

Even with our success in preparing majors for rhetorically effective public performances, we still must continually remind each other, our administrators, our students' parents, and our students why we emphasize publication so much. By embracing publishing as the key professional engagement in English studies, our students and faculty have a professional stage where we can employ our traditional skills and knowledge in order to become shapers and definers of the future profession.

TRANSFORMING UNDERGRADUATE WRITING MAJORS

There have been many attempts to redefine English studies and its contributions to society. One approach was an emphasis on building contemporary rhetorical and literary theories—in English we study texts in order to improve our theories. Another approach was greater emphasis on specialization of literacy research—in English we study texts in order to better understand cultures, genres, or even the cognitive science of reading and writing. Specific practical applications of English studies also came into prominence including programs in technical writing, new media studies, and the teaching of composition. One of the most bizarre results of these reform efforts was a growing split between literary and rhetorical studies. Some professors in English studied the reception of text (literary studies) while others studied the production of text (writing).

At Millikin, the English faculty avoided this split for obvious reasons. First, Millikin's mission has always emphasized a combination of professional and liberal arts. In the early 1990's, the English faculty conducted a study of English alumni, to see what the graduates were actually doing with their English degrees. The answer was very clear: many were professional writers, journalists, editors, English teachers, managers, lawyers, and graduate students or professors. There was no split between theory and practice in their careers. They were clearly engaged in both the reception and production of text. It was evident that there were many careers directly related to English studies; we needed to revise our curriculum at that time to enhance learning experiences for all English majors and directly prepare them for those careers.

While the Millikin University English writing major began in 1986 with a strongly recommended professional writing internship, students had no specific requirements other than to take six advanced writing courses. They exhibited little common knowledge or shared skills. Most knew a word processing program but clearly lacked basic technical knowledge of contemporary publishing and editing. They knew broad literary history but lacked knowledge of the intellectual heritage of rhetorical or contemporary writing theories. Based on this assessment study of the major, the Millikin English department faculty deliberately embraced integration of writing and reading in all of its programs, both within the department and through general education curriculum service. As a part of this effort, the English faculty redesigned and added several core curriculum requirements: Western Classical Traditions, Applying Writing Theory, and Senior Writing Portfolio.

In reconfiguring the Western Classical Traditions, which formerly emphasized reading great literary works from the ancient Greek and Roman cultures, faculty deliberately integrated the simultaneous emergence of rhetorical and poetic theories in ancient Greece. Students read some of the same texts as before, but the focus of discussion shifted to the emerging role of writing and the rhetorical act. Additionally, in redesigning a history of rhetorical theory course, Millikin faculty moved from emphasizing a survey of rhetorical theories to examining the ways contemporary rhetorical theories can be used and applied for research on writing, research on composition or rhetoric, and for direct use in professions such as teaching, editing, or publishing.

As a capstone requirement, in the fall of the senior year, the English writing major students integrate hands-on applications of broadly ranging curricular instruction. In the Senior Writing Portfolio course, students gather together the materials they have been shaping in various rhetorical discourses and reflect on their identities not only as consumers but, more importantly, as producers of text. In this way, students celebrate their accomplishments and recognize their multiple writing identities. Students realize the integration model as they articulate who they were, who they are, and who they want to become as writers. The classroom then becomes what James Berlin, in his study *Rhetorics, Poetics, and Cultures: Refiguring College English Studies*, terms a "site of discovery, not simply of recapitulation and transmission" (2003, 159). Drawing on past writing experiences, students shape their future writing identities through reflection on the integration of traditional disciplinary splits between poetic and rhetoric. As students engage in such reflection, they discover the ways in which private and public, theory and practice, reading and writing, teaching and scholarship, and the literary and rhetorical traditions work together to create a holistic view—not only of the student but, more importantly, of writers and their communities.

In light of the historical progression of the integrated model at Millikin, writing majors now have a range of integrated experiences. In the tradition of curriculum models like Carnegie Mellon's undergraduate English program and others described by Berlin, faculty in our program actively "decenter its curriculum, both in the theory that goes into its construction and in the non-hierarchical arrangement of its elements" (2003, 150). In doing so, we expose students to a variety of roles as readers and writers: the scholar, the cultural critic, the theorist, the creative writer. While a deliberate sequence emerges as we advise our students, Millikin English majors decide how to shape their experiences in the program. Some options are specifically guided by curriculum and others are elective, both within and beyond the major. New space is thus provided to prepare students for the workplace or for alternative graduate study in composition and rhetoric or creative writing. Such preparation asks students not only to allow the discourses in which they participate to shape themselves but also to deliberately and constructively shape discourses. Rather than creating narrow boundaries, this "polylogue" of integrated English studies creates the lived, synthesized experience of the whole student.

The holistic approach positions students as active, independent agents at the center of text production. However, as students discover their niche and work to explore their identities as writers, they may begin to resist the model of integration that helped them arrive at the decision to pursue a specific writing identity. While students are advised to continue their integration of reading and writing experiences, they often complain about having to take courses outside their narrowed scope of a writing concentration. This resistance to the integrated model, along with students' struggles to connect themselves to theoretical and rhetorical theories, signifies the prominent challenge faculty face as they work to move students beyond the narrow sense of identity that seemingly splits creative and professional writers.

One way the department has worked to meet such challenges is to introduce students early on to real-world practice with a variety of writing and publishing projects. Such breadth in experiences with advanced applications in writing theory helps students connect classroom learning and experiential learning. Publishing projects, in particular, provide a necessary forum where students draw on knowledge from a range of courses with the goal of making new contributions to the discipline. Under the umbrella of publishing, Millikin has found the key for bringing together theory, teaching, and poetic and rhetorical production. Rather than reinforcing the traditional splits among these, we see them as co-responsible elements that work together in the creation of the whole: the whole text, the whole student, the whole curriculum, the whole faculty member.

To accentuate the possibilities of such a holistic approach to learning, we ask students to engage in writing, editing, and publishing activities either loosely connected to or outside their advised set of courses. Such activities include writing for the school newspaper, the *Decaturian*, the department newsletter, *The Projector*, or the university alumni magazine, *Millikin Quarterly*; serving as an editor for the literacy magazine, *Collage*; completing a teaching internship with the first-year writing program; attending professional conferences, such as The Association of Writers & Writing Programs (AWP) and Conference on College Composition and Communication (CCCC); joining the Bronze Man Book publishing company; and serving as research fellows or writing center tutors. This broad range of experiential learning provides students with more opportunities to diversify and enrich their experience. Students who major in writing engage in learning communities beyond the classroom. These advanced opportunities for integrating theory and practice prepare our majors for a variety of professional opportunities.

REDEFINING THE FIRST-YEAR WRITING PROGRAM

As the writing major took shape, Millikin's general education program also underwent drastic changes in 1995. Under the old GE curriculum, the first-year writing program relied heavily on the process model and banned literature, under the assumption that students only needed intense instruction on mechanical and organizational writing skills and did not need to develop critical reading skills. There was a clear split between form and content. Students were taught to pre-write, write, and rewrite. On the other hand, incoming honors students, exempt from first-year writing courses under the assumption that they have mastered writing skills, took seminars that were literature-based surveys of western civilization.

Understanding the problematic nature of the split between composition and literature, the English department worked with faculty to embrace a new integrated model for first-year writing. According to Nancy DeJoy, former director of Millikin's first-year writing program and author of *Process This: Undergraduate Writing in Composition Studies*, "creating an approach that bridges the gap between reading and writing without setting aside the idea of process is vital as we respond to questions about the places and functions of reading in first-year writing classrooms" (2004, 70). Millikin faculty transformed the two-semester, skills-based, first-year writing sequence and the literature-heavy honors seminars into interdisciplinary courses renamed Critical Writing, Reading and Research (CWRR) I & II, required of traditional and honors students. This allowed us to integrate a broader conception of reception and production of text. All students would then benefit from a deeper understanding of the interrelated nature of reading and writing.

Bridging the gap between reading and writing allows faculty to reintegrate a wide variety of texts, including literature, into the curriculum of the first-year writing program, opening a wider range of texts to students. It also enables faculty to move beyond the skills-based, process model of the first-year writing experience and incorporate a wide range of experiences for students. Most importantly, this new model asks that faculty members view students, even and especially first-year students, as contributors and participants in the important academic disciplines of reading, writing, and research. We resist traditional curricular models so that students can contribute to rhetorical situations, conversations, and contexts. We invite students into the field as participants by asking them to write about "the histories, theories, pedagogies and practices informing their literacy educations" and to construct "their literacy experiences in writing classrooms" (2004, 16). Situating students as participants, we have been able to help them understand that what they have to say is important, that it can make a difference in the world. In this way, students are able to recognize their own positions as readers and writers and can locate themselves among the various discourses they encounter as they move forward as democratic citizens in a culturally diverse world.

According to Berlin, such a model helps students "establish their own agency in ongoing issues of public discourse . . . [and] engage the experts in debate to offer their own position, from their own perspective" (2003, 152). This new conception of the student has taken much effort to support. It was difficult for faculty members within the program and across the university to accept a new vision of the first-year writer. As was the case with Carnegie Mellon, "the commitment to integration has still not been worked out in the entire curriculum" (2003, 153). At first, some faculty resisted the vision of the student as contributor.

However, the majority of current faculty members embrace this model, and as new faculty members come to teach in the program, we see evolving and marked differences in the relationships faculty establish with first-year students. Those who recognize the importance of moving students toward a participatory understanding of their agency, toward what DeJoy calls "a critical understanding rather than mastery of the way things are" (2004, 19), see the difference such an approach makes in student attitude and performance in the classroom. When students are able to make the unfamiliar familiar by learning to examine and contextualize what they read and write, and to relate those examinations and contextualizations to their own identities as readers and writers, they are more likely to become invested in their own learning and discovery.

Significant curricular and instructional changes took place as a deliberate result of re-constructing the first-year writing program based on a model of integration. Re-conceptualizing notions of text allows faculty to integrate various theories of audience and purpose so that students are not simply practicing writing but also theorizing their roles as readers and writers in order to become more effective rhetorical communicators.

Whether taught by TAs or full-time faculty members, with a common text or not, the first-year writing program can benefit from this integrated model developed for the writing major program. Bringing a wider range of texts to the first-year writing program and to the undergraduate writing major is something all universities can embrace. The benefits of embracing the integration of rhetorical theories and practices into the first-year program and the undergraduate writing major are: 1) students engage in the reception and production of a variety of texts and rhetorical models; 2) students recognize their own agency as knowledge-makers; and 3) students engage in the fundamental, theoretical questions in English studies, such as what is text, who and what constitutes an audience, what do we mean by purpose, in what variety of contexts do we write, how does theory become a part of practice, why do we consume, produce and reflect on text? Using the model of integration to address these questions in both the writing major and the first-year writing program provides continuity of experience and a sense of autonomy for both students and English department faculty.

CULTIVATING ENGLISH WRITING FACULTY

Both transformations—that of the writing major and of the first-year writing program—redefine what it means to be an English faculty member at

Millikin. Because we are dedicated to developing innovative approaches for teaching writing, Millikin faculty look for creative ways to illustrate to students a wide array of conversations to enter alongside a broad range of rhetorical situations in which to participate. Such innovation requires flexibility, a generalist perspective and a strong investment in the teaching of first-year writing. We attempt not only to bridge the gap between poetics and rhetoric but to preclude the traditional split between teaching and scholarship. When faculty have the opportunity to bring their research interests into the classroom and can integrate their work in literary and rhetorical traditions, not only does the quality of the program expand, but faculty are provided agency to continue their own learning. Openness to new learning and to new concepts of text suggests that our faculty know how to learn. We are teaching ourselves and teaching others how to teach. As the department grows and changes, we continue to seek like-minded individuals unafraid to break out of narrow expertise on behalf of new learning, individuals who celebrate a multiplicity of voices, personalities, and identities in students, and who demonstrate genuine commitment to the tradition of integration we have successfully established at Millikin University.

The relatively small size of our department contributes a great deal to our success in these endeavors, while a larger faculty at a larger institution might encounter difficulties for implementation. The success of our model of integration depends on faculty members' willingness to embrace both generalist and personal expertise. A model such as ours, given time, proper implementation, and faculty buy-in, constitutes a reasonable way to productively bridge gaps in the discipline and effectively and ethically prepare students for writing in the real world. Though the career of the faculty member who operates within the specialization model of larger schools and departments may not reflect such a comprehensive integration of teaching and scholarship as ours, it is possible for faculty at any institution to show respect, curiosity, and commitment toward an integrated, synthesized student experience. Any institution can encourage their faculty to gain a better appreciation of the interrelated areas of expertise in English studies, and the best institutions will find ways to encourage collaborative efforts between faculty members with different and varying expertise. If institutions continue to create barriers that prevent faculty from crossing the borders of their areas of expertise, students and programs will suffer from ongoing turf battles, disrespect, and alienation of members in the English studies community.

REDEFINING GRADUATE PROGRAMS
IN RHETORIC AND COMPOSITION

In her review of Stephen North's prophetically entitled book *Refiguring the Ph.D. in English Studies: Writing, Doctoral Education, and SUNY-Albany's Fusion-Based Curriculum*, Beth Burmeister bravely proposes some questions that invite careful exploration of the models for defining and refiguring the field of English studies. One question proves both relevant and provocative: "what will we gain (lose) if we turn to undergraduate models for configuring new graduate pedagogy? For example, is it a natural extension that has simply been overlooked, or do we need to develop brand new models that may be more customized to fit graduate student expectations and desires?" (2000, 127).

This chapter is, in some ways, an extended response to her question. Writing major programs are not only housed in public and research universities but also in private and small colleges, but because "most graduate programs ignore the small college context altogether, leaving that context out of seminar discussions, advising conferences, and workshops designed for job seekers," graduates are often unprepared "for the cultural and institutional shift" (Taylor 2004, 54). While we are aware that our example comes from a small comprehensive four-year university, we believe that if graduate rhetoric and composition programs turn to this integration model at an undergraduate level for directions in future program planning, they will lose their half-century rhetoric and poetic split and gain more prepared and better positioned graduate students. They will also prove more effective in their encounters with those students who might in fact change the assumptions of the field. To collapse such an entrenched split takes collective effort and time. However, such an integration model will fit both graduate and undergraduate rhetoric and composition students' expectations and desires.

Unlike their predecessors ten years ago, who entered the graduate programs in rhetoric and composition with "limited or non-existent background in rhetoric and composition" (Brown et al. 2000, 11), undergraduate writing majors from this integrated model will arrive at graduate programs in rhetoric and composition prepared. Whether they want to develop further expertise in creative writing, writing theory and pedagogy, rhetorical theory, professional writing, new media or publishing, they will bring with them not only an earlier head start in advanced inquiry in their concentrated area but also a broader understanding about the various subfields within the field of rhetoric and composition. With more undergraduate programs better preparing their writing majors for a wide variety of professional and academic contexts, graduate programs may need to shift focus toward models of integration in order to effectively recruit and successfully meet the needs of new graduate students.

We suspect that the growth of undergraduate rhetoric and composition will feed graduate rhetoric and composition studies with higher quality and more prepared first-year graduate students. This preparedness may gradually bring changes to graduate rhetoric and composition programs' criteria for admission, scholarships, and research or teaching assistantships. The growth of these prepared students will perpetually restructure the student population in graduate programs in rhetoric and composition. Moreover, because of their exposure to various writing and rhetorical theories which are currently taught in graduate programs, these students will eventually challenge the existing rhetoric and composition programs to refigure their programs in four ways.

First, since new graduate students come with a good foundation of rhetorical and writing theories, the practicum for teaching first-year writing courses may need to shift their emphasis from basic rhetorical and writing theories to pedagogical theories and practices. Second, instead of focusing exclusively on training writing program administrators for larger institutions, future faculty initiatives should also address the institutional settings including smaller colleges. Third, with an integrated learning experience at undergraduate writing programs, the new generation of first-year graduate students will look forward to faculty mentors who embrace integration of rhetoric and poetic. Last, graduate programs should develop curriculum that will allow students to experience and explore integration in their advanced studies and research activities.

CONCLUSION: PERFORMING INTEGRATIONS IN ENGLISH STUDIES

Students—first-year, writing majors, graduate students—and English faculty at institutions big and small—are all called by this model to perform integrations of reading, writing, publishing, researching, and teaching. This call for all participants in English studies to perform integrations is not new or unique to Millikin University. Many scholars in English studies have envisioned a future that embraces integration. For example, as James Berlin argues, by reconfiguring the opposition between production and consumption of texts, this integration model will point out a direction for refiguring English studies, a direction similar to Stephen North's fusion model (2003). It also echoes Louise Phelps's belief that "the overall thrust of the field is generalist, meaning that the most characteristic features of its programs are the way they combine specialties and require students to perform integrations" (1995, 123). Some observers might notice that, at Millikin University, the English faculty are generalists who teach a wide range of courses and have become very good at "performing integrations," thus replicating themselves in their students by creating generalist English writing graduates interested in their own individualized mix of English studies. To which we respond, "That's right! Isn't it wonderful to be immersed in the rich professional life of reading, writing, editing, and publishing?"

The challenges of developing a new undergraduate writing major are very difficult to overcome because English faculty are so entrenched in traditions of specialization that alienate colleagues and reinforce a fragmented, disconnected learning experience for English students. Regardless of the ways in which institutions configure programs in rhetoric, writing, literature, culture studies, or literacy, their students are eager for a more holistic approach. The ideal undergraduate writing major model will encourage and invite students to celebrate all aspects of theory, research, and practice related to reading, writing, and publishing. Even in situations where the writing program is fragmented across the institution or across areas of expertise within the faculty so much that such integration is nearly impossible, the goals of integration can still be sought. The undergraduate writing major program should develop opportunities and means for the students to perform these integrations on their own.

What is the final message that this integration model of the undergraduate writing major provides to the field of English studies? We believe that all undergraduate writing majors need an integrated learning experience so that they can successfully perform such integration in their professional lives. They need to perform the integrations of reception and production of text. They need to perform the integrations of theory and practice. They need to perform the integrations of rhetoric and poetic. They need to perform the integrations of general analytical thinking within the context of particular professional rhetorical acts. These integrated performances will allow them to both participate and refigure our discipline of English studies.

REFERENCES

Berlin, James A. 2003. *Rhetorics, poetics, and cultures: Refiguring college English studies.* West Lafayette, IN: Parlor Press.

Brown, Stuart, Rebecca Jackson, and Theresa Enos. 2000. The arrival of rhetoric in the twentieth century: The 1999 survey of doctoral programs in rhetoric. *Rhetoric Review* 18.2:233–79.

Brown, Stuart, Monica F. Torres, Theresa Enos, and Erik Juergensmeyer. 2004. Mapping a landscape: The 2004 survey of MA programs in Rhetoric and Composition Studies. *Rhetoric Review* 24.1: 5-12.

Burmeister, Beth. 2000. Writing (into) the academic past, present, and future: Graduate students, curriculum reform, and doctoral education in English studies. *Composition Studies* 28.2:113–35.

Carpini, Dominic Delli. 2007. Re-writing the humanities: The writing major's effect upon undergraduate studies in English departments. *Composition Studies* 35.1:15–36.

Chapman, David, and Gary Tate. 1987. A survey of doctoral programs in rhetoric and composition. *Rhetoric Review* 5.2:124–86.

DeJoy, Nancy. 2004. *Process this: Undergraduate writing in composition studies.* Logan: Utah State University Press.

Howard, Rebecca Moore. 2007. Curricular activism: The writing major as counterdiscourse. *Composition Studies* 35.1:41–52.

Huber, Bettina J. 1996. Undergraduate English programs: Findings from an MLA survey of the 1991–1992 academic year. *ADE Bulletin* 115:34–73.

Kinneavy, James. 1971. *A Theory of discourse.* Englewood Cliffs, NJ: Prentice.

North, Stephen. 2000. *Refiguring the Ph.D. in English studies: Writing, doctoral education, and SUNY-Albany's fusion-based curriculum.* Urbana, IL: National Council of Teachers of English.

Phelps, Louise Wetherbee. 1995. Reproducing composition and rhetoric: The intellectual challenge of doctoral education. *Composition Studies/Freshman English News* 23.2:115–32.

Stygall, Gail. 2000. At the century's end: The job market in rhetoric and composition. *Rhetoric Review* 18.2:375–89.

Taylor, Rebecca. 2004. Preparing WPA for the small college context. *Composition Studies* 32.2:53–73.

Werner, Warren, Isabelle K Thompson, and Joyce Rothschild. 1988. A survey of specialized writing courses for English majors: 1975–76 to 1985–86. *Rhetoric Review* 6.2:204–17.

Young, Richard E., and Erwin R. Steinberg. 2000. Planning graduate programs in rhetoric in departments of English. *Rhetoric Review* 18.2:390–402.

3

RESTORYING DISCIPLINARY RELATIONSHIPS
The Development of an Undergraduate Writing Concentration

Lisa Langstraat
Mike Palmquist
Kate Kiefer

> *If we faculty who [develop advanced writing programs] are to succeed
> . . . not only must we be aware of the opposition we may encounter in
> our efforts at implementation, but we would also do well to respond
> constructively rather than defensively to that opposition. Program
> developers working in a political vacuum or playing the victim role—
> the downtrodden, unappreciated compositionist fighting on the side
> of Right—may otherwise find themselves with an exemplary program
> design that is never, or only briefly, implemented.*
> —Rebecca Moore Howard

These cautionary comments are all too familiar in both spirit and let-ter: Howard is reminding composition administrators that, rather than positioning ourselves as injured parties, compromise and savvy are abso-lutely vital if we are to build successful advanced writing curricula within English departments. Howard does not, by any means, deny the vexing struggles that faculty working to institute advanced writing programs have experienced. Indeed, this passage is preceded by rather chilling accounts of such struggles. Yet, there is something troubling about Howard's characterization of a composition "victim role," particularly since her essay carries significant weight as the introduction to one of the few recent book-length treatments of advanced composition, *Coming of Age: The Advanced Writing Curriculum.* Howard's depiction of the belea-guered, idealistic compositionist's defensiveness uncomfortably mirrors all-too-common responses to narratives of embattled departmental con-flicts; in fact, it seems to reflect the reaction of many English department faculty who prefer to interpret such conflicts within an interpersonal context, rather than one framed by competing narratives of disciplinary and institutional history.

Yet Howard's allusion to victim roles brings to mind a useful approach for exploring the conflicts associated with the development of advanced writing programs. In this essay, we argue that we might understand difficult disciplinary relationships and their subsequent negotiations by turning to research from victim advocates. In making this argument, we're not suggesting that the injustice of departmental hostilities and their resulting injuries are synonymous to the trauma experienced by crime victims. Nor are we suggesting that compositionists are always-already victims of that nefarious poetic-rhetoric split that so often devalues writing instruction; most of us are quite aware of the many privileges that come with PhDs in rhetoric and composition.[1] However, the conflicts and the resulting distress that many of us experience are real and have significant personal and material consequences. The emotional labor demanded of compositionists is unique.[2] And we *are* sometimes injured by institutional and disciplinary injustices that take their toll, so we need to articulate ways of negotiating that toll. Drawing from research on victim advocacy, we might locate better models of and metaphors for navigating the wearying challenges of the minor skirmishes and significant battles that mark the daily lives of many of us working to develop advanced writing curricula.

Indeed, when we review even the most basic scholarship from victim advocates, a central issue arises: expecting "closure" to the harms of injustice is a limiting and risky view of healing. As restorative justice activist Howard Zehr notes, the experience of profound injustice represents an attack on the foundational narratives—about order, knowledge, connection, and identity—that shape our sense of selves. In other words, when we experience intense professional conflicts founded on the devaluing of our profession, our sense of selves as scholars, teachers, and departmental citizens is dramatically challenged. Zehr explains that, after an experience of acute injustice, humans must "restory" their lives; we must learn

---

1. Considerable research on the growth of the field of composition, particularly the increasing number of tenure-track composition positions in comparison to other areas of English studies, is available. See, in particular, Horner's recent book, *Terms of Work for Composition: A Materialist Critique* and Bousquet, Scott, and Parascondola's *Tenured Bosses and Disposable Teachers: Writing Instruction in the Managed University.*

2. See Micciche, and Langstraat and Lindquist for a discussion of the emotional labor associated with composition administration.

"to reconstruct a new narrative, to put boundaries around the story of suffering, to be victorious over it. Victimization is essentially an erosion of meaning and identity, so we must recover a redeeming narrative that reconstructs a sense of meaning and identity" (2001, 83).

We find this principle or metaphor of restorying generative, recognizing as it does that negotiating conflicts and their harms is a process, rather than a narrative of closure with finite beginnings and endings. That we narrate the ongoing evolution of our restorying collaboratively speaks to the importance of a sense of community, both local and more public, in the process of that restorying. This essay explores our approach to restorying some noteworthy moments of conflict and negotiation in the development of a writing concentration within our English major. By connecting this restorying to larger disciplinary issues that face compositionists pursuing exemplary writing curricula, we hope to offer a structure for interpretation, a means of understanding the intensely rhetorical process of negotiating conflicting disciplinary orientations, and the toll they take on composition faculty. Recovering that "redeeming narrative" of which Zehr speaks has meant, to us, a process of rethinking the very purpose and mission of English departments, and our narrative of restorying speaks to the ways in which the presence of an advanced writing program can dramatically alter personal and professional identities in departments of English. We begin by offering a brief overview of our program, followed by "snapshots" of conflicted moments in its ongoing development and explanations of how we have restoried the role of composition within and beyond the department.

THE UNDERGRADUATE WRITING CONCENTRATION AT COLORADO STATE UNIVERSITY

In 1999, after two years of work by members of our composition faculty, the English department at CSU approved a new undergraduate concentration in "writing" and began the process of shepherding new course proposals through the university's curriculum approval process. As director of the composition program and its representative on the department's Executive Committee, Mike took on the primary work of developing the proposal and responding to questions about the concentration, drawing as often as possible on the longer institutional memories of colleagues Stephen Reid and Kate. When Lisa joined the CSU faculty in 2003, approximately twenty students declared the writing concentration within their English major. (Essentially, as we discuss in more detail below, each concentration serves as a distinct major.) Now, only four years later, the writing concentration boasts approximately seventy students who, given their responses to senior and alumni surveys, report professional success and satisfaction with their program of study. The writing concentration continues to grow; we have gained approval for several new courses, including Principles of Writing and Rhetoric, and internships in our writing center and Center for Community Literacy, and we have hired two new tenure-track rhetoric and composition faculty, bringing our faculty total to seven.

Our theoretical objectives for the program include offering students a strong sense of the history of writing and rhetoric; emphasizing the power of writing in community and public contexts; giving students a solid grounding in writing theories, including issues of audience, genre, and technology; blending that theory with writing practice through experiential learning opportunities; and demystifying, and thus preparing students for, an array of writing professions and activities. Our curriculum reflects these objectives in a variety of ways. A sampling of the concentration's courses includes:

- *Principles of Writing and Rhetoric,* a historically grounded discussion of rhetoric and writing theory;
- *Advanced Composition,* a technology-heavy course that focuses on theories of genre and style;
- *Topics in Literacy,* a variable content course that examines the politics of literacy in light of topics such as gender, race, and community literacies;
- *Writing Arguments,* which emphasizes writing for public audiences;
- *Writing in the Disciplines,* a series of courses, focused on writing about education, the social sciences, the humanities, and the natural sciences; and
- *On-line Writing,* which can be substituted for theories of new media.
- *Internship,* in CSU's Writing Center and Center for Community Literacy.

In addition, we offer a variety of writing course electives, such as *Nature Writing, Creative Non-Fiction,* and *Rhetorics of Popular Culture* and internship courses in our writing center, and our Center for Community Literacy. Students are, of course, also required to take a number of core courses in literature and literary theory, such as *Introduction to Poetry*, American and British survey courses, and critical theory.

As we have developed the concentration, we have certainly experienced the common struggles that other compositionists have voiced about the development of advanced writing programs. John Rampage, for example, in "From Profession to Discipline: The Politics of Establishing a Writing Concentration," identifies three primary challenges:

> Resistance from your increasingly embattled literature colleagues worried that you are encroaching on their curricular turf or poaching their majors; the necessity of collectively defining and enacting a disciplinary identity that is necessarily "impure" from the perspective of any one of the major theoretical versions of that identity subscribed to by writing faculty; the likelihood of having to debate "secession" (from the English department) . . . insofar as these moves have already been constructed by some theorists as logical extensions of the move to program status and necessary preconditions for full disciplinarity. (2000, 2)

In the next sections of this essay, we reflect on these challenges as we describe conflicted moments—and our process of restorying those moments—in the development of the writing concentration.

RESTORYING THE LITERATURE-CENTRIC MODEL OF ENGLISH STUDIES

English departments across the nation are facing the challenge of restructuring their philosophies and course offerings in light of the changing dynamics of English Studies. Our department is no exception. When we began conversations about a writing concentration in 1998, many in the department greeted this development with interest and even some enthusiasm. Indeed, the initial impetus for the proposal was concern about a recent decline in the number of English majors and the potential benefits of expanding the major to attract students who were interested in the study of writing. As the concentration solidified in the shape of a proposal, however, it led to conversations that were uncomfortable and, at times, trying for many colleagues. The key challenges addressed in those conversations were an understandable concern that the proposed concentration might encroach on other programs, as well as a lack of understanding about the discipline of rhetoric and composition. These challenges manifested themselves in discussions about how our department defined a "concentration," the name and substance of the proposed concentration, and the impact of the program on future department hires.

Our decision to propose what has become, essentially, a writing major, reflected our attention to the kairos of the moment. The decline in enrollments in the English major, had they continued, would have had negative material consequences for the department in terms of reduced budget and faculty lines. The department's Executive Committee's initial positive response to the idea of a writing concentration can be understood as situated within a pragmatic recognition of the changes in student interests and needs. The decision of the composition and rhetoric faculty to support the proposal, in contrast, can be understood not only within the context of local concerns about the material consequences of the declining number of English majors but also within the larger framework of a maturing discipline. During the Executive Committee's initial discussion about the waning numbers in the major, Mike noted the national trend toward the creation of a writing major and the potential benefits such a major would hold for both the department as a whole, as well as for faculty in composition and rhetoric.

Shortly after that early discussion, the composition faculty shared ideas, and Mike began developing a proposal. Soon thereafter, Mike recalls approaching the then-chair of the department, who had long been a strong supporter of the composition program and who was well aware of changes in the discipline of rhetoric and composition. The brief conversation that ensued revealed how deeply engrained was the literature-centric model in our department: Mike suggested that composition faculty were interested in developing a concentration that would be like the other concentrations in the department—English education, linguistics, creative writing, and literature. The chair responded by explaining that literature was not a concentration within the major but that it *was* the major from which other concentrations branched. Mike explained that he had a different vision of English studies, one that viewed literature, rhetoric and composition, creative writing, linguistics, and English education as a family of disciplines sharing an interest in the reading and writing of texts. After a brief conversation, the chair and Mike agreed to set that discussion aside for a moment, since it seemed likely to bog down the progress of the proposal.

Conversations about the proposal lasted for more than a year. The issue of whether the concentration should be viewed as a subset of literary studies simmered in the background, manifesting itself in expressions of concern about the official name of the concentration, its specific course requirements, and its impact on future department hires. Some faculty, for example, worried that students would find it difficult to differentiate between the "writing concentration" and the "creative writing concentration." Others were concerned that the title "writing concentration" might create misunderstandings with the journalism and technical communication programs, which are housed in another department. Over the years, we had come to an agreement that the English Department would not replicate courses offered in journalism and technical communication and that our sister department would not offer courses in creative writing.

In an e-mail message to Mike, the then-chair of the English department's Undergraduate Committee, which would need to approve the proposal before it could move to discussion by the Executive Committee, wrote:

> The Undergraduate Committee finally met today to talk about the writing concentration proposal. We approve of the idea of a concentration in the area of writing and would like very much to encourage you and the comp faculty to develop and refine it further.
>
> We still have certain problems with the specifics of the proposal which we hope can be resolved to everyone's satisfaction. One trouble we had was that "writing" seemed so general and undefined as to encompass nearly any/everything: writing on computers, expository composition, creative writing, technical writing, editing. Several members of the committee were bothered by what seemed a grab-bag approach, a little of everything for everybody. Could you refine what you mean by writing so that it is distinguished from creative writing on the one hand and technical communication (Dept. of Journalism) on the other? Several of us thought that the centering of the focus should be on what we mean by "Composition," even though we may not like that title. We thought this better summed up what we could do, where our faculty expertise lay, and how it differs from other departments and/or segments of our department. We tend to see this as a Composition concentration, no matter what we title it, and would like to see the course requirements etc. reflect more coherently the idea of composition as central. . . . What would you think of "Composition" or "Expository Writing" as a title for the concentration? (Swinson, personal communication, April 14, 1998)

In the same message, concerns were also raised about resources and new hires:

We are concerned that the concentration would require new hires in the area of composition studies and would like it formed so that we can offer the concentration with the staff we now have and without sacrificing courses/programs that we now offer.

Clearly, this communication illustrates an acknowledgment of the import of a writing concentration and a willingness to devote time and effort to its development. Yet, to a great (although not necessarily unexpected) extent, discussions about the proposal revealed a significant lack of awareness about the discipline of rhetoric and composition. One of the central concerns voiced by members of the department's Undergraduate Committee was that the notion of writing itself appeared to be a conceptual "grab-bag," such that the concentration seemed to have no center, no clearly defined perimeters. As we explain below, we addressed this concern with a carefully constructed rhetorical reply: we identified the writing concentration as an opportunity for students to study and practice writing within a humanities-based curriculum, and we invited interested colleagues to offer their perspectives about what such a curriculum might entail.

As the proposal moved out of the Undergraduate Committee and toward final approval by the Executive Committee, the issue of how to view the relationship between the program and the larger English major resurfaced. Historically, the other concentrations (creative writing, linguistics, English education) had been understood as variations on the literature major, rather than as programs on par with literature. By presenting the writing concentration as equal to and compatible with, rather than as a sub-category of, the literature major, we were challenging deeply held assumptions about the model of English studies on which our curricula and philosophies were based. The literature-centric model just a decade ago was so deeply ingrained as to be naturalized, but the pending approval of the writing concentration demanded an explicit articulation of that model, and that articulation led to significant changes. After the proposal was ultimately approved, the chair announced at a fall department meeting that we now had five concentrations, all sharing a common core of lower-division courses but differentiated by discipline from that point.

Clearly, the discussions incited by the writing concentration proposal compelled our department to revisit the theoretical assumptions that shaped our curricula. As Rampage foretold, we did experience "resistance from [our] increasingly embattled literature colleagues worried that [we] are encroaching on their curricular turf or poaching their majors" (2000, 2). There were certainly moments when we composition faculty felt not only disciplinarily marginalized but willfully placed in a service role, the "housekeeping" role that composition has so often inhabited. Responding with defensiveness—with the hurt that accompanies the denial of the intellectual rigor of one's chosen field, one's professional identity—was rather understandable. As we continued (and continue) to illustrate the viability of the writing concentration, as well as the field of rhetoric and composition more generally, we've had dramatic moments of gratification, such as the meeting when it became clear that the chair placed the writing concentration on par with literature and other concentrations in the department's range of fields. Hence, we, through careful planning and assiduous effort, were able to restory the initial disdain and lack of understanding for the discipline of rhetoric and composition. That restorying has not been an idealistic process of simply replacing a less acceptable narrative with a more acceptable one. It has engaged real material change and public sharing of competing narratives. To continue the metaphor of victimization and the process of restorying that experience (and, again, we want to emphasize that we are not claiming the same suffering as crime victims), consider the fact that the most common questions victims ask offenders in victim/offender mediation meetings is, "Why me? Why did you target me as a victim?" (Umbreit 2001, 53). And in the vast majority of cases, the offender explains that the crime was not "personal"; that is, the offender did not target the victim as a person, as an individual, and instead targeted an anonymous being or place. Many survivors of crimes report that this is both a liberating and daunting epiphany: liberating because as survivors of crimes come to understand that their individual personhood was not the target, they can often free themselves from the residual questions about whether they, as individuals with specific personalities and beliefs, were in some way responsible for the crime. But the epiphany is often daunting because, as Zehr explains, as it depersonalizes, it also creates a "crisis of relatedness," wherein general assumptions about whom we can trust and what kind of world we live in must be restoried (2001, 189). If we transfer this insight as a metaphor for the interpersonal and institutional dynamics of the workplace, we come to realize the importance of community support—especially amongst our composition faculty, but also amongst our colleagues in other fields of English who may also be feeling an erosion of identity and foundational narratives as they face vastly changing institutional and disciplinary dynamics. The restorying cannot be an individualized act but instead requires a community shift in thinking.

RESTORYING (AN IMPURE) DISCIPLINARY IDENTITY

Lest the passage of the writing concentration sound like a story with a entirely happy ending, with closure, we should note that this process of restorying has been anything but seamless. We continue to struggle with Rampage's insight: "the necessity of collectively defining and enacting a disciplinary identity that is necessarily 'impure' from the perspective of any one of the major theoretical versions of that identity subscribed to by writing faculty" (2000, 2) still shapes our writing concentration and our roles in that concentration.

The description of our writing concentration on our departmental Web site is a case in point:

> The Writing Concentration builds on departmental strengths in composition and nonfiction writing, as well as in technology-based writing and writing instruction. It is designed for students who wish to pursue the study of writing from a humanities perspective and particularly for those students who wish to combine the study of writing with the study of literature. The Writing Concentration offers students
>
> - The ability to study writing in a department that takes a humanistic approach to learning
> - The ability to study writing without sacrificing the study of literature
> - The ability to study a wider range of writing and writing theory than is possible in the department's creative writing concentration (http://www.colostate.edu/Depts/English/programs/con_writing.htm)

Certainly, this description reflects the institutional dynamics we negotiated as we put the writing concentration in place; it was vital to address the concerns of our colleagues in literature and creative writing as we articulated the program's name, goals, and curricula. Moreover, as aforementioned, because CSU's journalism and technical writing programs, housed in a different department, long preceded our writing concentration, we do not emphasize technical or professional writing per se. Our Web site overview of the concentration would seem to be primarily defined by a) what it is not (i.e., a technical writing program, a creative writing program) and b) in relation to literary studies (e.g., the emphasis on preserving the study of literature in the writing concentration). Beyond a defensive claim, "What we *really* do isn't necessarily captured in our Web site description," we see the description as evidence of the need to negotiate the institutional contexts in which we're operating. The writing concentration thus represents a hybrid of approaches, expertise, and objectives. In the ongoing effort to define and negotiate the position of the program, in the process of communicating its objectives and importance to the department, we opened up lines of communication, sparked conversations about implicitly understood values and goals.

The issue of writing internships reflects our attempts to negotiate that "impure" identity to which Rampage refers. Our composition faculty are firmly convinced that writing internships play a vital, integral role in any theoretically sound writing program. We recognize the import of experiential learning, bridging community and academic writing, and the professional opportunities that internships offer writing concentration students. Yet, when our writing concentration was approved in 1999, we faced a department-wide stipulation that experiential learning, such as internships, count as general elective credit, not as credit in the major. Since 2001, rhetoric and composition faculty raised the issue of internship credit repeatedly to the Undergraduate Committee, and finally, in 2006, proposals for two specific internships—an internship with CSU's writing center and one with our Center for Community Literacy—were passed. Like the negotiations about the writing concentration itself, the work of approving these two internships raised difficult questions of disciplinary and institutional assumptions and identities.

Rhetoric and composition faculty pressed for internship credit as part of the concentration because we believe that the combination of fully contextualized writing experience and carefully structured academic tasks give students greater insight into rhetorical principles than academic tasks alone. Resistance to fully-credited internships reflected the same concern expressed in the early stages of the writing concentration proposal: there was apprehension that internships would not be rigorous, that they reflected the "grab-bag" approach to disciplinarity, for the internship seemed to have no textual center, no body of knowledge on which a student's experiential learning would be based. Many members of the Undergraduate Committee expressed to Lisa, who participated in three years of conversations about the internships, their concern that the internships had the extraordinary potential to be both unstructured and unacademic. The notion of internships as not only rigorous but as integral to rhetorical training for writing concentration students seemed rather foreign to many faculty trained in a literature-centric model of education.

But the backdrop of these discussions about experiential learning in general and the internships in particular is equally important to understand. Just at the time we hoped to bolster our writing concentration with internship credits, the university as a whole was in upheaval over recommendations from the provost's office to regularize the teaching workload across departments and colleges. Part of this university effort included more carefully distinguishing between "typical" classroom courses—lectures, recitations, seminars, labs, called type A courses— and "independent" student credits, such as independent study, thesis, and internship credits, called type B courses. Under the hotly debated plan, faculty across the university could count type A courses in their workload but not type B courses. Although very few faculty members in English "counted" any type B courses in their workload, the general perception was one of devaluation of the mentoring and advising that faculty members did with graduate and undergraduate students, and internship courses fell into this category. Add to this mix the fact that much of the community literacy and other outreach efforts of department faculty had been largely extracurricular, such as a literacy through poetry initiative undertaken by graduate students working with children in elementary schools, book drives for local organizations, or engaged scholarship performed by individual faculty in the department. While graduate students, particularly those in the rhetoric and composition and communication development MA programs, participated in internships varying from work in our Center for Literary Publishing to local technology-based corporations, "internship" work for undergraduates were loosely defined projects that often included little direct faculty supervision and that merited only elective credit.

Our proposals for internships were met with skepticism on the part of the Undergraduate Committee for several years. We then changed our strategy. Rather than focusing on our own disciplinary values—about experiential learning, the import of engaged scholarship and understanding community literacies, the rhetorical complexities that internships demand—we produced detailed descriptions of specific "classes" for writing center and Center for Community Literacy internships. These descriptions clearly delineated the "class" activities that students would participate in—discussions of assigned readings on both theory and practice, sequenced writing assignments (both analytic and reflective) based on readings and experience in the internship setting—and the detailed evaluation they would receive. At that point, the Undergraduate Committee approved those two internships for credit toward the major, explaining that these particular internship classes were "adequately rigorous" to merit upper-division credit as type A courses.

Certainly both the writing concentration description on our Web site and the current status of our internship courses are theoretical hybrids, "impure" responses to institutional histories and constraints. But as we restory the narrative of composition's lack of rigor or lack of center— two of the most onerous misunderstandings that shaped the current form of our description and ongoing efforts to expand our internship programs—we also open more opportunities amongst composition faculty to discuss our own often-differing theoretical objectives for the concentration. Indeed, the ongoing process of educating our colleagues has forced us to articulate our own perspective: Should the writing concentration focus more on rhetorical history and prepare students for entry to graduate programs in rhetoric and composition? Should the emphasis on technology be further heightened? Should we stress current faculty expertise in community literacies? How should we differentiate ourselves from the technical journalism programs or even from literary studies? Rather than hunkering down in an "us against the rest" narrative, rather than languishing in a business-as-usual framework, we are constantly revisiting and revising our own positions, perspectives, goals. The result has been a writing concentration that is anything but comfortable with the status quo, one that is vital and responsive to student needs and objectives.

RESTORYING THE ROLE OF WRITING WITHIN AND BEYOND THE UNIVERSITY

Rampage's final forecast of the challenges that faculty developing advanced writing programs will face includes the extra-departmental concerns that shape university-wide notions of writing: "the likelihood of having to debate 'secession' (from the English department) . . . insofar as these moves have already been constructed by some theorists as logical extensions of the move to program status and necessary preconditions for full disciplinarity" (2000, 2). Currently, our debates about our upper-division writing curricula have less to do with secession from the English department and more to do with state-wide mandates and pressures, which have brought with them unexpected minor skirmishes and significant battles that directly impact our writing concentration curricula.

In the late 1980s, our state commission on higher education started to respond to legislative pressures to guarantee transfer credits between institutions. Significant battles indeed characterized the early efforts to agree on goals and curricula for the required first-year composition courses offered at all state institutions of higher education. As the years rolled by, however, programs drifted or changed direction radically, and changes in admissions policies and funding resulted in disparities between student populations. In just the past eighteen months, the two public Research 1 universities in Colorado (CSU and University of Colorado) have been mandated to require not just first-year composition but an additional writing course at the upper division. In addition to concerns amongst composition faculty across the state that the new advanced writing curriculum is just the first step in a competency exam to be aimed at the two-year institutions, we at CSU are facing a literal explosion of students in our upper-division writing course. Indeed, we face the prospect of phasing an additional four thousand students into our junior-level writing courses over the next three years.

Within this framework of the larger composition community across the state, the pressure to build consensus about appropriate criteria for the advanced writing requirement has added a great deal of strain to our department- and university-wide discussion of advanced writing curricula, which, of course, overlaps with our writing concentration curriculum. In addition to the pull on composition faculty resources as we administer an advanced writing program whose size will rival our first-year composition program, we (Kate, in particular) face the challenge of new faculty hiring, training, and evaluation, particularly since most of the advanced courses will be taught by non-tenure-track faculty in special instructor positions. And the initiative comes at what may be an unfortunate time. In the past year, we have been responding to another state-mandated requirement: the "GtPathways" initiative, which requires that all university core classes feature a writing-intensive component, such that writing assignments will constitute 25 percent of each student's grade in each core course. Since the university did receive considerable funding for TA lines to support faculty teaching these writing-intensive courses, composition faculty have been asked to coordinate many of the efforts to train and mentor these new TAs in the teaching and evaluation of writing. Given these mandates, we composition faculty find ourselves negotiating an intensified service identity in the English department and across the university. We have, like so many compositionists nationwide, assiduously resisted being identified primarily as service workers by emphasizing the intellectually dynamic nature of our writing programs through publications about administration work, by hosting the Writing Across the Curriculum (WAC) Clearinghouse Web site, by offering a vital and successful MA in rhetoric and composition, etc. Yet these mandates have had a contradictory effect on composition's status in the English department. On the one hand, many of our colleagues have become more aware of the university-wide demands on composition faculty's time and energies; on the other hand, the mandates have solidified for many our primary role as administrators pulled into the ongoing corporatization and regulation of the university.

More immediate, still, is the perception of many English department colleagues that the composition program at CSU is empire-building, that while the new mandates are certainly demanding administrative work, they nonetheless represent new opportunities for composition programs and faculty—opportunities for funding, resources, upper-administrative support, and visibility to which colleagues in other areas of English may not have. Indeed, in 2006, composition received funding for a tenure-track faculty line to work with the GtPathways initiative. Though the funding for that position comes not from the English Department's coffer but from the provost's office, there is nonetheless the feeling among some of our colleagues that the composition programs have grown at the expense of other programs. Indeed, this is a primary concern in the department: that these new initiatives will draw on English resources and will dramatically affect other departmental programs.

We composition faculty certainly feel a measure of beleaguered injury, given these new developments, their concomitant reaffirmation of our service role, the misunderstandings about composition's desire to expand our terrain, and the daunting department-wide concern about what may seem an unfair distribution of resources. We have only begun to write the identity narrative that will set the victim role aside in this case. The particular threads of this story will include using our writing program criteria and descriptions to build consensus among writing teachers and WPAs across the state about the values of our program and using specific syllabi and students samples from our courses to illustrate to writing teachers and WPAs across the state how we enact our values and set program standards appropriate for upper-division writing. On the department level, we continue to remind our colleagues about the origin of the mandated growth of the composition program, and we emphasize the budget lines that separate composition from English department funding.

We're hoping, too, that these current challenges will offer us more opportunity to forge a community of teachers who share goals and criteria for upper-division writing courses, as we are building an extensive and useful professional development program so that interested non-tenure-track faculty can further build their knowledge and skills—as well as their enthusiasm—for teaching advanced writing courses. Most important, we are crafting curricular innovations that will connect upper-division writing students with communities outside the classroom, whether those are disciplinary communities or the larger community of our city, through experiential and service-learning options in the writing classes. We see a real opportunity here to enhance our externship and internship programs further. We do not eschew our service role; neither do we see it as the sole focus of our work as rhetoric and composition specialists. Restorying this conflict will allow us over the next several years to implement a more robust range of offerings at the upper division—a development that will undoubtedly positively affect our writing concentration— and build community with teachers and WPAs statewide.

RESTORYING AND RESTORYING AND RESTORYING . . .

Our stories and experiences of the embattled dynamics of the role of composition in our own department pale in comparison to many of the disturbing tales included in Howard's discussion of the development of advanced writing programs in colleges and universities across the nation. Overall, we're luckier than many—when it comes to collegiality in our department and the fact that we have a strong support system in place amongst our seven tenure-track faculty in rhetoric and composition. We also understand that many of the injurious responses we've received from departmental colleagues over the years are due not only to vast misunderstandings about the field of composition, which still remains so foreign to many of our colleagues, but also to the outrageously limited resources that our department, like many English departments, have faced over the years.

Nonetheless, we find the metaphor of restorying injustice generative and a means to engage in a process of, yes, healing from the moments when we've experienced what Zehr identifies as the three central effects of experiences of injustice: disorder, disempowerment, and disconnection, all of which pose significant challenges to our sense of identity—professional and personal (2001, 189). If, as Howard suggests, many compositionists "play the victim role," this may occur because we often feel a profound sense of humiliation and frustration when our contributions to a department are recast as "empire building" or our identity as scholars is devalued as "not rigorous enough." As Zehr explains, the process of moving from isolation and shame to belonging and empowerment "requires us to re-narrate our stories so that they are no longer just about shame and humiliation, but are ultimately about dignity and triumph. Questions of meaning, honor, and responsibility are all part of this journey" (2001, 191). We hope that, by addressing our own experiences as we've wrangled with the three challenges in developing a writing concentration which Rampage identifies, we've contributed to this restorying for our own department and for others facing similar challenges. But restorying is restorying; it never allows for the finished narrative. With a community of compositionists as audiences and interlocutors, let the restorying continue. It's bound to impact our advanced writing programs in profoundly important ways.

REFERENCES

Bousquet, Marc, Tony Scott, and Leo Parascondola, eds. 2004. *Tenured bosses and disposable teachers: Writing instruction in the managed university.* Carbondale: Southern Illinois University Press.

Colorado State University Department of English Website: Writing Concentration. http://www.colostate.edu/Depts/English/programs/con_writing.htm. 10/11/2009.

Horner, Bruce. 2000. *Terms of work for composition: A materialist critique.* Albany: SUNY University Press.

Langstraat, Lisa, and Julie Lindquist. 2006. Learning discipline: Disciplinary grammars, emotion cultures, and pragmatic education. In *Culture shock: The future of graduate education in rhetoric and composition,* ed. Virginia Anderson and Susan Romano, 19–42. New York: Hampton Press.

Micciche, Laura. 2007. *Doing emotion: Rhetoric, writing, teaching.* Portsmouth, NH: Boynton/Cook.

Howard, Rebecca Moore. 2000. Introduction: History, politics, pedagogy and advanced writing. In Shamoon et al. 2000.

Rampage, John. 2000. From profession to discipline: The politics of establishing a writing concentration. In Shamoon et al. 2002.

Shamoon, Linda K., Rebecca Moore Howard, Sandra Jamieson, and Robert A. Schweger, eds. 2000. Coming of age: The advanced writing curriculum. Portsmouth, NH: Boynton/Cook.

Swinson, Ward. (April 14, 1998). "Writing Concentration." [email message]. Sent to Mike Palmquist.

Umbreit, Mark. 2001. *The handbook of victim offender mediation.* San Francisco, CA: Jossey-Bass.

Zehr, Howard. 2001. *Transcending: Reflections of crime victims.* Intercourse, PA: Good Books.

4

OUTSIDE THE ENGLISH DEPARTMENT
Oakland University's Writing Program and the Writing and Rhetoric Major

Wallis May Andersen

On May 7, 2008, the Oakland University (OU) Board of Trustees approved a proposal for a new major and minor in writing and rhetoric, the culmination of over ten years of effort by rhetoric faculty in the Department of Rhetoric, Communication, and Journalism. On June 1, 2008, the dean of the College of Arts and Sciences (CAS) officially launched the Department of Writing and Rhetoric as a stand-alone writing department.[1] The writing program's independence and the development of its major intertwine. Initial independence allowed the faculty to create curriculum based on contemporary disciplinary thinking, and that curricular focus persisted through its time in a blended department, flowering in the proposal for the major. Moreover, the program's initial independence led to widespread faculty involvement in institutional service and administrative activities. The service and administrative work has been instrumental, though sometimes very subtly, in raising the writing faculty and program out of the second-class citizenship all too common for writing programs, regardless of their reporting lines. Now, as a department in the College of Arts and Sciences, with a major of our own, we can compete effectively with most other academic programs on campus, having our own representatives in the governance bodies and making our own case for resources.

INSTITUTIONAL CONTEXT

The writing program at OU has never been a part of the English department, for reasons rooted in institutional history. Founded as Michigan

---

1. The new (to the position) dean of the College of Arts and Sciences spent much of the 2007–08 academic year splitting rhetoric off from communication and journalism as a major element in achieving his long-range CAS goals. His passion came largely from the many years he spent as a senior member of the rhetoric faculty.

State University (MSU)—Oakland, OU admitted its first class of 570 students in 1959 and became an autonomous state regional institution in 1970 (Oakland University Timeline n.d.). Today it offers a full range of degrees and enrolls some 18,000 students—dramatic growth given its fifty-year existence. But it began as a liberal-arts-focused "honors" college for MSU with significant emphasis on the visual and performing arts. Faculty were recruited from top graduate schools across the country, and these "charter faculty" were deeply involved in setting curricular and academic policy. From today's perspective, active involvement of faculty from many disciplines in writing instruction and policy-setting appears very desirable, but the OU reality reveals significant drawbacks when such involvement is not guided by faculty with expertise in rhetoric and composition studies.

A WAC-LIKE APPROACH TO FIRST-YEAR COMPOSITION (FYC)

Initially at OU, no first-year writing courses were established. Instead, writing instruction was incorporated into first-year interdisciplinary seminars known as Freshman Exploratories, taught by charter faculty as part of their discipline-based coursework. These Exploratories were, according to both charter faculty and students enrolled in the early years, exciting and rewarding educational experiences. From the mid-1960s through the 1970s, each student was required to take two semesters of Exploratories, the first element of a three-part "series of courses designed to provide a broadening, intellectual experience in liberal education" required of all students:

> These Freshman Exploratories[,] taught in seminar-sized classes, offer an opportunity for the student to explore a wide variety of liberal subjects, and are intended to develop the student's ability to think, to discuss, and to write intelligently and critically. Freshman Exploratories satisfy the University requirements for freshman composition. Freshman Exploratories may be selected from the areas of Literature, Western Institutions, Fine Arts, Social Sciences, non-western Civilizations, Science and Mathematics. No two exploratories may be selected from the same area. (*Oakland University Catalog* n.d., 25)

Writing instruction was ancillary to the subject of the exploratory, folded into courses such as From Atom to Adam; Historical, Sociological, and Literary Perspective on the Black Experience in America; and Politics and Literature, taught by faculty from, respectively, the departments of biology, history, and English (*Registrar record books*Winter 1969, Fall 1969,

Winter 1970). As a result, faculty across the institution came to regard themselves as experts in writing instruction, with the unfortunate result that when writing instruction was moved to separate coursework, at a time when the discipline was professionalizing, faculty with little composition studies disciplinary experience wrote the charge to the new program.

ESTABLISHING A WRITING CURRICULUM

By the late 1960s, it became clear to OU faculty and administrators that more focused, systematic writing instruction was needed. Since no faculty positions existed for writing, decisions about writing-coursework requirements and placement were made primarily in OU's governance forum known as the University Senate, composed of faculty, administrators, and staff. In the senate minutes of 1972, formative voices include the dean of the College of Arts and Sciences, who was a historian, the dean of the School of Education, and faculty members from engineering, English, philosophy, history, political science, speech communication, chemistry, and psychology.[2] First, the senate acknowledged the need for separate writing coursework, "discontinu[ing] the use of Freshman Exploratories to teach writing and substitute[ing] . . . a proficiency standard" (Oakland University Senate 1972, April 5). Admissions testing would evaluate student writing for "proficiency," and one senator (from history) commented that "out of her considerable experience in teaching freshmen composition, not more than 20% of the students [could] proceed without further instruction in writing." Senators saw evaluation of writing as the work of the entire faculty, not of the English department: "the Advisory Committee on the proficiency standard was . . . a University-wide committee . . . intended to include predominately Arts and Sciences faculty, but [also] at least one member from each of the other Schools and Colleges" (1972, April 5). Following this decision, the university, after much senate meddling, created a writing program named the Department of Learning Skills and housed it administratively in the provost's office. Both the name and the senate charge reveal a lack of disciplinary knowledge and a reductive approach to writing instruction that has haunted the program for over thirty years and has clearly been an impediment to the acquisition of new faculty and to the progress of our major proposal.

---

2. Most of these faculty had taught the Exploratories.

The writing curriculum itself, both First-Year Composition (FYC) and developmental, was created in the 1970s by newly hired learning skills faculty, who were engaged in the emerging composition and rhetoric discipline, though initially they were MA- rather than PhD-credentialed. Because the program grew out of a cross-curricular program where writing instruction was not seen as a function of the English department, the coursework was not focused on literature. After nine years, the program was renamed rhetoric, aligned administratively with the then-tiny communication and journalism programs, and moved to the College of Arts and Sciences.

Since the three disciplines largely operated as separate programs for curriculum and because writing was not housed in the English department, the writing curriculum remained focused on rhetoric and composition.

EXPANDING THE WRITING CURRICULUM BEYOND THE FIRST YEAR

The Learning Skills (LS) period (1972–81) found the writing program responsive to the evolving national disciplinary approaches to writing pedagogy and curriculum. Largely a first-year program, the LS courses included basic writing, reading, and (predominantly) Composition I and II. The administrative linking with communication and journalism in the early '80s was largely helpful for curriculum, despite myriad political problems, not the least of which was allocation of tenure-track lines. Communication and journalism both had upper-division classes and majors, and rhetoric faculty began to pursue that goal, both to offer the institution's students more writing instruction and to expand their teaching variety.[3]

In the late 1980s, probably the most significant drawback to not being a part of the English department became apparent: turf wars. English asserted that it "owned" all upper-division writing, that rhetoric was formed and destined forever to be a lower-division program. (Only very recently did the English department faculty member who mounted the most adamant opposition apologize to me for what he sees now as a misguided attack on the rhetoric program and faculty.) Had we been departmental colleagues, we could not have proposed courses without department support, and English faculty would then have been our allies rather than our opponents. On the other hand, had we been in English, the writing program might never have been permitted to grow

---

3. While a few of the writing faculty were occasionally invited to teach upper-division courses for other programs, in the main the faculty taught Composition I and II.

beyond its role as a service program, would likely have emphasized writing about literature, and would have even fewer composition and rhetoric faculty than it does. English has offered several writing classes in addition to its creative writing program, and virtually all of those classes have been staffed exclusively with part-time "Special Lecturers" or full-time "Special Instructors."[4] No tenure-track position for writing has ever been pursued by the English department, and the English department writing instructors are primarily that department's MA-credentialed graduates who studied literature exclusively.

The rhetoric program won the turf war over upper-division coursework largely due to the political astuteness of the Department of Rhetoric, Communication, and Journalism (RCJ) chair: when rhetoric was ready to propose 300-level courses in the late 1980s, I was strategically placed on the college curriculum committee to handle the vicious battle. Had the writing program not been represented on the CAS curriculum committee, we would surely not have been permitted to create upper-division classes at that time. Throughout our curriculum development work, such strategic service work has been instrumental in our prevailing, though often not without great trouble. Our later experience showed that we probably should have tried to continue representation on the CAS curriculum committee, as every course we proposed was sent to the English department for review and approval, while when English created two or three writing courses in addition to its creative writing courses, the rhetoric faculty were never consulted.[5]

FINDING AN AUDIENCE FOR UPPER-DIVISION WRITING CLASSES

The curriculum victory that allowed rhetoric to create such courses as Rhetoric (RHT) 320, Peer Tutoring in Composition, and RHT 334, Ethnographic Writing, established a foundation for developing our major proposal but was an empty victory: rarely in the ensuing fifteen years could we develop sufficient enrollments to mount the classes because typically they were merely general electives rather than graduation requirements. Rarely were we able to convince our department chair and dean that one of the classes should be taught despite enrollment of under ten students.

---

4. By faculty contract, a "Special Lecturer" is a part-time faculty member who teaches sixteen or more credits per year and a "Special Instructor" is a full-time faculty member whose credentials are not appropriate for a tenure-track position (*2006-09 Agreement*).
5. Most of these courses have been transferred from English to our new Writing and Rhetoric Department by the dean.

Membership on major university committees helped significantly in raising the profile of the rhetoric program. And because many of these committees limit membership to one person from any department, we were able to serve on committees that also had an English representative—a distinct advantage in helping us develop audiences for our upper-division courses. In the late 1990s, when I chaired the university General Education Committee, the university began revising its general education program. As the general education revision process moved forward, another senior rhetoric faculty member served on the committee's Task Force 1. The new general education structure, which came into the catalog in 2005, requires two "intensive writing" classes in addition to FYC.[6] Whether or not the presence of rhetoric faculty in the initial revision work was a catalyst, having rhetoric faculty on these key committees built respect and acceptance for the program. Importantly, the increasing national interest in improving writing led to a program with many opportunities to attract students looking to fulfill requirements to RHT upper-division courses. As soon as faculty were invited to submit courses for general education certification, we applied for "intensive writing" status for most of our 300- and 400-level courses, and we have seen enrollments jump dramatically.

Yet another strategy we used to improve enrollments, particularly in classes that are cross-listed as graduate classes, has been to encourage our part-time faculty to enroll. Those who lack training in rhetoric and composition benefit by becoming more current with disciplinary research, at little cost because Special Lecturers by OU's American Association of University Professors (AAUP) contract have a tuition benefit of two free courses (eight credits) per year.

CREATING THE MAJOR PROPOSAL

Having broken through the 300-level ceiling, we strategically pursued creating upper-division courses to serve as the basis for our major, knowing that the approval process for individual classes is much less onerous than for program proposals. The CAS curriculum committee approves courses; major proposals go through a full, complex governance process, passing through at least five committees before going to the board of trustees.

Rhetoric faculty began working formally on a major proposal in 1997–98. Talk about the major continued, but there was insufficient

---

6. The prior graduation requirement was simply "writing proficiency" documented by a 2.0 or better in Composition II. Please see "Framework" for the complete new program.

faculty time and energy to move it forward into a formal proposal for many years, given our severely limited number of tenured/tenure-track faculty. We would do some tasks but then teaching, service, and sometimes politics would intervene. We created a mission statement; we gained approval for several individual courses. We drafted and executed a survey of alumni about the importance of writing studies in the professional world. During that time, the Conference on College Composition and Communication (CCCC) offered two extremely valuable workshops on creating a major (in 2001 and 2002), which I attended. And in 2000, Boynton published *Coming of Age: The Advanced Writing Curriculum* (Shamoon, et al.). Both the workshops and the book assisted us in refining our proposal concepts in line with national disciplinary trends and our institutional context.

Within the institution, periodically, we would gather information on the proposal format (which did keep changing). I talked several times with the assistant dean who controlled the CAS curriculum committee agenda. We deliberately kept the idea of the major-proposal-in-progress in front of administrators and faculty friends, though it aroused no great enthusiasm the way I recall a Studio Art proposal did. As I reflect on the problems we had winning approval for the proposal in the CAS curriculum committee, I conclude that part of the difficulty was simply the newness of the discipline: faculty from other departments had never encountered a writing major other than a BFA/creative writing degree, so were not predisposed to support one.[7]

We were careful to bow to institutional pressures; it has been most helpful that several of our faculty have held administrative appointments and chaired or been members of the major university committees, so we have generally been aware of what the hot buttons are. After we had created and obtained approval for individual upper-division courses, we attempted to see that they were taught at least once. At OU, new programs which require significant new funding are rarely approved by university committees and the Board of Trustees. We were under pressure to show that our major would not require either new faculty at the outset or significant change in a faculty teaching commitment to FYC. With most courses approved and taught at least once, we could say honestly that "no new faculty will be required to start up the major" and that tenured and tenure-track faculty would continue their FYC commitment.

7. We were told that one member of the CAS curriculum committee was harsh on our proposal simply because his program's proposal the prior year had been roundly criticized.

THE MAJOR CURRICULUM

Of course, no proposal goes through governance, at least at OU, without considerable revision. Being open to such revisions and receptive to the often-misguided objections of faculty committee members from other disciplines, some of who have unrelated axes to grind, is essential. Since our goal was to win approval, we were compliant rather than defiant. Moreover, several years had passed between the initial drafting and the committee response, years which saw some significant personnel changes and increasing disciplinary emphasis on technology. The final approval of the writing and rhetoric major owes much to the sterling efforts of the two newest tenure-track hires and the tenured faculty member chosen to lead the new department, the three of whom revised the major's structure and coursework into attractive, contemporary disciplinary tracks including new media and writing studies.

The design draws on national disciplinary principles. Writing and rhetoric faculty have incorporated insights from CCCC workshops on the major dating back to 2001, the book *Coming of Age: The Advanced Writing Curriculum*, Kathleen Blake Yancy's 2004 chair's address at CCCC in San Antonio, CCCC presentations on majors in rhetoric and composition (e.g., Giberson 2007), the spring 2007 issue of *Composition Studies* about writing majors, and this collection of how writing majors develop in institutional contexts. Moreover, the OU writing faculty have been active in CCCC and other national disciplinary bodies since the 1970s; our planning for a major reflects that disciplinary focus. Early documents exploring coursework for the proposal for a major (dated 1997–98) include Writing in the Electronic Media and Contemporary Rhetorical Criticism and limit majors to eight credits from rubrics such as COM (Rhetoric and Public Address) or ENG (Business Writing).[8] Had our program been a part of the English department, the course list, even in its early stages, would have likely been much more a hybrid with creative writing, professional/business writing, and possibly some literature courses, rather than a course of study based on current disciplinary strands.

Students majoring in writing and rhetoric will take a twelve-credit, three-course core: WRT 160, Composition II (or equivalent); WRT 340, Issues in Writing and Rhetoric; and WRT 394, Literacy, Technology, and Civic Engagement. Majors then choose one of three tracks: Writing for the

---

8. By historical accident, business writing was housed in the English Department; effective June 2, 2008, the dean has moved it to the Writing and Rhetoric Department.

Professions, Writing for New Media, or Writing as a Discipline. Each track has one required course and three electives. Students take two additional electives (either WRT classes numbered 200 or higher or, with advisor approval, such courses from other departments as ENG 383, Workshop in Fiction, or JRN 200, Newswriting) and a culminating WRT capstone course.[9] The appendix gives the full list of courses in each track.[10]

OVERCOMING SECOND-CLASS CITIZENSHIP

An associate dean at one point suggested we submit a proposal just for a minor, since that approval process at OU is much simpler than for a major, and then in a few years submit a new proposal for the major. We decided against proposing just a minor for two reasons: the amount of work required to prepare the proposal was much the same, and we were certain that arguments for tenure-track positions for a minor would be trumped by other departments' needs in their majors. Approval of the major signals that the writing and rhetoric program has achieved equal status with other university departments and programs. The road has been long and difficult, but we probably would not ever have arrived had we been a part of the English department. From the initial creation of the Department of Learning Skills, the program had overtones of remediation, due both to its name and charge and to the broader faculty's involvement in setting policy for the writing program. I remember a conversation with an English department chair a few years ago, discussing ways our faculty might work together. He offered the possibility that some rhetoric faculty could teach an occasional English class; I countered with the opportunity for English faculty to teach the occasional writing class. His response? "I don't think our faculty would want to do THAT," clearly seeing it as a step down in contrast to the "treat" offered to rhetoric faculty of teaching an English class.

Further, once the writing program was established, the institution and faculty from other disciplines continued to regard writing instruction as something faculty members from any discipline could do: disciplinary expertise was not essential. Staffing has long been problematic. We have a much larger percent and number of contingent faculty than any other OU program, and many of our part-timers came from the

9. Since OU has primarily four-credit classes, a major of forty credits consists of ten classes.
10. For the full program, see http://www4.oakland.edu/?id=5836&sid=32, tab 13, attachment A.

English department's literature-based MA program, developing some composition and rhetoric expertise through our annual spring seminar workshops and other professional development activities. Tenure-track lines have been few and far between—in large part because without a major we were unable to make the argument that we needed to fill a particular "slot" with disciplinary expertise.

Historically, a budget crisis in the early 1980s reinforced the institutional perception that writing was not a discrete discipline, despite the number of rhetoric faculty who either had completed or were completing doctoral work and who were specializing in rhetoric and composition studies. With inadequate enrollments in other departments, OU chose to save tenured positions by assigning faculty from across the university to teach FYC in lieu of some courses in their own programs. Thus the rhetoric program saw tenured faculty from departments as diverse as modern languages, philosophy, music, and political science teaching FYC. Unlike those who taught the Exploratories, these faculty were given some training by OU's compositionists and were teaching FYC rather than integrating writing instruction into courses based in their own disciplines. Many grew to understand the complexity of the task, but few, if any, ever expressed any feeling of inadequacy for the work, particularly those who were abject failures. Within a very few years, university enrollments grew and the "cooperating faculty," as they were termed, gravitated to their home departments, leaving, unfortunately, with the sense (both for themselves and among administrators) that, really, any OU faculty member could teach FYC and (for some) the unenlightened notion that FYC instruction was primarily about "correctness."

As a result, both our course proposals and our major proposal have received scrutiny over the years by non-disciplinary faculty and some powerful administrative staff who consider themselves at least as expert as we, an attitude they would be most unlikely to take with chemistry, say, or theatre. Herein arises perhaps the largest benefit that might have accrued had the writing program been affiliated with English: English faculty were among the most severe critics as we developed the proposal, and their position heavily influenced the CAS curriculum committee. Had we been in the English department, the English faculty would likely have been allies if they had believed in the major, rather than seeing the writing program, as so many of them have for so long, as a service program only. Equally likely, though, is that the literature faculty would have suppressed the idea at the outset.

The residual belief that diverse Oakland faculty and administrators are experts about writing programs has continued to impede our development. Today, for example, among our English department colleagues, too many regard writing instruction as what inexperienced TAs do until they earn their PhDs and find full-time literature positions. Even the College of Arts and Sciences Committee on Instruction, in its initial response to our proposal for a major in rhetoric and writing, inquired, "Might the department want to budget for graduate assistants, perhaps from the [totally literature-based] English M.A. program?" (Elvekrog, 2007). Another example comes from the former chair of the linguistics department. In response to a request from us for a letter of support to accompany the first submission of our proposal, he objected to the entire course plan, offering in a March 2007 e-mail comments such as: "The use of various new technologies does not represent a content area," "A foundational course in writing ought to be an English grammar course," and "Suppose you remove RHT [XXX] from the core courses and add COM 311, Rhetoric and Public Address. . . . This way, you could appeal to the long history of rhetoric 'as an independent discipline'" (Binkert, 2007). Would we have found more understanding and academic support for our discipline if housed in an English department, as so many writing programs have been? Knowing the institutional politics, I think we would have fared differently but likely still would have been second-tier in allocation of positions and support for creating upper-division coursework—and, perhaps, would have been encouraged into creating a hybrid major or restrained from creating a major at all. Helpfully, institutional memory is fading due to retirements, and the writing faculty are gaining recognition across campus as disciplinary experts.

LOOKING AHEAD

Undoubtedly, the writing and rhetoric program faculty are excited about the new era unfolding: holding separate department status, offering a major and minor. Although the current dean explicitly disagreed that having a major was essential to becoming a department, creating the proposal and having sufficient tenured and tenure-track faculty to mount the coursework gave, I believe, more institutional legitimacy to his proposal to move the program into its own CAS department. A deep concern for senior faculty steeped in institutional history was the possibility that the new department would be created before the major completed its journey through governance, with the result that the program would then have some of the status and resource issues of the LS and RCJ periods. Importantly, that worry was resolved this spring. Now we can build on our disciplinary coursework, pedagogy, and research, which have their roots in the establishment of OU's independent writing program at the auspicious time when the rhetoric and composition studies discipline was emerging. The program now looks like an equal player with the other College of Arts and Sciences units, with the opportunity to make the case for tenure-track positions and for less reliance on part-time faculty, to seek grants and other development sources of support, and perhaps to pursue a graduate degree.

REFERENCES

Curriculum: Michigan State University–Oakland. 1959, May 22. Office of the Vice President for Academic Affairs and Provost, Oakland University, Rochester, MI.

Framework: General Education[1,2,3,4]. N.d. The foundation for success: General education at Oakland University. http://www2.oakland.edu/gened/framework.cfm. (accessed June 25, 2007).

Giberson, Gregory A. 2007. The undergraduate major and the future of rhetoric and composition. Paper presented at the annual meeting of the Conference on College Compositionand Communication, New York.

Oakland University Catalog 1966–67. N.d. . Rochester, MI.

Oakland University Senate. 1972. Minutes. http://www3.oakland.edu/oakland/frames.asp?main=http://www.oakland.edu/senate/ (accessed February 26–June 25, 2006).

Oakland University timeline. N.d. http://www3.oakland.edu/oakland/aboutou/popups/history_timeline.htm (accessed May 22, 2007).

Registrar record books. N.d. Office of the Registrar, Oakland University.Rochester, MI.

Shamoon, Linda K., Rebecca Moore Howard, Sandra Jamieson, and Robert A. Schwegler, eds. 2000. *Coming of age: The advanced writing curriculum*. Portsmouth, NH: Boynton/Cook.

2006–09 Agreement AAUP: Between Oakland University and the Oakland University chapter, American Association of University Professors. 2006. Rochester, MI.

Writing major. 2007. *Composition Studies* 36, no. 1 (Spring).

Yancy, Kathleen Blake. 2004. Made not only in words: Composition in a new key. *College Composition and Communication* 56, no. 2 (December):297–328.

APPENDIX
The Oakland University Writing Major Curriculum

Core *(12 credits):*

WRT 160 Composition II *(or equivalent)*

WRT 340 Issues in Writing and Rhetoric *(new course)*

WRT 394 Literacy, Technology, and Civic Engagement *(new course)*

Students will choose one of the following tracks for their major course work and complete both the required course and three of the electives from that track. One of the elective courses may be chosen from another track with the permission of the WRT department chair:

Writing for the Professions *(16 credits):*

WRT 331 Introduction to Professional Writing *(required; new course)*

WRT 305 Advanced Writing: Various Themes *(new course)*

WRT 332 Rhetoric of Web Design *(under development)*

WRT 335 Writing for Human Services Professionals

WRT 341 Rhetoric of Professional Discourse

WRT 350 Service Learning Writing

WRT 380 Persuasive Writing

WRT 382 Business Writing

WRT 381 Scientific and Technical Writing

WRT 460 Writing across the University: Language and Disciplinary Culture

Writing for New Media *(16 credits):*

WRT 330 Digital Culture: Identity and Community *(required)*

WRT 305 Advanced Writing: Various Themes (*new course*)

WRT 231 Composing Audio Essays (*new course*)

WRT 233 Digital Storytelling (*new course*)

WRT 320 Peer Tutoring in Composition

WRT 332 Rhetoric of Web Design (*under development*)

WRT 364 Writing about Culture: Ethnography

WRT 381 Scientific and Technical Writing

Writing as a Discipline *(16 credits)*

WRT 320 Peer Tutoring in Composition *(required)*

WRT 305 Advanced Writing: Various Themes (*new course*)

WRT 341 Rhetoric of Professional Discourse

WRT 342 Contemporary Rhetorical Studies

WRT 350 Service Learning Writing

WRT 364 Writing about Culture: Ethnography

WRT 365 Women Writing Autobiography

WRT 380 Persuasive Writing

WRT 414 Teaching Writing

WRT 460 Writing across the University: Language and
        Disciplinary Culture

5

"BETWEEN THE IDEA AND THE REALITY . . . FALLS THE SHADOW"

The Promise and Peril of a Small College Writing Major

Kelly Lowe
William Macauley

> . . . *most students conclude that the field of English studies entails the study of literature and, to a lesser extent, the teaching of composition.*
> —Janice Lauer, "Rhetoric and Composition"
> in *English Studies: An Introduction to the Discipline(s).*

There is a certain intellectual and emotional appeal to an undergraduate writing major: majors bring students and advisees and money and tenure-lines and your name in the graduation bulletin. A writing major can also indicate that, finally, your institution recognizes writing as a legitimate academic field rather than simply a set of skills to be (quickly) mastered in the service of other majors or as a secondary consideration to "content." So, what could possibly be wrong with a writing major?

Plenty, as it turns out. Our argument is simple: there is nothing wrong with a writing major *per se*. However, there is a lot that *can go wrong* with a writing major and we feel, in our experience in creating, maintaining, and finally leaving a writing major at a small liberal arts college, that we have seen much of what is good about a major and the many pitfalls, traps, and other mishaps that can occur in the development of a writing major at a small college. Whether you are working to begin a writing major or you are sustaining one, we hope that a discussion of some of the issues that presented themselves in our work in developing a writing major will be helpful in supporting yours.

We write this not out of a sense of sour grapes (although, in an effort at full disclosure, it is important to acknowledge that our various levels of dissatisfaction with the writing major led to both of us seeking and finding employment elsewhere), but in the hope that others can learn from our experiences.[1] We can also now, more than two years later, recognize our own culpability in how things went. We write this with the knowledge that nothing is perfect and that, for many, a bad writing major is better than a number of professional alternatives. Finally, we write this with the knowledge that the number of writing majors around the country is growing and that we are not interested in inveighing against any sort(s) of historical inevitability.

That said, we would like to present a case study of one writing major at one school at one time, tracing the development, maturity, and eventual decay of the first iteration of the program. We are most interested in articulating the peculiarities of doing so at a small, somewhat selective, liberal arts school where, as common assumptions might have it, things should be "easier" if for no other reason than there are fewer worries; fewer faculty, smaller majors, and less red tape should, one posits, make change easier. We will present this information in the form of a cautionary tale: We got what we wanted, in a sense, but the price we had to pay for what we got was, in retrospect, far too high.

BACKGROUND: LITERATURE AND WRITING

Before we talk in specifics about our own experiences with a writing major, it is important to take a brief look at the history of the teaching of writing in American colleges and universities. This history is important because the parallels between the development of the teaching of writing and the development of the study of writing are manifest. What we ran into, in short, was the central problem discovered by many of the historians of the discipline: how do you take a second-class subject like writing and keep it from becoming a second-class major? In some sense, of course, this history is as old as education—the turn toward rhetoric as a model for modern composition studies tries to tap into the powerful idea that all education has its roots in the teaching of reading, writing, speaking, and critical thinking.[2] And it does. But the departmental separation of rhetoric from literature in the late nineteenth century has

---

1. Disclosure number 2: Soon after we left, the department made significant changes to the writing major, changes that one or both of us had been advocating for several years. While our intellectual vanity wants to take credit for these changes, chances are they were made independent of our departure.
2. McComiskey's introduction to *English Studies: An Introduction to the Discipline(s)* does a far better job arguing this than we can.

led to the current *de facto* hierarchy: literature and the study of text as primary, writing and the production of text as the subordinate.[3]

Lest we stand accused as raving paranoids, the written histories of the discipline commonly called English and/or English studies seem to bear out the premise that writing is something that has always been the poor stepchild of literature. Gerald Graff's important history of the discipline has often been faulted for only mentioning composition and the teaching of writing a few times. The fact that Graff is telling the truth about the relationship between the teaching of writing and the study of literature only makes it more uncomfortable to consider the strange relationship between the two areas.

In a wonderful way, James Berlin's *Rhetoric and Reality: Writing Instruction in American Colleges*, in offering a strong counter-narrative to Graff's work, seems to, at the same time, confirm the argument that, in Berlin's terms, rhetoric and poetic, while forming the core concerns of an English department, are often featured in a dominant/subordinate relationship. Berlin's argument that "the devalorizing of the writing course in the curriculum was the result of the convergence of a remarkably complex set of forces" (1987, 21), makes for a wonderful story and, at the same time, lays the groundwork for the current sense of anxiety that pervades many rhetoric and composition faculty. Indeed, the story, in brief, is one of opportunism—that, as Berlin argues, seems to revolve around the simple argument that anyone can teach writing, and only the chosen few can teach literature. For instance, Berlin writes that "establishing the entrance test in composition suggested that the ability to write was something the college student ought to bring with him from his preparatory school" (1987, 23) and that

> In order to distinguish the new English department professor from the old rhetoric teacher or the new composition teacher, a new discipline had to be formulated, a discipline based in English as the language of learning and literature as the specialized province of study. (1987, 7)[4]

Robert Scholes makes this same argument in *The Rise and Fall of English*, where he explains:

---

3. We don't want to overstate things—the complicated nature of creative writing seems to wander throughout this tale; it's a subject we'll address throughout.

4. It is important to note, in the above, the use of "professor" and "teacher" in the two disciplinary conceptions Berlin presents.

English departments need composition as the "others" of literature in order to function as they have functioned. The useful, the practical, and even the intelligible were relegated to composition so that literature could stand as the complex embodiment of cultural ideals, based upon texts in which those ideals were so deeply embedded as to require the deep analysis of a trained scholar. Teachers of literature became the priests and theologians of English, while teachers of composition were the nuns, barred from the priesthood doing the shitwork of the field. (1998, 35–6)

Thus, we end up where we are today in so many schools and universities.

Recently (and fortuitously for the writing of this essay), the ugly specter of the literature v. writing divide has shown itself again. As has become an almost yearly ritual, the Writing Program Administration Listserv (WPA-L) online discussion board was consumed, for several weeks in March 2007, with a discussion of the metaphorical War between the States that is rhet/comp/lit. The narrative begins, as it often does, with a story about the different assumptions that faculty sharing the same departmental space often have about the work that one another do. To wit:

So . . . I went to a meeting today where we discussed the development of a new track in rhet/comp at the MA level. According to our track, a student could finish the degree without ever taking a graduate-level literature class . . . although they could take lit if they wanted. The comment was made that this would be okay if we were offering an MA in Rhet/Comp, but since we offer an MA in English with a track in rhet/comp no student should get their degree without taking literature because "literature is the foundation of English."[5]

And so begins a three-week series of e-mails that starts with a discussion of the statement that "literature is the foundation of English" and ends with a discussion of writing programs "divorcing" themselves from literature programs/departments.[6] Perhaps most troubling in this discussion is the realization, soon reached by Elizabeth Wardle, that a "divorce" between rhet/comp and literature isn't always the best solution because "splits were not necessarily resulting in stronger disciplinary standing for rhet/comp."[7] What Wardle has found is something we will address

---

5. Roxanne Kirkwood, posting to WPA-L, March 12, 2007, http://lists.asu.edu/cgi-bin/wa?A0=WPA-L.
6. Scott Rogers, posting to WPA-L, March 18, 2007, http://lists.asu.edu/cgi-bin/wa?A0=WPA-L.
7. Elizabeth Wardle, posting to WPA-L, March 18, 2007, http://lists.asu.edu/cgi-bin/wa?A0=WPA-L.

below: mainly that a writing major inside a strong English department is often, especially in a small school where new tenure lines are infrequent, a far better solution than going it alone. (At our former institution, one to two tenure lines a year for the entire school was the usual. Due to budget issues, there were no new tenure lines for several years during the ten years this study addresses.)

WHY A MAJOR IN WRITING? WHY NOW?

In the original planning documents for the writing major, we made four fairly basic claims having to do with how the major would work both within the department (in concert with the existing major in "English," which was, as many above argue, a major in literature) and within the curricular goals of the college. These claims as originally presented to the department and then to the college, were as follows:

> the concern to help students become better writers has perhaps never been so widely shared across all disciplines and between professional academics and people in many other careers;
>
> the demand—at the secondary and college level—for talented and trained teachers of writing and rhetoric has increased (even as the market for teachers of literature has become increasingly competitive);
>
> in recent decades, the field of English studies has rediscovered its roots in rhetoric and has increasingly recognized rhetorical research and pedagogy as equal in value to work in literature (in practice, it has always been difficult to separate literary study and rhetoric);
>
> the increasing demand in the corporate world not only for trained technical writers, but for all future career professionals to know how to write for business and technical fields. In a survey of nearly 2,000 recent graduates of business administration programs, 88% of respondents indicated that being able to write well is crucial to advancement, and that almost 25% of on-the-job time is spent writing. (Storms 1983, 13)

And here is where the trouble began. The department, at the time it discussed this major, was comprised of nine faculty: seven whose primary mission was to teach literature, one whose primary duty was to teach creative writing (although she had some academic preparation in rhet/comp), and one whose background was in rhetoric, composition, and program administration.[8] The one rhet/comp faculty had a two-course release (from a four/four annual teaching load) to run the writing center, develop the at-the-time new Writing Across the Curriculum (WAC) program, and solidify the summer assessment and placement program for first-year composition. All full-time, tenured and tenure-track faculty were to teach at least 50 percent of their load in first-year composition, although, as we'll see, this didn't always happen.

There was a lot of initial excitement about the major—faculty in the department felt that the major would take students away from the communications department and bring more students to literature and creative writing. There was, at the time, no discussion of what effect a writing major might have on the literature major.

The writing major, as originally developed, had students take a wide variety of classes, many in literature, including the two-semester Foundations course, which would be tweaked to serve as the foundation for all English department majors. Writing majors took a new course, a hybrid history and theory of rhetoric course called Rhetoric for Writers (to differentiate from the rhetoric courses taught in the speech/communications department) and a Senior Portfolio course which was an opportunity for senior writing majors to explore, in-depth, an area of writing which best reflected their intended field(s) of expertise. All well and good.

What happened next should be a familiar story. After lengthy discussions in the department about staffing, intention, and curriculum, it was determined that all writing majors should take a minimum of twelve hours of literature courses (a period, a genre, an elective, and another category which students most often fulfilled by taking literary theory); students also had to take either linguistics and/or history of the language. And nine hours of writing.

The irony was not lost on the writing faculty: a writing major where students took *over half* of their hours in literature (the Foundations course was entirely focused on literature and literary analysis) seemed less writing *major* and more a writing track or literature lite. Of course, as the story goes, we were just happy to be at the grown-ups' table. The major (called, perhaps prophetically, "English without books" by one colleague) was passed unanimously by the department and the faculty

---

8. There were four adjuncts who taught primarily first-year composition. They were not invited to department meetings and had no input into the major.

and was put into place in the fall semester of 1996. As is the case with so many opportunities in academe, the department may have jumped into a major without thinking through the long-term consequences—Kelly was a brand-new hire, the college's first in rhet/comp, and there may well have been a "honeymoon period" involved. That said, whatever the reasons, writing became a major at our college.

And it was a success. Within three years, the number of writing majors was equal to the number of literature majors, and within ten years, writing majors had exceeded the number of literature majors. This is when the sniping began.

As the writing majors began to outnumber the literature majors in literature classes, tension started between students and faculty. Typical comments heard across campus included "writing majors aren't very strong in the literature classes" and "the writing major senior projects are not as strong as those of the literature majors." Sympathetic colleagues from other departments pulled us aside to commiserate. Students ended up in tears in our offices after being told that the writing major was no good and wouldn't get them into a good grad school or land them a good job.

Other problems also presented themselves at this time, which exacerbated these many, albeit common, issues. We continued to hear from administrators (there were five deans in the ten years we were there) that they recognized the "significant levels of dysfunction" in our "deeply divided" department, which fueled our optimism for change. Administrative acknowledgement of our dysfunction, however, did not seem to bring with it any will to help the rhet/comp faculty find the balance they were looking for.

Within the department, we tried to force a number of changes to move each side toward some understanding. For instance, the introduction to the major's course was team-taught every year, over two semesters, by a pair of English department faculty. Until the last two years of our time at the college, it had usually been taught by two lit faculty. However, in an effort to bridge the growing divide between lit and writing, as well as meet the needs of students who were pretty evenly divided between the two majors, the course was team-taught by one lit person and one writing person. The problem this presented, of course, was manifest in the design: it was, for instance, the only team-taught course on campus where the teachers were *assigned* to teach it (as opposed to other courses which were team-taught because two faculty members shared an interest in multiple approaches to a subject). In the two years that one of us taught the course, the writing faculty member often sat quietly in the corner while the literature faculty "introduced" students to the "discipline" of English studies. The end result of this division of labor was, in retrospect, disastrous— students caught on very quickly to the fact that literature faculty had the power, due to their "expertise," to silence writing faculty during any discussion of literature. Discussion of writing, as is shown above in Berlin's discussion and as we demonstrate below, was a different matter.

Other, less formalized, efforts were made to bring the teaching of our senior majors together—to bring to their capstone a balance of writing and lit. These efforts sometimes resulted in cooperative capstone presentations, sometimes in capstone classes meeting together. There is no question that efforts were being made in good faith.

However, it just seemed like too little, too late. At this distance or closer, it is impossible to say what made these efforts less than healing. Was there just too much frustration within the department for these Band-Aids to help? Did the courses perpetuate the hierarchy in even more personal ways? Had the writing folks given up? Was there just too much evidence that these efforts were disingenuous? Although most, if not all, of these options were considered and discussed at some point, there was just no way to tell.

The question of why these conflicts continued when we all had ample opportunity to discuss and address them, unfortunately, involves some speculation. While there is a certain vanity that argues that of course the literature faculty were jealous of our success, there is no empirical proof of this. And while there is some anecdotal evidence that the writing faculty "copped an attitude" about the necessity for changes, we rest easy in knowing that whatever divisions there ended up being seem indicative of the kind of split that Berlin and Scholes describe in their respective histories of the discipline—that much of the discomfort the literature faculty felt was not jealousy so much as a misunderstanding of the mission of writing with/in a larger English studies curriculum. For instance, the unease that many in literature felt about the writing majors' senior portfolio projects—that they weren't as "serious" as the literature majors' twenty-page critical paper—is indicative of a *way of seeing* English studies that is fairly narrow in its focus. This unease, we would argue, is simply a deeper unease that manifests itself with students as proxies; the unease is born out of what Bruce McComiskey argues lies at the heart of the debate between literature and rhet/comp:

For example, scholarship in English education and rhetoric and composition is often "pedagogical." While pedagogical scholarship is highly valued in the disciplinary structures of English education and rhetoric and composition, in the context of tenure criteria based in literary studies, it is worth less than theoretical criticism. (2006, 29)

So it then stands to reason that students who are being taught and evaluated based upon their ability, as seniors, to produce a piece of "theoretical criticism," are judged as working harder than those students engaged in senior projects having to do with pedagogy or creative writing, as most of the writing majors were. We did wonder at times if they were right, but, consistently, we looked at the amount of work students did in each major, and they were certainly comparable in terms of difficulty.

So the writing major, in part, fell victim to a certain kind of success—an increasing number of majors—which carried with it some less comfortable questions: those having to do with personnel decisions and curricular and departmental priorities. This success, and again we are supposing to a certain extent, was explained away by our colleagues as due in part to the fact that the writing major was more "fun" and less "serious"—primarily because the production of texts, even multiple drafts in multiple genres, was viewed as less challenging than the theoretical engagement with literature.

By fall of 2001, when Bill arrived on campus, there was already interest in revising the writing major, in hopes of making it more focused on writing. In fact, Kelly had been arguing for some time that continued development was not only necessary but useful. Bill found himself in three different kinds of conversations about the writing major. In his on-campus interview conversations, he was told that the writing major was growing and that continued development was expected, to which he was encouraged to contribute. In private conversations with several literature faculty members, he was told that the writing major was unfocused and declining, not worthy of his time or energy. In yet another kind of conversation with various groups outside of the English department, he was told that the writing major was a target for the English department because they really didn't want to teach writing at all (with the exclusion of Kelly).

It is perhaps informative in our cautionary tale to try and pinpoint where the divisiveness about the revisions of the major began. One area of long-standing tension was that the students enrolled in the writing major

were taking the vast majority of their coursework in literature; this curriculum, however, had left the literature faculty very satisfied with the writing
major as it stood, and thus any desire they had for change was relative.

While it is easy to say in retrospect, it is important to understand that
there was no malice toward literature classes being included in the writing major; as a department, we all believed in the importance of both
reading and writing to both the English and writing majors. However,
after initial research by Bill, we discovered rather quickly that writing
courses comprised less than half of the curriculum in the writing major
(56 percent literature). This fact alone wouldn't have been so bad, but
we also discovered that the literature major only asked students to take
one writing course, which could be a creative writing course, the department's Advanced Writing course or its Business and Technical Writing
course. This seemed, to the writing faculty, an odd contrast and distribution of courses and resources.

Of course, there were significant contextual issues to be considered, a
point to which we will return later in the chapter. To wit: more than two-
thirds of the permanent faculty in the English department, in 2001, had
a background and/or training in literature, and, while they did assign
writing in their courses, they taught few writing courses. Their expertise
was needed in their areas of interest as well as in the general education
introduction to literature courses (a significant part of the department's
obligation to the college's general education curriculum). Although
some might argue the point (as, in fact, we did), *teaching writing* and
assigning writing are not exactly synonymous activities. That left the
majority of the writing courses, both for the majors and, significantly, for
the rest of campus, to the two of us, along with a complement of visiting
and adjunct faculty members. It is also important to note that both of us
had significant administrative duties that hampered our ability to teach
the full range of courses we needed to.

Almost from the start, Bill was not particularly careful about sharing
his perceptions of the writing major with Kelly and, to be truthful, part
of what attracted him to the college was the opportunity to develop the
writing major. Because Kelly had worked long and hard to make the writing major happen, it was often difficult for him and Bill to discuss revising the major without feeling criticized and/or Bill feeling misled about
the department's intentions about the writing major (as Kelly was one
of the two initial interviewers Bill met at MLA the winter before). This
is due, in no small part, to Kelly's personalization of the major—from

1996–2001, Kelly had been the only full-time faculty member working on/with the major and, by Bill's arrival in 2001, any critique of the program, constructive or otherwise, was seen by Kelly as a personal attack.

We knew that we had to protect our working relationship and our growing friendship, so, many times, when things got a little tense around revisions of the writing major, we had the good sense to leave it alone for a while. Having said that, there was never a time during Bill's four years at the college, or Kelly's ten years, when revision of the writing major was not a primary focus of departmental discussions, even if action and/or movement on revision was not. In retrospect, we are sure that the other members of the department must have been exhausted by our unrelenting insistence on talking about it.

In fall 2001, Bill's first semester on campus, it seemed clear and necessary to him that the department should consider what it was doing in terms of resources and majors. The department seemed split into two camps: folks who wanted the writing major to change and become more focused on writing and others who seemed tired of hearing about it and/or were happy with the writing major being 56 percent literature. But the conversations continued—one would focus on specific courses and the next on the relationships between the majors, then back to specific courses. Bill discussed with Kelly the need to break this trend and proposed looking at the distribution of resources in relation to courses and majors. So Bill prepared a report on resource allocations within the department.

At that time, the most salient points were these:

- More than half of the courses offered by the English department were first-year composition courses (57 percent)
- Writing majors and English majors were nearly equal, 46 percent and 54 percent of English department majors, respectively
- Ratio of literature sections offered to writing sections offered: 1:2
- Ratio of tenured literature faculty to tenured or tenure-track writing faculty: 2:1

A lot of this should not be surprising; this is a more than a twice-told tale. And it makes sense based on the resources in place.

However, not less than three years later, writing majors had overtaken English majors (51 percent and 49 percent of English department majors, respectively), and there had been some improvement in the ratio of literature sections to writing sections: 1:1.5. Even so, the lit/writing faculty ratio remained unchanged at 2:1. The data made it impossible to ignore the fact that the writing major was growing and the English major was declining, which, and again we're supposing here, certainly must have been disconcerting for the lit folks.[9]

Here, unfortunately, is where we dip again into the murky world of *perception*. While both of us were party to a number of public discussions of the major, we realize that some of what we describe below is in part a we-said-they-said argument. We have done our best to ground our discussion in personal recollections as well as with conversations with students who were, unfortunately, involved far more than anyone would have liked in the growing turmoil surrounding the major.

The most common response of the literature faculty to discussions of the writing major was that the writing major was too *unfocused*. We never did get to a good definition of what "unfocused" meant. It may be, as was discussed briefly above, that since the writing major didn't resemble the kinds of sequencing that went on in the literature major (i.e., first you take an introduction to the major, then follow with courses on British and American periods, literary genres, and critical theory, ending with a senior project), the literature faculty couldn't recognize it. It could have been considered "unfocused" because it allowed students to construct a sequence of courses that had seemingly nothing to do with one another. Or it could have been considered "unfocused" because the work that the students were doing involved a more product-based curriculum—that the literature major, wherein students were being taught theories and frameworks, was somehow more tightly focused than a writing major where students were, strangely enough, often just writing.

Despite all of the discussion about focus, however, prior to our departures (both at the end of the spring 2005 semester), the department had not been able to see the relationship between the lack of development of the writing major and its seeming lack of focus.

For both of us, it seemed a no-brainer—40 percent of the courses listed by the department were writing courses, and more than half of

---

9. An interesting number to consider here is that the total number of majors stayed relatively the same—so our hope of growing the total number of English majors was not coming true; what seemed to be happening is that many students who either were literature majors or potential literature majors ended up graduating as writing majors. We have no way of knowing why this might have happened.

the majors in the department were writing majors; yet 62 percent of the courses offered in the catalog were literature courses while only 18 percent of the courses offered in the catalog were writing.[10] The two sets of data just didn't add up.

Fall of 2003 saw the arrival of a new rhetoric and composition faculty member. Kelly and Bill did their best to keep him informed but protect him from the discord. He was bright enough, so we couldn't hide it from him, and, when we did work together toward revision, he was a full participant in our discussions even when he was not outspoken departmentally or publicly. He was able to come away unscathed and has had great success in working with the rest of the department since our departures, and he has proven much more successful in working with his colleagues in literature. He has indeed managed to see a very significant revision of the writing major sail through the department and the college. Our hats are off to him and our former colleagues.

One issue that at least Bill had not foreseen was that, even though he shared an English department with other English faculty, his work was considerably different from what the majority of his colleagues did. Many conversations within the department equated the assigning of writing with the teaching of writing just as, in the other direction, he had many times equated assigning readings with teaching literature. Bill realizes that, had he recognized the need, he could have done much more to work with the literature faculty. The irony is not lost on him now—he complained about his lit colleagues not understanding what he was saying and doing while he was not explaining his goals clearly or sharing the reasons for his actions.[11]

But he had a lot on his plate. Beyond struggling with a major and departmental discord, it took a great deal of energy and attention to keep our newest colleague informed while working hard to not sour him on the department before he even had a chance to get to know his new colleagues and to encourage his participation in decision making while guarding him from actions and roles that we thought would prove detrimental. We worried, too, that we were being too paternalistic, though our new colleague seemed to welcome our insights and council.

10. The other 20 percent of courses offered within the catalog could not be neatly fit into either literature or writing, usually because these courses were rhetoric courses, special topics courses, team-taught courses offered as interdisciplinary courses, and/or team-taught courses staffed by faculty from both groups.

11. In some ways Kelly had it easier—as a rhetorical theorist, he was able to make some connections with those in the department who taught literary theory.

With increasing numbers in the writing major and declining numbers in the literature major, as well as increasing numbers of writing courses needing to be offered and staffed and declining enrollments in literature courses, it seems clear now just how complicated all of this was. Could we have done more to build relationships? Sure. Could we have done more to invite our colleagues into what we were doing and wanted? Maybe. Would either have made any difference? No way to tell.

SOME TENTATIVE CONCLUSIONS

Any number of speculations are possible about why things played out the way they did. In retrospect, Bill can see that he was a little too eager to get in there and change things, based on a range of discussions within the department and elsewhere. This did nothing to improve the chances of greater harmony between lit and writing at the college while at the same time causing significant tension with Kelly. Kelly, by the time Bill arrived, was frustrated and tired of being the focal point for both the lit faculty's complaints about the writing major and their unwillingness to do anything about those complaints themselves. The messages we seemed to be receiving were thus: *Kelly, the writing major is problematic and you have to change it, but we will decide what the problems are and when and how those changes will occur, if at all. Bill, you change the writing major because it is too unfocused but, again, we will not define "focus" nor will we let you have any control over said process.* The real problem lay, however, in the fact that there was never a time when anyone within the English department said that they were satisfied with the writing major in terms of its construction, focus, or purpose, even if their lack of action in changing it indicated otherwise. The writing major was there. It was consistently attracting students, even increasing numbers of students, but the English department never seemed able to reconsider its design in any effective way. We could never get it focused to our collective satisfaction. We could never agree on its purpose. The reasons for this are a mystery to both of us. There was, in our last year, even some discussion of moving the major to another department, which seemed a more productive option, at least to Bill and our new colleague, than continuing to beat our heads against the wall in the English department. Kelly thought otherwise and continued to hope that we could work things out within the English department. Maybe we should have just left well enough alone. Maybe not.

The worst part of it all, really, was that the students were not blind to these conflicts. Indeed, it was surprising to us just how much the students, both in writing and in literature, were able to sense the tensions with/in the department. It was never our intention to drag students into the fray, and, for the most part, we, as a department, did an okay job of this. We, as a collective whole, could have done better. But, then again, that can be said about the whole endeavor.

SO WHAT HAVE WE LEARNED?

There are a number of lessons to be taken away from our experience with/in a growing writing major. Here are the key things we learned:

1. There needs, if at all possible, to be a "critical mass" of interested faculty from the jump. While it's obviously dicey to argue for positions where there is no major or minor to feed, the if-you-build-it-then-we-can-hire attitude is problematic. As our experience showed us, even hiring a second and then a third rhetoric and composition faculty member did very little to make our daily lives and the lives of our students much better. Indeed, what happened to us, in short, was in large part a neat little piece of circular rhetoric: writing can be taught by anyone; (because of necessity) writing majors can be taught by literature faculty; because anyone can teach these courses, they must not need specialized training; any major that doesn't need specialized training must be "weaker" than one that does; therefore, the writing major is weak. This argument, perhaps, wouldn't have been so devastating if there had been two or three writing faculty there to begin with or a departmental commitment to writing as a major and, by extension, as a discipline.

2. A second issue we ran into is also related to hiring. One of the issues we had in hiring a second, and then a third, writing faculty member was that the stakes seemed so high—that we were doing more than hiring another faculty member. Because this faculty member would be, at times, *the only other person on campus who recognized what we were doing,* the issue was fraught with much deeper issues of collegiality and indeed friendship. As we recognized right away, we had a relationship that was both professional and personal—questions of how to disagree professionally while at the same time maintain a personal friendship were difficult to answer.

3. Our third realization was that we needed to build the major and then hire for it. Let us explain. In 2003, we were given the opportunity to add an additional rhetoric and composition faculty line to the department. Ongoing discussions of the major were put on hold, indefinitely, in order to bring the new hire in and let him or her help construct the new major, as was the case when Bill was hired. This sounded good on paper. What we did was spend another two years going around the same turf, bringing the new colleague "up to speed" on where things stood and encouraging him to fully participate in building the new major. The reality of the situation was that the new hire had ideas of his own that needed to be integrated into the existing major, thus necessitating another two-year cycle of potential revisions to the major, discussions in the department, and despair on the part of Bill and Kelly (even though our own efforts to "protect" the new hire may have contributed to this despair and our new colleague's inability to recognize the reality of that despair). As well, constructing the major would have allowed us to be focused in our hiring, knowing exactly who we were looking for instead of casting a wide net and hiring the best person available, whether or not they 'fit' into what we were doing or intended to do. In fact, we never really knew whether the new hire 'fit' or not because the state of the revisions at that point was so unclear. In retrospect, he is a better fit than either of us turned out to be.

4. One final exhortation or realization: Build a place for the new major in the minds and working lives of the department as well as the college or university, one that calls for their relying on it. It was clear that a number of folks didn't "get" the writing major, which may or may not have been by choice, especially given the English department's institutional reputation for being resistant to teaching writing. Because the college did not have to rely on the writing major for any reason, they did not have to care about its success or failure. However, if a major like this is going to work in a small English department and/or a small college, folks other than those who will be working in that major need to have a vested interest in its success. The success of the major has to be essential for them too.

There may well be no way past the difficulty highlighted above: that there are significant differences in how writing, including both the study and teaching thereof, is perceived both within and outside an English department. The fact that many teachers of writing are interested in things that go beyond a particularly recognizable specialty makes many, if not most, conversations in an English studies program difficult. If one faculty member is a Hemingway scholar and another looks at quantitative analysis of first-year composition errors, there is not only little common ground but a sort of built-in hierarchy that seems to only be encouraged by a departmental ethos that places theoretical work above either quantitative research and/or meta-analysis.[12]

It's a delicate balance—and there is no way that our narrative can prepare any department for taking on something like this. However, that balance must be tended with careful, gentle, and attentive hands and minds—a tough balance to maintain and one for which both of us now have a much higher appreciation.

REFERENCES

Berlin, James. 1987. *Rhetoric and reality: Writing instruction in American colleges, 1900–1985.* Carbondale: Southern Illinois University Press.

Graff, Gerald. 1989. *Professing literature: An institutional history.* Chicago, IL: University of Chicago Press.

Lauer, Janice. 2006. Rhetoric and composition. In McComiskey, 2006.

McComiskey, Bruce, ed. 2006. *English Studies: An introduction to the discipline(s).* Urbana, IL: National Council of Teachers of English.

Scholes, Robert. 1998. *The rise and fall of English.* New Haven, CT: Yale University Press.

Storms, C. Gilbert. 1983. What business school graduates say about the writing they do at work: Implications for the business communications course. *ABCA Bulletin* (December: 13–18).

12. And, to be fair, this ethos is often driven by tenure and promotion guidelines that place theoretical work above other kinds of work.

6

THE WRITING MAJOR
AS SHARED COMMITMENT

Rodney F. Dick

*[O]ur responsibility to the English major . . . [is] to get him [sic] to read
with understanding and pleasure the monuments of English literature.*
—Herbert Weisinger, "The Problem
of the English Major," *College English*

*What is needed is a paradigm shift from thinking of English as a field to
thinking of it as a discipline.*
—Robert Scholes, *The Rise and Fall of English:
Reconstructing English as a Discipline*

*English Studies can move from being a set of unrelated sub-disciplines to
a powerful collection of integrated (structurally separate but functionally
interrelated) disciplines with a coherent and collective goal that does not
compromise each discipline's unique integrity . . . the analysis, critique
and production of discourse in social context.*
—Bruce McComiskey, *English Studies:
An Introduction to the Discipline(s)*

In 1945, Herbert Weisinger and his colleagues at Michigan State University felt they had reason to worry about the state of the field of English studies. To summarize the complaint using his own words: "The first and most serious charge which I shall lay against the present method [of preparation] is that the major can complete his work without having studied many of the important works in the history of English literature" (342). Weisinger's solution, of course, is a list of great works that should be read from "cover to cover" and a six-semester curriculum guide, providing teachers with an order to present the readings to students and the number of course hours to spend teaching each work (738 total hours). There is no doubt that what is meant by *English studies* as a field or as a discipline has changed quite drastically over the past half century. And, while English studies no longer means solely the study of literature and literary theory, it may be misleading to imply that there ever was a unified discipline called English. As Gerald Graff notes, "The quest for a precise definition of the discipline of English has been a persistent one since the founding of English Studies as an academic subject about a century ago" (1996, 15). In fact, Graff argues that the literature versus composition rift is only the latest in a series of arguments that mark a tumultuous history of English studies as a discipline. The re-introduction of rhetoric and the introduction of composition and writing studies to English departments have only redefined the players in the "us" versus "them" debate in the field of English and in English departments across the nation.

At present, continued efforts to redefine composition as a discipline and writing as an academic endeavor (Bloom, Daiker, and White 1996; Yancey 2004) have forced English departments that house writing programs (reluctantly or not) to reexamine the relationship between literature and writing. In their study of how specialized writing courses have affected English departments, Chapman, Harris, and Hult (1995) found that while many schools did experience tension between literature and writing faculty, several other schools indicated a rapprochement between the two:

> In these programs the dichotomy of literature versus composition, *theoria* versus *praxis*, *techne* versus *humanitas* seems to be giving way to a synthesis of writing and reading as mutually supportive activities intended not merely to refine human sensibility but to enable and empower students in the academy and beyond. (427)

While most of the professionalization of writing faculty occurs at larger, public research institutions—through graduate programs and research and scholarly pursuits (Brown, Meyer, and Enos 1994)—many undergraduate writing programs exist within much smaller, private and liberal arts colleges and universities. And while some of the students who major in writing will enter graduate school, many more will enter the professional world or become English or language arts teachers in middle and high schools. Additionally, some scholars critique the assumption that the default goal of studying writing should be to reproduce students who are sympathetic to our "cause" rather than making ourselves and our expertise useful to them (Bullock 2000, 21). As we develop curricula that better attend to the changing nature of composition and writing studies, it is equally necessary that our faculty who make commitments to teaching within these writing majors and English departments at smaller schools remain open to engendering the study of *an* "English" that values writing and literature, rhetoric and theory, producing and consuming texts, rather than forcing students to accept the disciplinary fault lines between rhetoric and composition and literature, "us" and "them." As Chapman, Harris, and Hult argue, "The challenge we face is not simply to replace the old hegemony of literature with a new hegemony of composition but to construct a new English department" where the two are "mutually valued and mutually supportive activities" (1995, 429). Other scholars agree with a wider context for English studies.

In their "intellectual history" of composition studies, Nystrand, Greene, and Wiemelt (1993) argue that the development of composition studies needs to be understood in a broader context that affects linguistics, literary studies, and theory as well as composition. Moreover, Robert Scholes concludes his book *The Rise and Fall of English* by proposing that the new English should be a discipline "based on rhetoric and the teaching of reading and writing over a broad range of texts" (1998, 179). Finally, in the most recent, and perhaps compelling, reevaluation of the field of English studies, Bruce McComiskey argues that English studies can grow from a group of unrelated sub-disciplines to an integration of interrelated disciplines *if and only if* they share a coherent and collective goal:

> I propose that the goal of this integrated English studies should be the analysis, critique and production of discourse in social context. And all of the various disciplines that make up English studies—linguistics and discourse analysis, rhetoric and composition, creative writing, literature and literary criticism, critical theory and cultural studies, and English education—contribute equally important functions toward accomplishing this goal. But there must be constant dialectical contact between the specialized disciplines and the larger project of English studies in order to curb further separation and divisiveness. (2006, 43)

This prompt to redefine the role of writing in English studies has also prompted other scholars to historicize, theorize, and postulate about the shape of "a" writing discipline (Shamoon, Howard, Jamieson, and Schwegler 2000; Carpini 2007; Lowe 2007; Newman 2007). And the trend toward recognizing, refining and redefining a "writing" discipline shows no signs of waning.

The writing major at Mount Union College has undergone significant revision in the past years, especially as the writing and literature faculty have reexamined what it means to have a writing major in response to a larger liberal arts imperative. This chapter will discuss this re-envisioned writing major and argue that at such small, liberal arts schools the success of a writing major may lie in the embracing of a disciplinary "middle ground" of English studies rooted in a shared commitment to literature *and* writing, rhetoric *and* theory, producing *and* consuming texts. Moreover, such a shared commitment does not threaten the intellectual or professional integrity of rhetoric and composition as a valid or salient academic pursuit. Writing majors, minors, and concentrations within English departments can and should be recognized as locations having the potential to bridge institutional mandates toward professionalization and liberal arts endeavors toward humanistic education, rather than as divisive forces threatening to make the study of English less "liberal artsy." Likewise, writing studies within traditionally literature-based English departments can and should recognize the potential in and build upon the position of liberal arts privilege afforded by the connection to literature.

THE BEGINNING OF A "WRITING" CONCENTRATION AT MOUNT UNION COLLEGE

In its first iteration in 1987, the writing concentration (termed a "writing minor") in the English department at Mount Union College consisted of fifteen credit hours and included two courses in English language, two "writing" courses, and one experiential course.

Fig 1. Writing Minor 1987

Language (6 cr.)

> EH 235: Practical English Grammar
>
> EH 390: Structure of the English Language

Writing (6 cr.)

> EH 240: Business and Technical Writing
>
> Either EH 215: Creative Writing *or* EH 245: Advanced Writing

Experiential (3 cr.)

EH 499: Internship in English

Robert A. Schwegler (2000) argues that a curriculum is a "set of practices and material conditions" more than simply a collection of courses (25). The formation of the writing minor at Mount Union College constituted a specialization more than a collection of courses that share a disciplinary prefix. In its initial iteration, the "shape" of the minor made an argument for a writing specialization emphasizing the study of the English language and its application through practice and apprenticeship. For instance, the language courses for the writing minor included a 200-level "practical application" of grammar, punctuation, conventions, and usage in addition to a 300-level course titled Structure of the English Language, focusing on the structure of modern English with an emphasis on grammatical analysis.

Along with an understanding of language through syntax and grammar, the writing minor included a component of "practice" constituted through writing courses. And there was some flexibility included between creative or advanced writing. The creative writing course, defined in the 1987-1989 catalogue as an "exploration of the creative process," including the "directed writing of short stories and poems," provided broad coverage of the creative writing process and the most popular genres (1987, 99). Additionally, the "advanced" writing course emphasized the "development of skills" needed to generate and organize ideas, edit text, and adapt writing to various audiences (99). Essentially, advanced writing was an advanced "college writing"—more of the same only harder. Both "general" writing courses existed prior to the constitution of the writing minor and were included as an either/or option in the English (literature) major. Without question, though, the creation of business and technical writing as the first "specialized" writing course shows the expectations for and direction of the writing minor. Unlike the two general writing courses, like most other courses in business and professional and technical writing (especially those found in liberal arts colleges), the course was defined as the study and application of writing genres within business, industry, and the basic sciences emphasizing genres and writing situations "related to employment" (99). And, to some extent, the course can be seen as much as a "service" course for students majoring in more pre-professional programs (such as business, management, and accountancy) as one belonging to the English department, faculty, and students. However, the business and technical writing course was added to the English curriculum concurrently with the formation of the writing minor, as was the course in "practical" grammar, though the other courses, including creative and advanced writing and the English-language course, had been part of the existing English major and minor. As part of an English department emphasizing the study of language, literature, and literary history, a writing minor focusing on attaining and applying practical language and writing skills seems less humanistic but is typical of writing courses in English departments throughout the 1980s (Werner, Thompson, and Rothschild 1998).

Moreover, a comparison of course offerings between 1983 and 1993 indicates that, except for the introduction of the one course in business and technical writing, no changes to the English department curriculum contradict this bifurcation of specializations within the English department.

Table 1. Course Breakdown (1983–1993)

		100-level	200-level	300-level	400-level	Total
1983–1987	LT	1	9	9	5	24
	WR	1	2	0	0	3
	ED	0	1	3	0	4
	LA	0	0	1	1	2
1987–1993	LT	1	9	10	3	23
	WR	1	3	0	0	4
	ED	0	1	0	0	1
	LA	0	1	1	1	3

The other curricular changes made to the English department at Mount Union College during the same period show that the department and its faculty were consciously and actively thinking about ways to reformulate the curriculum to better reflect the state of the field. And these curricular changes—combining two 400-level Shakespeare courses into one, replacing courses on Chaucer and Milton with a major authors course, and adding a course in the English Renaissance—resulted in an overall reduction of one literature course and an increase in one writing course. However, the overall effect of the addition of a specialization in writing on the English curriculum was less perceptible than that caused by the reformation of the literature emphasis. This is shown by the clear disparity of courses devoted to each specialization (23 to 4) and by the fact that the number of language and linguistics courses (3) nearly equaled the number of writing courses (4).

In the years directly following the formation of the writing minor in the English department, two additional curricular changes reflect the status of writing as a specialization: the relocation of educational methods courses from the English department curriculum to the department of education and the creation of a separate English as a Second Language (ESL) writing course to support an increasingly internationalized student body. This course, along with similar courses covering communication and reading, shared the English prefix (EH) but were listed separately in the course catalogue under the ESL program. No further significant curricular changes in the writing specialization occur until the fall of 1993, the year after the English department hired its first "writing" specialist.

THE FIRST "MINOR" REVISION: TOWARD A WRITING SPECIALIZATION (1993)

Though the writing minor was provided a loose skeleton in 1987, the curricular alterations occurring before the 1993 academic year began to add flesh to a more rigorous writing specialization. This emerging specialization was due, in part, to significant changes occurring in the English department as a whole, including the expansion of the major to 36 and the minors to 18 credit hours and the focused separation of the one upper-division linguistics course into two discrete language-emphasized courses (introduction to linguistics and history of the English language). Other curricular changes resulted from a real expansion of courses dedicated to and created specifically for a specialization in writing. The most significant of which included the separation of the generic creative writing course into two (focusing on the study and crafting of short fiction and poetry) and the creation of a course titled "Teaching Writing and Rhetoric."

Fig 2. Writing Minor Revision 1993

Language (6 cr.)

    EH 235: Practical English Grammar

    Either EH 385: Introduction to Linguistics *or*
    EH 405: History of the English Language

Writing (9 cr.)

>*Either* EH 216: Writing Short Fiction *or*
>EH 217: Writing Poetry
>
>EH 240: Business and Technical Writing
>
>*Either* EH 245: Advanced Writing *or*
>EH 300: Teaching Writing and Rhetoric

Guided Elective (3 cr.)

>*Either* Additional Language *or*
>Additional Writing *or*
>EH 499: Internship in English

Overall, the changes, though rather significant in that they expanded the choices offered to students choosing to specialize in writing as a minor field of study, offered support for the already-established direction for the writing minor as a grafting together of creative and professional writing, language and linguistics, and pedagogy. Other, more subtle, changes allowed students flexibility of foci. For instance, students interested in pursuing "professional" writing did not have to take as many pedagogy courses; future teachers could opt out of the internship in favor of additional language or writing courses. Creative writers could take more courses in creative writing. The tenor of the concentration, though, in this newer iteration still rested in the combination of these foundational areas. Finally, the inclusion of the first upper-division writing course marked a departure of sorts—as the implication of upper-division courses in the college-wide curriculum is that such courses offer focused and in-depth studies rather than a general introduction.

Table 2. Course Breakdown (1993–1997)

		100-level	200-level	300-level	400-level	Total
1993–1997	LT	1	10	14	4	29
	WR	3	4	1	0	8
	ED	0	1	1	0	2
	LA	0	1	1	1	3

One final change proffered by the curricular revision between 1993 and 1995 was the creation of a writing across the curriculum (WAC) program. The writing initiative, unveiled during the 1995 academic year, was a combination of WAC and writing within the disciplines (WID), consisting mainly of a requirement that all students complete "writing-intensive" (W) courses from three disciplinary areas across the curriculum. In addition to the extra-departmental consequences—every department in the college was responsible for developing and teaching their own writing-intensive courses—because the first step of the WAC initiative was a writing assessment, the English department added two additional college writing courses (one for basic writers and one for advanced writers) to create a three-tiered college writing hierarchy.

Finally, to facilitate and support the increased demand on faculty as they learned to teach more and specific writing-intensive courses in their areas of specialization and to support students' fluency and success developing and honing writing skills, the first writing center was established. More than simply departmental changes, the creation of a WAC program and writing center can be seen as reflecting the importance of writing and writing-based initiatives on an institutional scale. However, the work was begun in and by faculty in the English department and, by large part, the formation, implementation, and maintenance of the institutional writing initiatives was overseen by a writing specialist in English. Moreover, perhaps because of the need to support and develop the writing initiatives, the English department hired a second, full-time tenure-track writing specialist. Along with the growth of the writing curriculum, such administrative developments attest to the growing need for and stature of writing specialists, both in the English department and at the college in general. And the momentum brought about by these curricular changes, as well as the expertise offered by the two writing specialists within the English department, would continue for the next two years, culminating in the inception of a writing major in 1997.

THE FIRST "MAJOR" REVISION: SPECIALIZATION AND THE "WRITING MAJOR" (1997)

One significant change to the writing specialization at the level of the minor from 1993 to 1997 was the inclusion of a "departmental core" comprising a sophomore sequence designed to introduce all students to the study of English. This sequence, titled "Human Experience in Language and Literature" (perhaps aptly given the moniker HELL), was created and implemented in the curriculum for the English major and minor in 1993. The curricular changes sparked by the creation of the writing major, however, which included the inclusion of the HELL sequence for the new major, also brought about its inclusion in the minor. A second significant curricular change concomitant with the new major was the inception of four new writing-specific courses, including the department's first course in rhetorical theory and application, two lower-division genre courses (drama and nonfiction), and the senior capstone course (the senior portfolio) for writing majors paralleling the senior capstone for the English major, a college-wide general education requirement.

Fig 3. Writing Minor Revision 1997

Departmental Core (6 cr.)

> EH 295: Human Experience in Language and Literature I
>
> EH 296: Human Experience in Language and Literature II

Rhetoric (3 cr.)

> EH 225: Introduction To Rhetoric For Writers

Language (3 cr.)

> *Either* EH 385: Introduction to Linguistics
> *or* EH 405: History of the English Language

Writing (6 cr.)

> *Either* EH 216: Writing Short Fiction *or*
>
> EH 217: Writing Poetry *or*
>
> EH 240: Business and Technical Writing *or*
>
> EH 243: Writing Drama *or*
>
> EH 245: Advanced Writing *or*
>
> EH 247: Reading and Writing Literary Nonfiction *or*
>
> EH 300: Teaching Writing and Rhetoric *or*
>
> EH 499: Internship in English

Despite the new courses, because of the decision to include the departmental sophomore sequence, the overall effect on the writing minor was a reduction in the number of both language and writing credits required (from 6 to 3 and 9 to 6 credits, respectively). The decision by the department faculty, including both writing and literature specialists, to maintain a departmental "core" experience for all students, though not inherently undermining of either the study of literature or writing, did prove to have consequences for both areas of emphasis. This decision can be interpreted as a reflection of an interest to stay rooted in a shared commitment to the pursuit of English studies while also remaining sensitive to the need to address the growing specializations in the field. As was the case with the writing minor, the inclusion of the departmental core (constituting 6 credit hours) affected the number of credit hours required in specialized writing courses.

Fig 4. Writing Major 1997

Departmental Core (9 cr.)

>   EH 295: Human Experience in Language and Literature I

>   EH 296: Human Experience in Language and Literature II

>   EH 435: Senior Portfolio

Rhetoric (3 cr.)

>   EH 225: Introduction to Rhetoric for Writers

Language (3 cr.)

>   *Either* EH 385: Introduction to Linguistics *or*
>   EH 405: History of the English Language

Literature (9 cr.)

>   Period Course

>   Genre Course

>   Literature Elective

Writing (9 cr.)

>   Professional Writing:

>>   Print Media (in comm. dept.)

>>   Broadcast Media (in comm. dept.)

>>   Nonfiction/Belle Lettres:

>>>   EH 240: Business and Technical Writing

EH 245 Advanced Writing

EH 247: Reading and Writing Literary Nonfiction

Creative Writing:

EH 216: Writing Short Fiction

EH 217: Writing Poetry

EH 243: Writing Drama

Teaching Writing:

EH 210: Children's Literature

EH 235: Practical English Grammar

EH 300: Teaching Writing and Rhetoric

Experiential/Directed Study (3 cr.)

Either EH 450: Independent Study in English *or*
EH 499: Internship in English

Moreover and perhaps more reflective of the desire to maintain a sense of shared commitment to a traditional literature-driven English studies was the decision to require an equal number of credit hours of literature courses as writing courses for the new writing major (9 credits). And, as is the case at most institutions and with most new areas of specialization, the new writing major also reflected an attempt to collect together existing courses in addition to filling gaps by creating new courses, especially given the institutional resistance to create new curricular areas without a demonstrated need and without demonstrating that existing resources (including faculty) can handle the changes. The decision to include already-existing courses in print and broadcast media (both located in the communication department) as options for new writing majors can be interpreted as a reflection of this need. Moreover, one can also read the decision to maintain a core of already-existing language, literature, and general English studies courses as staples of the new writing major as more sensible, given the institutional resistance to the creation of new areas of study without demonstrating that courses can be taught by existing faculty using existing resources. In short, the decisions make sense, practically and politically, regardless of whether one could interpret the new writing major as appeasement, as a negotiation, or as a true commitment to shared curricular efforts.

And it is more likely the case that the curricular decisions were influenced by appeasement, negotiation, *and* commitment to a shared vision. The shape of the writing specialization from its inception as a minor in 1987 reflected a commitment to balancing an introduction to the field with the need to offer direction and allow specialization. The reiterations a decade later were no different. For instance, the newer minor and major still incorporated a grafting together of literature, language and linguistics, theory and pedagogy, professional and creative writing, and experiential learning and application, many of which were commitments of the first iteration of a writing specialization in 1987. And changes to the writing specializations in the years after the creation of the major and revision to the minor in 1997 reveal the desire to hone the concept and address the curricular issue of specialization without violating the "shared" commitment, rather than revise it significantly. The most significant proof of this occurred in 2000 with the reclassification of the rhetorical theory course as an upper-division theory course, paralleling the 300-level critical theory and practice course for the English major and minor, and the addition of an upper-division writing workshop.

Table 3. Course Breakdown (1997–2006)

		100-level	200-level	300-level	400-level	Total
1997–2006	LT	4	10	18	5	37
	WR	3	9	1	1	14
	ED	0	2	1	0	3
	LA	0	1	1	2	4

Further evidence of a shared curricular vision for all writing and literature students is the significant revision of the content for and direction of the shared sophomore sequence (HELL). When created in 1993 for English majors and minors, the courses were intended as an introduction for students to a more traditional vision of English studies rooted in foundational approaches to literature and literary topics and concepts. According to the 1993-1995 course catalogue, EH 295 was:

> An exploration of three influential twentieth-century approaches to literature: the new critical emphasis on tradition and individual talent, Northrop Frye's understanding of literature as universal archetype, and more recent views of literature as the making of meaning through self fashioning and the exploitation of difference.

The second course in the sequence, EH 296, was defined in terms less driven by the overt study of literature and more open to a collective, inclusive vision of English studies:

> An introduction to three current topics in English studies: the growing role of English as a global language, the relationship between language and politics, and a speculative discussion of the future of English studies and the humanities.

As the writing specialization gained curricular momentum, and with the inclusion of the sophomore sequence as a departmental requirement for students pursuing the study of both writing and literature, the intention and direction of the sequence was revised, perhaps as an attempt to mediate to some degree the exclusively literary tenor by more explicitly appealing to the study of an English studies more generally, as the 2001-2002 catalogue descriptions for the two courses illustrate (emphasis added):

> EH 295W The Human Experience in Literature and Language I. This is the first of the two foundation courses for *English and writing majors and minors.* Enrollment is limited to these majors or minors. The course is an exploration of the traditional understandings of literary genres and historical periods *as well as an introduction to the discipline and current issues of English studies.*
>
> EH 296W The Human Experience in Literature and Language II. This is the second of the two foundation courses *for English and writing majors and minors.* Enrollment is limited to these majors or minors. The course is an exploration of three influential 20th century approaches to literature (such as the new critical emphasis on tradition and individual talent, the understanding of literature as universal archetype, structuralism, reader-response theories and/or more recent views of literature) and an application of those approaches.

The changes, though overtly recognizing the curricular desire for an inclusive vision of an English studies broader than the study of literary and literary theory, can be seen as a curricular manifestation of a growing tension in the department—between writing and literature faculty—over the distribution of resources, the commitment to a true shared curricular vision, and the status of writing as a valuable and valued specialization within English studies.

And there is curricular evidence to support the contention that the English department was more concerned with overt appeasement than a true re-envisioning of the curriculum as a shared commitment valuing as equal the study of writing and literature. As early as the first iteration of the writing specialization in 1987, the terminology reflects this tension; the study of literature—here termed "English"—was paralleled with a study of writing, as if the study of literature was seen as the default of the English department, while writing was an addition to rather than an equal and equally valid specialization within English studies. This terminology was carried over with the creation of the writing major (as opposed to the default English major). Moreover, each significant revision of the curriculum (in 1993 and 1997) involved an equally (if not more) significant revision to the English/literature specialization as well.

Table 4. Course Breakdown (1983–2006)

		100-level	200-level	300-level	400-level	Total
1983–1987	LT	1	9	9	5	24
	WR	1	2	0	0	3
	ED	0	1	3	0	4
	LA	0	0	1	1	2
1987–1993	LT	1	9	10	3	23
	WR	1	3	0	0	4
	ED	0	1	0	0	1
	LA	0	1	1	1	3
1993–1997	LT	1	10	14	4	29
	WR	3	4	1	0	8
	ED	0	1	1	0	2
	LA	0	1	1	1	3
1997–2006	LT	4	10	18	5	37
	WR	3	9	1	1	14
	ED	0	2	1	0	3
	LA	0	1	1	2	4

Fig 5. Course Changes to Literature and Writing Curricula (1987–2002)

	Literature			Writing		
Date	Add(+)	Subtr(-)	Change	Add(+)	Subtr(-)	Change
1987	425 Major Authors	412 Shakespeare	411 Shakespeare to 410 Shakespeare	240 Business and Technical Writing		
		415 Chaucer				
		420 Milton				
1989	315 English Renaissance			110 ESL Writing		
1993	295 HELL I		355 Modern Drama to 350 20th Century Drama	216 Writing Poetry	215 Creative Writing	
	296 HELL II		360 Modern Poetry to 20th Century Poetry	217 Writing Fiction		
	320 Voices of Native Americans			300 Teaching Writing and Rhetoric		
	321 Voices of Canadian Americans					
	322 Voices of Spanish/ Portuguese Americans					
	325 Gender and Literature					
	420 Critical Theory and Practice					
1995				100i College Writing Intensive		
				120 Honors College Writing		

1997	130 Introduction to Poetry	105 Understanding Literature	320 Voices of Native Americans to 255 Voices of Native Americans	225 Introduction to Rhetoric for Writers		300 Teaching Writing and Rhetoric to Practicum in Peer Tutoring
	135 Introduction to Fiction	322 Voices of Spanish/ Portuguese Americans	321 Voices of Canadian Americans to 257 Voices of Canadian Americans	243 Writing Drama		
	140 Popular Literature	330 Restoration and 18th Century Literature	325 Gender and Literature to 265 Gender and Literature	247 Reading and Writing Literary Nonfiction		
	260 Post-Colonial Literature	425 Major Authors	340 Romantic Literature to 332 Neoclassical and Romantic Literature	435 Senior Portfolio		
	326 Women and Literature		345 Victorian Age to Victorian and Early 20th Century Literature			
	328 Medieval English Literature		420 Critical Theory and Practice to 310 Critical Theory and Practice			
	352 Post-modernism					
	356 Auto-biography					
	371 Early American Literature					
	372 19th Century American Literature					

	373 20th Century American Literature					
	413 Chaucer					
	440 Topics in African-American Literature					
	442 Topics in Gender and Literature					
1999					110 ESL Writing to FE 110 ESL Writing	
2000				417 Writing Workshop		225 Intro to Rhetoric for Writers to 325 Rhetoric for Writers
2002	147 Introduction to Literary Nonfiction					
	270 American Regional Literature					
	335 The Literary Essay					

For example, during the curricular revision for the period leading up to the 1997 major, the addition of four writing-specific courses for the writing minor was accompanied by the increase of six literature courses, including five upper-division courses. And the curricular revisions in 1997 and the decade following the creation of the writing major, which gave rise to six additional writing-specific courses (including two upper-division courses), was accompanied by an increase of eight literature courses, including five upper-division courses. Moreover, additional curricular changes (including revisions to existing courses more than simply the addition of new courses) reveal the extent to which each period of significant curricular revision to the writing specializations also involved significant revisions to the literature specializations. Overall, the curricular revisions between 1987 and 2006 resulted in thirteen new literature courses and eleven new writing courses, totaling thirty-seven literature and fourteen writing courses. However, during the same period, a total of forty-two changes were made to literature courses, compared with sixteen changes to writing courses. Even in the period leading up to and following the creation of the writing major (from 1997 to 2006), changes to the literature courses numbered twenty-eight, compared to eight for the writing courses. During every major period of curricular revision and at every level of the curriculum, including general education courses, lower-division introduction courses, and upper-division specialty courses, more additions and changes were made to literature than writing courses in the English department. There were a variety of other factors, however, that suggest that the issues surrounding the growing problems with the writing major in the English department at Mount Union College in the period from 1997 to 2006 could not be simply reduced to resistance to threats by outsiders to an established literature faculty and an established literature major; it is much more likely the result of a confluence of interrelated factors.

The curricular evidence detailed above offers proof that the English department and its faculty, as a group, committed greater effort to revisions to the literature curriculum than to writing. Logically, though, there were more literature courses than writing courses, more literature faculty than writing faculty, and a longer history in the department for the literature major and minor than the writing major and minor. In short, the writing major was newer, represented a smaller part of the curriculum, and had fewer specialists among the faculty. Added to this, as with any new area of specialization, was the expectation that the writing major should face considerable growing pains in the first several years. Complicating this was the relative newness of the writing specialists in the faculty, mixed with faculty turnaround, an almost universally expected trend in academia today. The first writing specialist was hired in 1992, and the second in 1995. And while both these individuals played an instrumental role in the formation of the writing major, the most senior writing specialist left the department after the 1997–1998 academic year, leaving one full-time specialist on the faculty until 2001. The number of full-time tenured and tenure-track writing faculty increased to three when I was hired in 2003, constituting nearly one-third of the department faculty (three of ten). Yet, during the same time, the literature faculty underwent no changes (no hiring, firing, retiring, or replacement).

The relative instability caused by the frequent faculty changes by writing specialists in the department cannot be ignored as a factor. Moreover, as newer former graduate students, being educated in a climate of growing tension and a widening bifurcation between literature and rhet/comp as warring disciplines, there was, to some degree, an expectation for, if not a true "obligation" to, reproducing the disciplinary tension.

In addition, there was an introspective turn by the writing specialists in the department. The initial writing major had been formed. The writing program, comprising an initial writing assessment, a revision of the college-writing hierarchy, a WAC program, and a writing center, had been established at the college and had, by 2001, become successful within the college landscape as a whole. This, to some extent, allowed, if not demanded, that the writing specialists turn their efforts inward, toward a revision, reconsideration, and refinement of the writing curriculum. This introspection, mixed with the complexity of a writing specialization in relation to the relative simplicity of a literature specialization, inevitably lead to a questioning of every decision made during the formation of the original major which, when combined with the idiosyncrasies, personality, and leadership differences of the faculty, lead to an almost unavoidable, if not predictable, fracture. This fracture occurred in the spring of 2005 when two-thirds of the writing faculty left the department and the college, accepting faculty and administrative positions at other institutions.

THE WRITING MAJOR AS SHARED COMMITMENT: THE CURRENT ITERATION (2006)

Many of the concerns that lead to the fracture in the department were voiced if not uncovered during the English department program review that began during the summer of 2004 and concluded with a report by an external evaluator, published in October of 2004. Citing a unique balance between writing and literature at a small liberal arts school, the reviewer indicated that a key to solving the problem was not submission to "acrimony" but "mutual appreciation" (Risden 2004, 10). A first step, he proposed, was the presentation of a "unified front" from the English department to the college and the students. (11) Also, he suggested the need for the faculty to overtly address the commonality between our subdisciplines—a shared appreciation of language and its role in contributing to and making sense of the human experience. At the same time, it was necessary to introduce rather than avoid the "issues" that split, separate, and complicate the relationship between literature and writing; this process, he argued, would also uncover that English studies is more than literature and/or writing (it is inclusive of linguistics, literature, rhetoric and composition, creative writing, English education, and critical theory). In fact, as Graff, McComiskey, and Scholes (among countless others) have argued, the history of an "English" disciplinarity is wrought with, and to some degree depends upon, such strife. The key to emerging successfully from the fire, according to the reviewer, was to engage in conversation and dialogue rather than sink into stasis, complacency, and monologic thinking. However, before any significant action could be taken, the tension in the department had reached a boiling point— resulting in the departure of two of the three writing specialists.

By the spring of 2005, months after the publication of the report, the English department began, two specialists down, to revise the writing curriculum and rebuild the writing faculty, under the auspices of this renewed and reinvigorated mission to create a more-than-superficial shared curriculum for both literature and writing in one English department. This newer iteration, unveiled during the fall of 2006, was an attempt to address the two major concerns that to some degree plagued the older iterations: the establishment of true magnanimity between writing and literature in relation to faculty, students, and curriculum; and a revision that recognizes both the majors and the multiple concentrations as a shared commitment, one that seeks out areas of overlap and dialogue that have historically made English a vast and varied field of study.

The first of many major changes to the writing specializations, and to the department as a whole, involved paying closer critical attention to the language used to define and describe the areas of focus within the department. The decision in 1987 to add a second minor in "writing" while leaving the "English" major and minor unchanged (instead of altering the specializations in name to "literature" or something related) was probably a practical decision. It was a "new" invention for the department, an experiment of sorts, and required less curricular change—every curricular change progresses from the department to the committee on academic policies, then to the full faculty for a vote. And one change is two fewer than three. However, when the writing major was created in 1997, the naming structure carried over as well, creating the impression that the English department offered two majors and minors: ENGLISH and writing. Intentional or not, a hierarchy was created, and this hierarchy was perpetuated for nearly a decade. The 2006 reiteration, though, addressed this issue by naming two specializations: English: Literature and English: Writing. And this change was also a conscious attempt to overtly argue that the two specializations, writing and literature, are both sub-disciplines of and simultaneously rooted in English studies.

Additionally, in revising the majors and minors, a second effort was made to rename, and by renaming redefine, the space shared by the two sub-specialties. While previous iterations of the majors and minors set aside courses that literature and writing majors and minors shared (i.e., as departmental core courses), the new iteration attempted to recognize and acknowledge the content of this shared space and name it. The result was a common section called "Language, Theory and History," which included courses in literature and literary criticism, language and linguistics, and critical and rhetorical theory. Moreover, new courses, such as "Issues and Methods in Rhetoric and Composition" and "Literacies" were created for both majors, as was an upper-division rotational-topics seminar in language, theory, and history. Other courses already part of the established majors and minors, such as the sophomore sequence (HELL I & II), and a newly combined "theory" course—grafting together critical and rhetorical theory—were folded into this newly crafted shared space for all majors and minors.

Fig 6. Writing Major Revision (2006)

Language, Theory and History (15 cr.)

> EH 295: Human Experience in Language and Literature I
>
> EH 296: Human Experience in Languages and Literature II
>
> EH 310: Critical Theory and Rhetoric
>
> LTH Electives:
>
>> EH 319: Issues and Methods in Rhetoric and Composition
>>
>> EH 340: Literacies
>>
>> EH 385: Introduction to Linguistics
>>
>> EH 390: Seminar in Language, Theory, and History
>>
>> EH 405: History of the English Language
>>
>> EH 444: Seminar in Linguistics
>>
>> Approved 200+ Level Literature Courses

Writing (12 cr.)

> Professional Writing:

>> EH 240: Business and Technical Writing

>> EH 245: Argumentative Writing

>> EH 330: Theory and Practice of Editing

>> EH 391: Seminar in Professional Writing

>> Journalistic Writing (CM 250W, 255, 256, 350)

> Creative Writing:

>> EH 216: Writing Short Fiction

>> EH 217: Writing Poetry

>> EH 243: Writing Drama

>> EH 247: Writing Literary Nonfiction

>> EH 392: Seminar in Creative Writing

Practicum/application (9 cr.)

> PA Electives:

>> EH 300: Teaching Writing

>> EH 301: Writing Center Practicum (around 1 cr.)

>> EH 302: Calliope Practicum (1 cr.)

>> EH 317: Writing Workshop

>> EH 450: Independent Study

>> EH 499: Internship

>> EH 435: Senior Portfolio (SCE)

Fig 7. Writing Minor Revision (2006)

Language, Theory, and History (9 cr.)

> EH 295: Human Experience in Language and Literature I

> EH 296: Human Experience in Languages and Literature II

> LTH Electives:

>> EH 310: Critical Theory and Rhetoric

EH 319: Issues and Methods in Rhetoric and Composition

 EH 340: Literacies

 EH 385: Introduction to Linguistics

 EH 390: Seminar in Language, Theory, and History

 EH 405: History of the English Language

 EH 444: Seminar in Linguistics

 Approved 200+ Level Literature Courses

Writing (6 cr.)

 Professional Writing:

  EH 240: Business and Technical Writing

  EH 245: Argumentative Writing

  EH 330: Theory and Practice of Editing

  EH 391: Seminar in Professional Writing

  Journalistic Writing (CM 250W, 255, 256, 350)

 Creative Writing:

  EH 216: Writing Short Fiction

  EH 217: Writing Poetry

  EH 243: Writing Drama

  EH 247: Writing Literary Nonfiction

  EH 392: Seminar in Creative Writing

Practicum/application (3 cr.)

 PA Electives:

  EH 300: Teaching Writing

  EH 301: Writing Center Practicum (1 cr.)

  EH 302: *Calliope* Practicum (1 cr.)

  EH 317: Writing Workshop

  EH 450: Independent Study

  EH 499: Internship

Emphases from the older iterations of the writing specialization, such as language and linguistics, pedagogy, and professional and creative writing, were reformed but still evident in the revised curriculum.

First, the "artificial" bifurcation between creative writing and professional writing was tamed a bit, offering one larger category for writing courses, here defined as area or genre courses. Under this section, equal weight is given to the two concentrations present from the inception of the writing specialization in 1987. Moreover, each section was expanded to include a combination of revised and new courses, at both the lower- and upper-division level. In fact, overall, the department added nine new, writing-specific and shared courses, all at the upper-division level. At the same time, even though several of these courses were created as shared courses—additions to the curriculum of both literature and writing students—the revisions to the majors and minors resulted in a net reduction of one literature course. This marked a change from previous curricular reiterations in that significant revision to the writing specialization also resulted in an equal, if not more significant, revision of the literature specialization. The 2006 major/minor revisions produced eleven changes to the literature curriculum, including seven course revisions, two subtractions, and two additions. In reality, the two new courses (the literacies course and the rotational-topics seminar in language, theory, and history) were both shared courses. In short, the revision produced no new literature courses. In contrast, thirteen alterations were made to the writing curriculum, including eight new courses (two shared) and revisions to five courses.

Table 5. Course Breakdown (1997–Present)

		100-level	200-level	300-level	400-level	Total
1997–2006	LT	4	10	18	5	37
	WR	3	9	1	1	14
	ED	0	2	1	0	3
	LA	0	1	1	2	4
2006–present	LT	4	10	17	5	36
	WR	3	9	10	1	23
	ED	0	2	1	0	3
	LA	0	1	3	2	6

Fig 8. Course Changes to Literature and Writing Curricula (2006–Present)

	Literature			Writing		
Date	Add(+)	Subtr(-)	Change	Add(+)	Subtr(-)	Change
2006	340 Literacies	370 Modern Novel	310 Critical Theory and Practice to 310 Critical Theory and Rhetoric	300 Teaching Writing		120 Honors College Writing to Advanced College Writing
	390 Seminar in Language, Theory and History	375 American Novel	335 The Literary Essay to Studies in the Literary Essay	301 Writing Center Practicum		245 Advanced Writing to Argu-mentative Writing
			350 20th Century Drama to Studies in Drama	302 Calliope Practicum		300 Issues in Compo-sition Studies to 319 Issues and Methods in Compo-sition Studies
			356 Auto-biography to Studies in Auto-biography	330 Theory and Practice of Editing		325 Rhetoric for Writers to 310 Critical Theory and Rhetoric
			360 20th Century Poetry to Studies in Poetry	340 Literacies		417 Writing Workshop to 317 Writing Workshop
			365 English Novel to Studies in the Novel	390 Seminar in Language, Theory and History		
			380 American Short Story to Studies in Short Story	391 Seminar in Pro-fessional Writing		
				392 Seminar in Creative Writing		

Two additional curricular changes, both alterations of courses, also support the contention that the latest revision to the writing major and minor reflected a substantive shift in the status between the two specializations in the English department, and that one main purpose was to create and nurture a "middle ground" exposing students studying writing and literature students to a shared English experience. First, the revisions to the required sophomore sequence (HELL I & II), intended as an introduction to the department, the faculty, and the field of English studies, addressed concerns raised by both faculty and students regarding a literature-bias, cited in the 2004 external report issued following the department assessment. In fact, the intention of the revised course is made explicit in the syllabus from the first class taught after the major revision (2006–2007):

> English Studies has traditionally been a diverse field, responding to the multiplicity that is characteristic of human experience. At the same time, people in the fields of English language and literature share much in common. The purpose of EH 295 and its sequel, EH 296, is to introduce students of English language and literature to the ranges of ideas studied in the discipline while also presenting a common body of knowledge, critical methods and professional standards. The two courses are organized to introduce recent developments in thinking about language, literature, rhetoric and writing with an emphasis on ideas and issues of continuing value and concern. In other words, we're going to teach you how to be English majors.

And the required reading list, pairing Terry Eagleton with Jim Berlin, Harvey Graff with Janet Emig and Walter Ong, shows a commitment to theorists, scholars, researchers, and writers across the disciplines. Finally, the decision was made to fuse together the two theory courses (rhetorical theory and critical theory) into one shared theory course. The purpose of this course is to introduce both literature and writing students to the major concepts and periods of critical and rhetorical theory so that they can develop a historically-informed understanding of contemporary critical and rhetorical issues. Together with the other curricular changes, the revision to these three core departmental courses supports the contention that the latest revision is a truer attempt to embrace a disciplinary "middle ground" of English studies rooted in a shared commitment to literature *and* writing, rhetoric *and* theory, producing *and* consuming texts.

More significantly, in the two years following the revision (including the 2007–2008 academic year), seven of the new writing (and shared) courses were taught at least once (including the literacies course, professional editing, the two practica, the seminar on language, theory, and history, teaching writing, and the seminar in professional writing), indicating not just a lip-service attempt toward curricular change but a substantive effort to support the redesigned writing specialization.

THE FUTURE OF THE WRITING MAJOR

One way or another, a significant factor leading to the creation of the first writing major at Mount Union College in 1997 was a desire to address the changing needs of students educated as English majors and seeking employment as teachers and professional writers. In many ways, for students who wish to pursue the production of texts as a career, a major in writing makes sense. Students are exposed to a wider variety of rhetorical situations for analyzing and producing texts; students can professionalize as writers and gain more practical and varied experiential knowledge than studying literature alone can afford. In fact, in an alumni survey conducted in 2005, nearly 30 percent of English department graduates indicated they were pursuing a career in the professional sector (Office of Institutional Research 2005). Additionally, when asked about courses they would have found helpful or beneficial to their careers, the English alumni often cited "professional" writing courses (such as editing and new media writing), as well as other and a wider variety of "writing" courses. To some degree, the 2006 revision was a further attempt to

Table 6. Breakdown of English Students by Major and Minor

AY (Fall)	EH	EH Majors	EH Minors	EH: Lit.	EH: Lit. Majors	EH: Lit. Minors	EH: Writ.	EH: Writ. Majors	EH: Writ. Minors
1998	50	30	20	44	28	16	6	2	4
1999	47	33	14	33	23	10	14	10	4
2000	52	43	9	33	29	4	19	14	5
2001	55	42	13	29	23	6	26	19	7
2002	50	39	11	25	20	5	25	19	6
2003	55	39	16	28	23	5	27	16	11
2004	70	57	13	40	35	5	30	22	8
2005	57	44	13	22	18	4	35	26	9
2006	49	35	14	20	16	4	29	19	10
2007	55	40	15	22	20	2	33	20	13

Table 7. Breakdown of English Graduates by Major

AY (Fall)	EH Grads	EH: Lit. Grads	EH: Writ. Grads
1998	17	15	2
1999	7	6	1
2000	11	8	3
2001	25	15	10
2002	14	7	7
2003	16	6	10
2004	11	7	4
2005	14	4	10
2006	9	1	8
TOTAL	124	69	55

address these apparent curricular gaps as well as offer a writing curriculum that reflects current trends in writing theory and practice.

Moreover, statistics on the number of majors, minors, and graduates in the English department since 1998 (one year after the first writing major was established) reflect a growing popularity of writing as an option for students. In fact, in 1999, just two years after the constitution of the writing major, nearly one third (30.3 percent) of the students in the department were declared writing majors. Two years later, in 2001, writing majors constituted 40 percent of the English graduates, a trend that has continued to the present day. In 2006, 59.2 percent of the students in the English department were writing students: 54.3 percent of majors were writing majors, 71.4 percent of the minors were in writing, and 88.9 percent graduated with a BA in writing. Since 2001, 55 percent of the English graduates (49 of 89) were writing majors. And there is no indication that the popularity of the writing option for English students (at either the level of a major or minor) is waning. Moreover, the rehiring of both full-time tenure-track writing specialists lost in 2005 is further evidence of the institutional and departmental support for and value of writing. Obviously, there is and will continue to be a need to hire more writing specialists and to teach more and more frequent writing courses, as well as to expand course options for students in English departments. Less obvious is the need to better articulate how best to expose all English students to texts and methodologies specific to writing and emphasize commonalities between issues and theories pertinent to the study of writing and literature. Such efforts will continue to affect and be effected by larger disciplinary trends.

Historically, the field of English has always experienced identity tensions (e.g., theory versus practice, literature versus composition). And the position of writing in English departments has frequently been at the epicenter of these tensions. Ideologically, writing as a sub-discipline has been "used" by English faculty and departments to garner institutional support for the pursuit of English and the existence of literature as more than merely a service to general education. From the creation of first-year writing at Harvard in the early 1900s to the formation of basic or remedial and ESL writing as an assuage to the open admissions era in public higher education to the creation of writing programs (including WAC and writing centers) to "deal with" writing in the disciplines and across the curriculum, composition has historically been used to reposition English departments as valuable and valued sites of important and valid work. We are, however, in a new historical moment.

Many colleges and universities are being "forced" to rethink how the liberal arts and humanistic education can be successfully redefined in the face of a changing applicant pool and work force. Parents want their children to be educated in smaller, libera- arts-based settings, but they also want assurance that the one-hundred-thousand-dollar education will result in a job. Students want this same assurance. Balancing the benefits of a liberal arts degree with the pragmatism of a pre-professional program is key to the survival of traditionally humanistic disciplines, like English. Writing studies can provide this bridge. In light of such larger, institutional mandates to redefine curricula for an adaptive and adapting workforce, many traditionally humanistic disciplines (e.g., philosophy, history, and English) need to redefine their objectives to account for a more professionally-driven student population or face the real possibility of disciplinary extinction. For English departments, we need to recognize the foundational role of writing studies (e.g., literacy, rhetoric and composition, professional writing, and English education) in reshaping English as an academic area of study that both promotes traditional humanistic endeavors and is sensitive to the impetus to professionalize. Writing majors, minors, and concentrations within English departments can and should be recognized as locations having the potential to bridge institutional mandates toward professionalization and liberal arts endeavors towards humanistic education, rather than as divisive forces threatening to make the study of English less liberal artsy. Likewise, proponents of writing studies within traditionally literature-based English departments can and should recognize the potential in and build upon (rather than undermine) the position of liberal-arts privilege afforded by the connection (however tenuous) to literature.

There is no simple answer to the question, "Where does the writing major go from here?" Instead, every revision must be made rhetorically, as an answer to a question that considers the needs of the students, the capabilities of the faculty, and the direction of and trends marking the discipline(s). And all of these considerations are and always must be mediated by the needs, limitations, strengths, and mission of a particular institution. In a liberal arts setting, within an English department that shares students and a curriculum, the students require not acrimony and animosity, division and bifurcation, but magnanimity and dialogue, unity and cooperation. Our goal must be to continue to develop and refine curricula that better attend to the changing nature of composition and writing studies, meet the needs of our students, and also engender the study of a discipline that resists being labeled as *either* rhetoric and writing *or* literature and literary theory. As Robert P. Yagelski argues, "English as a discipline is ultimately about language, which is a vehicle by which we understand ourselves and act in the world" (310). Recognizing the power and potential of such a middle-ground approach is a position that few in English studies can disagree with or afford to ignore, regardless of sub-disciplinary affiliation.

REFERENCES

Bloom, Lynn Z., Donald A. Daiker, and Edward M. White, eds. 1996. *Composition in the twenty-first century: Crisis and change.* Carbondale: Southern Illinois University Press.

Brown, Stuart C., Paul R. Meyer, and Theresa Enos. 1994. Doctoral programs in rhetoric and composition: A catalogue of the profession. *Rhetoric Review* 12.2:240–51, 253–389.

Bullock, Richard. 2000. Feathering our nest? A critical view from within our discipline. In Shamoon et al. 2000.

Carpini, Dominic Delli. 2007. Re-writing the humanities: The writing major's effect of undergraduate studies in English departments. *Composition Studies* 35.1:15-36.

Chapman, David, Jeanette Harris, and Christine Hult. 1995. Agents for change: undergraduate writing programs in departments of English. *Rhetoric Review* 13.2:421–34.

Graff, Gerald. 1996. Is there a conversation in this curriculum? Or, coherence without disciplinarity. In *English as a discipline, or, Is there a plot in this play?*, ed. James C. Raymond, 11–28. Tuscaloosa: University of Alabama Press.

Lowe, Kelly. 2007. Against the writing major. *Composition Studies* 35.1: 97-98

McComiskey, Bruce, ed. 2006. *English studies: An introduction to the discipline(s).* Urbana, IL: National Council of Teachers of English.

———. Introduction. In McComiskey 2006.

Mount Union College. 1987. Mount Union College catalogue 1987-1989. Alliance, Oh.

———. 1993. Mount Union College catalogue 1993-1995. Alliance, Oh.

———. 2001. Mount Union College catalogue 2001-2002. Alliance, Oh.

———. 2005. Mount Union College English department alumni survey results. Office of Institutional Research. Alliance, Oh. Duplicated.

Newman, Glenn. 2007. Concocting a writing major: A recipe for success. *Composition Studies* 35.1:1–65.

Nystrand, Martin, Stuart Greene, and Jeffrey Wiemelt. 1993. Where did composition studies come from? An intellectual history. *Written Communication* 10.3:267–333.

Risden, Edward L. 2004. Report on the October 2004 review of the English department of Mount Union College. St. Norbert College, De Pere, Wis. Duplicated.

Scholes, Robert. 1998. *The rise and fall of English: Reconstructing English as a discipline.* New Haven, CT: Yale University Press.

Schwegler, Robert A. 2000. Curriculum development in composition. In Shamoon et al. 2000.

Shamoon, Linda K., Rebecca Moore Howard, Sandra Jamieson, and Robert A. Schwegler, eds. 2000. *Coming of age: The advanced writing curriculum.* Portsmouth, NH: Boynton/ Cook.

Weisinger, Herbert. 1945. The problem of the English major. *College English* 6.6:342–46.

Werner, Warren W., Isabelle K. Thompson, and Joyce Rothschild. 1998. A survey of specialized writing courses for English majors: 1975–76 to 1985–86. *Rhetoric Review* 6.2:204–17.

Yagelski, Robert P. English education. In McComiskey 2006.

Yancey, Kathleen Blake. 2004. Made not only in words: Composition in a new key. *College Composition and Communication* 56.2:297–328.

7

DANCING WITH OUR SIBLINGS
The Unlikely Case for a Rhetoric Major

David Beard

If the overall thrust of this book is to account for the possibility of a "writing major," it takes its place alongside other anthologies (for example, Shamoon, Howard, Jamieson, and Schwegler's *Coming of Age: The Advanced Writing Curriculum*) and special issues of composition journals (the spring 2007 edition of *Composition Studies*, for example). My own take on the major writing curriculum is grounded by my belief that the rhetorical tradition is integral to the research agenda for composition studies, useful for composition pedagogy (in the service and major curricula), and foundational to our claims of disciplinarity. Rhetoric is part of our future and integral to our past. As such, this essay builds upon my own enthusiastic contribution to *Coming of Age* (written with Arthur Walzer), an essay that argued for courses in rhetorical theory in the writing curriculum.

This essay differs from that earlier work in that it advances a new claim: As much as rhetoric is part of the core of our discipline, it is also our greatest liability. As we build undergraduate major curricula, we must be wary of the history of rhetorical study in the twentieth century in a broad, disciplinary sense and a local, institutional sense. That history inflects the politics of the writing major in the twenty-first century.

RHETORIC IN THE TWENTY-FIRST CENTURY

The measure of rhetoric's success in the academy can be measured in terms of research, to be sure. The number of journals with rhetoric as a primary focus has multiplied (*Rhetoric Review, Rhetorica, Rhetoric Society Quarterly, Advances in the History of Rhetoric, Philosophy and Rhetoric*). The number of journals that include rhetoric as a subfield is swelling (*Quarterly Journal of Speech, Communication Studies, Technical Communication Quarterly, College Composition and Communication*). Book series in rhetoric are vital and doctoral programs are gaining in professional visibility.

But, in a controversial essay, David Fleming challenges us to rethink the revival of rhetoric in the academy in terms not of the flowering of research but in terms of the flowering of curricula:

> A better test for the revival of rhetoric in English departments would be the flourishing of an undergraduate major: In the past, this is what rhetoric was: three to four years of intense study and practice, sometime between the ages of (about) fifteen and twenty, organized to develop the discursive competencies and sensibilities needed for effective and responsible participation in public life. (1998, 173)

While Fleming writes with English departments in mind, his claims could also apply to communication programs. In both types of programs, research in rhetoric may be stronger than undergraduate curriculum. Rhetoric, which at the level of research may sustain freestanding journals, conferences, and professional associations, may in these undergraduate majors be circumscribed to a handful of required courses or free electives.

Fleming's essay is complicated, first of all, because it fails to connect the study of rhetoric with the economic realities of the university. Few universities will justify the expense of a new major by virtue of preparing students for public life; some demand for connection to the marketplace drives arguments for new majors at nearly any institution.[1] Second, it fails to recognize the extent to which rhetoric is already integrated in those larger majors: English, writing, technical writing or technical communication, speech communication or communication studies. Rhetoric may already be in the curriculum, though in a dispersed and fragmented way.

This essay talks about the future possibilities of rhetoric and the advanced composition curriculum—as well as the curricular and administrative challenges that face the advanced composition curriculum with rhetoric at its core. It identifies those challenges by looking historically at the fate of rhetoric in the undergraduate curriculum. In the first third of this essay, I narrate the process by which rhetorical production

---

1. As a group of respondents (Peggy O'Neill, Nan Stevens LoBue, Margaret McLaughlin, Angela Crow, and Kathy S. Albertson) to Fleming's essay noted, "[We] need to prove that students who graduate with a major in rhetoric are employable" ("A Comment on 'Rhetoric as a Course of Study,'" 274).

is systematically devalued in favor of critical consumption in English and in communication. This process leads to fragmentation, as multiple departments come to claim some aspect of rhetoric. Amid such fragmentation, the historical paradigm cases of rhetorical majors are no longer possible. The dispersal and diffusion of these paradigmatic majors (merging the oral and written, the productive and critical) is recounted in the second third of this essay. The result will clarify that the shape of rhetoric in the writing curriculum at the undergraduate level depends on the shape of its siblings at any given institution.

Given these historical conditions, the final third of this essay questions the efforts to seek disciplinary autonomy for rhetorical studies. Such autonomy is already manifest in research, and that has been the basis for arguments for curricular and departmental independence. This essay problematizes the search for autonomy, a valuable goal for research but at best a problematic one at the undergraduate level. Instead, it proposes that rhetoric scholars must work at the intersections and must develop curricula that respect the local conditions at each institution. That may mean configurations unlike anything seen before.

THE HISTORICAL FRAGMENTATION OF RHETORIC IN THE UNDERGRADUATE CURRICULUM

Fragmentation may be the norm in rhetorical education. Most (though not all) universities differentiate departments and programs in speech communication (or communication studies) from departments and programs in written communication (or English or composition). Both of these types of departments *can* lay claim to rhetorical study, though not all do. There are communication programs that are entirely social scientific in orientation and so free of rhetorical work, just as there are composition programs rooted in the empirical, qualitative tradition of composition studies instead of the rhetorical tradition.

The fragmentation of rhetorical majors is the subject of some scholarly inquiry; Thomas Miller (2005) and Brian Jackson (2007) have both attempted to assess the place of rhetoric in composition and communication departments. Miller found that interdisciplinary collaboration in rhetoric was more likely to occur at smaller institutions (indeed, at the smallest scale of institution, communication and composition were sometimes housed in the same department, enabling such collaboration), while Jackson finds that rhetoric is more likely to take a prominent place in the curriculum in larger institutions.

In both Jackson's and Miller's cases, however, it is clear that neither field, broadly demonstrated, has a full commitment to rhetoric. It is statistically very possible to find programs in composition and in communication without courses in rhetoric. By analogy, it would be impossible, I think, to envision an English department without a course in British literature or a psychology department without a course in developmental psychology. Those are areas of those fields that are embedded in the discipline's very identity. Rhetoric is not so embedded. The ultimate conclusion of Miller's and Jackson's research might be that rhetoric is everywhere in possibility but nowhere by necessity.

What is the source of this fragmentation and marginalization of rhetorical studies? Using the University of Minnesota—Duluth (UMD) as a case study, I outline one process, over eighty years, by which rhetoric became dispersed among three departments. The result is, in concrete, curricular form, the fragmentation of rhetorical studies. One department, at the turn of the twentieth century, included both written and oral communication of both poetic and rhetorical discourse, but over the length of the twentieth century, courses in rhetorical performance were systematically diminished and marginalized, resulting in the creation of new departments and the redistribution of courses and programs.

First Schism: Speech and English

UMD is a typical regional institution, born of a state teachers college (or normal school). Its first majors were oriented toward the K–12 teaching curriculum, so no major in rhetoric found its place alongside English, math and the sciences. Instead, all things rhetorical could be found, initially, in the English department.

In the 1920s, curricular change resulted in the lowering of the course numbers of specific courses in performance (both oral and theatrical) from advanced undergraduate level to the first-year level. I believe that this change manifested the preference, among the bulk of English faculty, toward consumption of texts over performance. James Berlin argues that, consonant with the values of American culture since the nineteenth century, English departments have valued the consumption of texts over their production (1984 and 1987). This valuation of consumption mirrors the cultural practice of the upper and middle classes of American society, for whom consumption (i.e., shopping, the acquisition of goods) is a marker of status. The upper-division courses in English at UMD taught critical consumption of texts, both written and oral or theatrical; the production and performance of those texts was confined to the freshman level.[2]

This curricular shift resulted, eventually, in the development of the Department of Speech, where the performance courses in oral interpretation, theatrical production, and public speaking were restored to the center of the major curriculum. Arguments for the epistemic distinction between speech and writing (outlined and critiqued by Mailloux in *Disciplinary Identities: Rhetorical Paths of English, Speech, and Composition* and by William Keith in *Democracy as Discussion: Civic Education and the American Forum Movement*) were intimately bound to the value given performance against consumption. Course descriptions that become the core of the speech program are redrafted to emphasize the performative. A course in Oral Interpretation appears on the books to replace English 202, Reading and Speech, at UMD.

Course Description, *Reading and Speech*	Course Description, *Oral Interpretation*
The problem is that of assisting students to realize more fully the possibilities of enjoyment afforded by a sympathetic study of literature and by the attempt to give it adequate oral expression. (UMD *Bulletin*, 1935–1936)	Fundamentals of the oral interpretation of different forms of literature are studied. Practical platform training in both interpretation with the book and impersonation is given through the medium of modern and classical selections of humorous and dramatic nature, 'character' and dialect studies, and one-act plays. (UMD *Bulletin*, 1936–1937)

The difference between these two course descriptions is worth discussing. In the English curriculum, skill in reading literature aloud enabled "enjoyment" and "sympathetic study of literature." Oral reading was a tool for critical consumption. In the speech curriculum, effective performance is its own goal.

A Second Schism: Journalism and Mass Communication

The division between written and oral discourse served to distinguish the two departments for decades.[3] In the 1970s, the Department of

2. In the 1980s, the Department of English again faced schism over the place of rhetorical performance; this time, courses in written rhetorical performance were separated from the other courses in English into the newly formed Department of Composition. (Notably, creative writing remained anchored to the literature program in the English Department; it really is *rhetorical* performance that is isolated, not all writing practice.) The division between consumption and production, composition and literature, was manifest again.

3. Such friendly division was threatened when both departments moved to appropriate the term "Communication[s]." In the 1970s, the Department of English offered a

Speech became the Department of Communication, following a national trend that eventually culminated in changing the name of the national association from the Speech-Communication Association to the National Communication Association in the 1990s. Communication, as a defining term, opened speech departments everywhere to discourses outside the oral: broadcast media, new media, and mass communication broadly.

Within that new department of communication, however, we saw again the marginalization of rhetorical performance: courses in writing and production for mass communication were identified as journalism courses, while courses in the analysis (critical consumption) of mass communication were fully integrated into the major curriculum in communication. There is some cause for analogy with the changes in the department of English in the 1920s: again, critical *consumption* of media was segregated from rhetorical *production.*

Following faculty retirement and curricular refocusing in the Department of Communication, the courses carrying a journalism designator were eventually moved from the communication department to the Department of Writing Studies. To this date, courses in media literacy and the critical study of media effects are located in Communication; courses in media production (from basic news reporting to advanced audio production for broadcast and new media writing) are located in the Department of Writing Studies.[4]

A quick analysis of the majors in English and communication at UMD demonstrates the impact of this curricular fragmentation. Both of these majors contain rhetorical classes (in communication, rhetorical history or criticism is required; in English, it is an elective and at least touched upon in courses in literary theory), but none of them produces a full understanding of rhetoric's broad utility as a *heuristic and productive* as well as *critical* toolkit. Most of the courses in rhetorical production (professional writing, editing, broadcast and print journalism) are housed in the Department of Writing Studies.

---

minor in communication*s* (indicating a kind of mass communication program that included a hybrid of courses in practical writing and in, for example, the analysis of propaganda). That minor was eliminated when the Department of Speech changed its name to the Department of Communication, and its courses were used to build the mass communication wing of the new Communication Department.

4. The Department of Writing Studies is now a hybrid: faculty in composition and rhetoric teach alongside faculty in journalism and in linguistics. Notably the only department with significant commitment to rhetorical performance, as of 2007, the Department of Writing Studies has no undergraduate major and has faced a complicated set of challenges in implementing that major or courses with the term "rhetoric" in the title.

The narrative at UMD is not atypical. Aspects of this timeline may have been more or less accelerated at other schools, and the particular departmental configurations may have varied slightly. Many schools experience the schism between *media studies as a subfield of communication criticism* and *journalism as a field of rhetorical production* faster than it was experienced at UMD, for example. Other universities never see freestanding departments of writing studies develop. (For example, Thomas Benson [2003] tells the story of similar disciplinary fragmentation at Cornell from the perspective of its rhetorical scholars in the Department of Speech and Drama, where they taught and researched alongside a freestanding Department of Communication in the College of Agriculture.) Regardless of the unique configuration at any one school, the end result (the fragmentation of rhetorical theory, criticism, and performance among two or three or more academic departments) is typical.

Even more typical is the mechanism that enables or drives such fragmentation: the systematic diminishment of rhetorical production in favor of rhetorical consumption.

BUILDING A MAJOR FROM AN INCOMPLETE RHETORIC

The posture that a major or department can lay claim to teaching the rhetorical tradition while systematically devaluing rhetorical production is a typical one. Even in what could be a flagship undergraduate program in rhetoric, we see those processes of diminishing rhetorical production at work. University of California, Berkeley operates a major in rhetoric; it is not housed in a department of English or communication. But nonetheless, this rhetoric major is imbalanced; it seems to recognize rhetoric as a hermeneutic tool far more than it does rhetoric as a productive art. The goals of the major are described in this way:

> Rhetoric majors are trained in the theory and history of rhetorical practice. With a grounding in argumentation and in the analysis of the symbolic and institutional dimensions of discourse, Rhetoric students study how meaning and persuasion function in a wide variety of specific contexts—from legal discourse and philosophical argumentation, to literary narratives and popular media culture. The major includes courses in three different areas of study:
>
> • History and Theory of Rhetoric
> • Public Discourse
> • Narrative and Image
> • (http://rhetoric.berkeley.edu/rhetoric_major.html)

This is a rich and energetic description promising the best of literary rhetoric, civic rhetoric, and the history of rhetoric's tradition. Nonetheless, the curriculum is weighted in much the same way that curriculum has historically been weighted: against rhetorical practice. To borrow terms derived from Dominic Delli Carpini (2007), if rhetorically centered majors are typified by an appeal to praxis, gnosis, or some combination of the two, the Berkeley major is grounded entirely in the gnosis that typifies the English and communication majors described above—a gnosis that undervalues praxis. Once the student enters the upper division, in which the three areas of study dominate, courses in the productive aspects of rhetoric become scarce (see appendix for a list of the classes in the areas of study at UC Berkeley).

Rhetorical theory and criticism becomes the culminating experience for students in those majors, an experience that Brian Jackson calls into question. According to Jackson, the teaching of rhetorical criticism cannot be taken for granted as inherently more civically minded than the teaching of literary criticism. Jackson claims that "rhetoricians who advocate critical-analytical courses for rhetoric education must consider how teaching a student to be a rhetorical critic is a service to the *polis*" (2007, 189).[5] Courses in rhetoric without a connection to the productive skills that are a service to the polis are a disfigurement of what rhetoric can be and so are unhelpful models for the advanced composition curriculum.

Some writing programs take rhetorical theory as the authorizing and foundational force. But the development of those courses and curricula is not without political risk; rhetoric is at once the prized possession and the diminished stepchild of many academic departments.

Proposing a course in rhetoric can lead to tense battles with multiple departments, doubly so if that proposal calls into question whether another unit has enacted real stewardship of all that the term "rhetoric" implies. Phrased bluntly, to the extent that rhetoric signifies a body of theory and critical reading strategies, it may be claimed by multiple units. To the extent that it names a body of practice, it is shuffled into the lower division or excised from the curriculum altogether. But the claim of neglect of practice on the part of *another* unit is poor

---

5. The intellectual position called "rhetorical hermeneutics" has been vulnerable to these very arguments. Steve Mailloux has rebutted these criticisms (that his turn toward "cultural rhetorics" turns rhetoric into a variety of literary criticism) in *Disciplinary Identities*; Gaonkar accuses the project for the rhetoric of science of being thinly veiled literary criticism without respect for the productive aspects of its Aristotelian roots in Gross and Keith's anthology, *Rhetorical Hermeneutics: Invention and Interpretation in the Age of Science*.

political grounds for claiming rhetoric for a new program in advanced composition.

Rebecca Moore Howard (2007) makes a strong argument that the creation of a writing major can be conceived as "counterdiscourse"—that the existence of a writing major can lead to a reconfiguration of institutional values around writing, literacy, and rhetoric. Such a project Howard calls "curricular activism" (42). And while I endorse Howard's goals, I admit a certain anxiety—you cannot enact curricular and institutional change without enacting curricular and institutional resistance. Indeed, Tony Scott tells us that "curricular innovations need to be imagined in conjunction with fundamental institutional changes" (2007, 89). Resistance to those institutional changes is predictable, based on the historical patterns identified in this essay. It takes a strong and empowered composition faculty to seek to build the bridges necessary to create a major (given institutional politics) while simultaneously challenging institutional norms.

THE LOST HISTORICAL CONTEXT OF RHETORICAL MAJORS

There are a handful of unique institutions where rhetoric majors have occurred—historical, institutional experiments of value for what they can tell us about the conditions necessary for a rhetoric major. Two of these experiments occurred in the contexts of freestanding departments of rhetoric, and both happened at the University of Minnesota. They demonstrate what is possible if a major in rhetoric is developed without the administrative pressures of a relationship to a larger department of English or communication. They demonstrate the balance of the productive and the critical, the academic, technical, and civic that is possible in an organic major in rhetoric.

Rhetoric in Flower: The Major in the First Department of Rhetoric at Minnesota in the College of Sciences and Liberal Arts (SLA)

The nineteenth-century Department of Rhetoric and Public Speaking (R&PS) on the Twin Cities campus of the University of Minnesota was energetically ahead of its time. If the twenty-first century is a time of rapprochement among rhetorically centered disciplines, the University of Minnesota manifested a synthesis of rhetoric and aesthetic, of written and oral in its R&PS.[6] As such, it manifested all that can be sought of a rhetoric major, allowed to develop unfettered by a sibling discipline.

R&PS was developed from an initial, freestanding department of rhetoric and elocution. The nineteenth-century context associated "elocution" with professional, persuasive speakers with an emphasis on personal expression; "public speaking" was selected as an alternative term that placed weight on the public and civic aspects of oral communication.[6] But regardless of its title, the department offered a full array of courses. For example, as the Department of Rhetoric and Elocution, the faculty offered courses in written and oral performance, in debate, in the history and criticism of oratory, and in the history and theory of criticism of both art and literature.[7]

R&PS was, at its largest, staffed by two professors, five assistant professors, and ten instructors. Those faculty were responsible for what would seem, even by today's standards, an innovative rhetoric major, integrating theory, practice, and an engagement of the civic power of rhetoric. The catalog identified the courses offered by R&PS in the early twentieth century in a number of ways:

- Introductory courses (Composition and Rhetoric, Exposition, Description and Narration, and Exposition and Argument). By their titles, these courses manifest the principles of current-traditional rhetoric and its division of discourse.

- Courses for engineers (Composition for Engineers and Technical Writing). These courses are ahead of the curve, in terms of the widespread acceptance of courses in both writing in technical disciplines and professions.

- Advanced courses in writing defined by genre (Short-Story Writing, Essay Writing, Dramatic Technique).

- Advanced seminars (Seminar in Writing and Seminar in Rhetoric)

- Public speaking (Argumentation and Debate, Intercollegiate Debate and Oratory, and Interpretive Reading). Here, the public/civic work of rhetorical production was most clear.

---

6. This history of the rise of the term "public speaking" against "elocution" is traced in Keith's *Democracy as Discussion*.

7. See the *Bulletin of the College of Science, Literature and the Arts, 1905–1906* (University of Minnesota 1905). Of special note was the role of Maria Sanford, the first woman professor in the state of Minnesota and a professor of rhetoric and elocution, in establishing both the debate courses and the criticism courses. A statue of Sanford resides in the National Statuary Hall Collection in Washington, D.C. Thanks to the staff at the archives of the University of Minnesota for bringing her to my attention.

Minnesota's offerings were as exciting, perhaps, as any at the turn of the century—the twentieth or the twenty-first. Taken together, in their diversity of rhetorical performance and nod toward rhetorical theory, the nineteenth-century curriculum in rhetoric was innovative. And the major was even more innovative, in that it pulled supporting elective courses from complementary units: English, philology, philosophy, Latin, Greek, advanced modern language courses, history, and the social sciences (University of Minnesota 1914).

If, in the twenty-first century, we continue discussions of Big Rhetoric as an interdisciplinary field that encompasses theories from other disciplines and which can be used, in part, to explain the dynamics of knowledge in politics, art, and a variety of academic fields, in the nineteenth century, there was at least a tacit understanding of the interrelations we explore today. They were nascent, they were undeveloped in any sense of a research agenda, and they did not last, but they were there.

Rhetoric Diminished

After the merger of the departments of English and R&PS in 1920, the rhetoric major changed radically. The combined new Department of English held five full professors, three associate professors, and five assistant professors, and among that faculty, there was desire to see *all* classes in the department fill. As a result, the rhetoric major became even more embedded in the courses offered in this remolded department of English. Among the changes: the Seminar in Rhetoric (in which students read rhetorical theory) dissolved and freestanding courses in criticism collapsed into extant courses in literary criticism. Additionally, all rhetoric majors were now prescribed six credits of coursework in literature selected from the following:

- Two quarters of nineteenth-century prose, or
- Two quarters of eighteenth-century prose, or
- Two quarters of seventeenth-century prose

Beyond these requirements, students also selected an emphasis that yoked courses in writing in a genre with courses in literature in that genre. For example, a student might have selected Versification as six credits of courses in rhetoric, accompanied by courses in the work of famous author-lyricists through the literature program (University of Minnesota 1920).

This restructuring of the major had three primary effects. The first administrative impact is a radical restriction on student choice. The rhetoric major lost its independence from literature; yoking writing courses with period and genre courses in literature became a way to funnel students interested in writing and speaking into literature classes. Second, by eliminating the seminar in rhetoric and replacing it with courses in literary prose and other genres of literature, it created the illusion that one learns to write by reading literature, rather than by studying rhetoric as an art. This illusion would rest at the basis of composition instruction for decades, at Minnesota and at other institutions, because it replicated the ideology of consumption that lay beneath English curriculum. (Only in literacy and literary circles does this misperception exist, it seems to me; no one believes that driving makes someone an effective automotive engineer or that eating makes someone an effective chef.) Finally, any possibility of seeking supporting courses in Philology, Philosophy, Latin, Greek, advanced modern language, History, or the social sciences (as outlined in the 1914 catalog) are eliminated in the revised major. Today, we know that rhetoric includes all these areas of study, but this change in the major in rhetoric closed off that recognition. Rhetoric became entirely a subfield of English at Minnesota, and its contours were radically altered until it was finally dissolved into the English major entirely.

Rhetoric Revived: The STC Program in Rhetoric in the College of Agriculture

The Department of Rhetoric in the College of Agriculture at the University of Minnesota traced its history to 1907, but because it was located on the St. Paul campus and because it was initially part of the School of Agriculture, it flew "under the radar" while the Department of English and R&PS were being merged in the 1920s. There were, then, two departments of rhetoric at the University of Minnesota for a brief period in the first decades of the twentieth century.

The Department of Rhetoric in the College of Agriculture offered no major for decades; it existed to serve general education needs for agriculture majors. And the College of Agriculture required more liberal education courses than most units at the university. For example, the communications movements of the 1950s and 1960s (described by Crowley in "Communications Skills and a Brief Rapprochement of Rhetoricians") led to a College of Agriculture requirement for undergraduate majors to take nine credits of Communication I-II-III, with "integrated assignments in reading, listening and speaking" as well as writing. The college also required courses in public speaking and in exposition.

Outside the production-oriented communication courses, the department of rhetoric also offered introductory humanities courses in the Enlightenment, the Industrial Revolution, and the Age of Darwin, in addition to traditional courses in literary history and genre. It offered advanced courses in communication: listening, technical writing, and discussion. It offered advanced humanities courses in Individualism, in Religion in American Thought and Experience, and in Nationalism in American Thought and Experience (*College of Agriculture, Food and Human Ecology Catalog*, 1969–1971). This diversity of courses became the raw material for the eventual Scientific and Technical Communicaton major in the college.

The reasons for this commitment to rhetorical education, in its fullest sense (as both training in communication strategies and critical reading of the humanistic tradition) can be attributed to both an ethical mission and a status anxiety. On the one hand, there was immense anxiety that agricultural students, typically hailing from rural areas, might need extra training in effective communication skills. On the other hand, agriculture programs were both highly technical and integral to the social and economic fabric of the state. The university participated in the land grant mission, in which those trained in the techniques and technologies of agriculture were to contribute to the community. The College of Agriculture ensured that those who understood the science of agriculture could communicate that science to others and communicate the importance of that science in the public or political sphere. The civic component of rhetoric was reinforced in the department not only by the rhetorical tradition but also by the mission of the land grant, agricultural university.

When the department of rhetoric created its technical communication (later scientific and technical communication) major in the 1970s, it couched the major in the language of business:

> Technical Communication is defined as the application of modern communication techniques to the dissemination of technical knowledge in industry, business, education and government. The technical communicator develops the channels of communication that run from scientist and engineer to management and to the consumers of the products and services provided by technology. (University of Minnesota 1975)

Despite the pragmatic bent of the description in the course catalog, the major was clearly constructed from the same commitment to the broad rhetorical principles at the heart of the extant undergraduate service curriculum. Table 1 summarizes the distribution of credits in the undergraduate program, including liberal education courses, listed in quarter-system credits. Additionally, I note which categories could include courses offered by the Department of Rhetoric.

Table 1. Technical Communication Major Requirements
(Source: University of Minnesota 1975)

Course Area	Credits Required
Communication, Language, Symbolic Systems	21 credits (16 from the Department of Rhetoric)
Physical and Biological Sciences	18 credits
Man and Society	16 credits (some of which could come from the Department of Rhetoric)
Artistic Expression	20 credits (some of which could come from the Department of Rhetoric)
Technical Communication, subdivided into: Writing & Editing Media Communication Graphic Communication Organizational, Managerial and Training Communication Communication Theory and Research Oral Communication	60 credits (some of which could come from the Department of Rhetoric)
Technical Electives	20 credits
Other Electives	25 credits
Total:	180 credits

Over thirty years, the major retained that broad understanding of rhetoric as both communication strategy and communication theory, embedded in knowledge of cultural values. Table 2 offers a summary of the major program requirements in 2006, listed in semester, rather than quarter, credits.

Table 2: Scientific and Technical Communication Major Requirements
(Source: University of Minnesota 2007 http://www.rhetoric.umn.edu)

Course Area	Credits Required
Introduction to Scientific and Technical Communication	2 credits in Rhetoric

Written, Oral and Visual Communication	19 credits in Rhetoric
Theory and Research	11 credits in Rhetoric
Science, Technology and Society	6 credits in Rhetoric
Internship	3 credits in Rhetoric
Electives	5 credits in Rhetoric
Total:	46 major credits in Rhetoric

This major curriculum is likely to change; the Department of Rhetoric has been collapsed into a new Department of Writing Studies that will exist within the College of Liberal Arts, and its agricultural context will be erased. The land grant mission will fade from view and the undergraduate curriculum will be forced to exist in the same college as its siblings in Communication and English. Whether the civic component will remain, and whether the synthesis of communication in oral, written, and visual forms can be sustained, is yet to be known. This is not the first time that a department of rhetoric has been dismantled at Minnesota, but history tells us that the closer rhetoric is brought to its siblings, the more sharply it is defined in contrast to them, rather than in its own fullness.

The lesson taught by the history of the University of Minnesota, then, is that fully rhetorical majors, embracing the written and oral, the critical and productive, simply may not be possible in the modern university. The fully rhetorical major only exists in a context external or prior to the disciplinary fragmentation that typifies the modern university. If we do not recognize that reality, our efforts to design a major in rhetoric and composition are stymied from the start.

RHETORICAL RESEARCH AND THE RHETORICAL MAJOR

The first two sections of this essay set out, through historical and contemporary examples, two central points about the place of rhetoric in the undergraduate curriculum. First, multiple disciplines lay claim to rhetoric as a conceptual field, but the fact that rhetoric contains both critical and productive modes has resulted in its fragmentation, as disciplines and departments that seek to grasp the critical power of rhetoric sometimes devalue the productive component. This is the context in which we struggle to define our own writing majors.

The second point follows from the first, in that it is clear that the scope of rhetoric is shaped by the location of rhetoric within an institution. When rhetoric is allowed to flourish in a freestanding department, something amazing can happen, in terms of synthesizing all that rhetoric can be. When asked to sprout alongside a program in literature or even a program in communication, rhetoric can be circumscribed in ways that tell us as much about rhetoric's sibling than the rhetorical tradition itself. The historical moments in which freestanding rhetoric programs can exist are vanishing, and we are left to build our majors in the vacant lots of the academy between literature, speech, philosophy, and other disciplines.

There are two implications of this historical analysis. First, the steamroller that is driving forward the declaration of rhetoric and composition's disciplinary independence needs to be reconsidered in terms of its implications for undergraduate teaching. If rhetoric and composition is its own discipline, do undergraduate majors inevitably follow? Second, if you believe that undergraduate majors are inevitable, how do we address the historical circumstances that make rhetoric unstable as an intellectual field in the modern university? How do we build our majors on the scraps of land in the academy that remain for us?

Should All Disciplines Have Freestanding Undergraduate Majors?

In 2004, the Consortium of Doctoral Programs in Rhetoric and Composition proposed that "rhetoric and composition" be given status as an "emerging field" in National Research Council categorization. Such a request is tantamount to requesting recognition by external institutions as a freestanding discipline. The consortium's claims are threefold:

1. Rhetoric and composition is a discipline dating from 1963 and with doctoral programs of its own.

2. Rhetoric and composition has its own subdiscipline of technical and professional communication, reinforcing its claim to disciplinary status.

3. As a discipline it is distinct from English, from communication and from creative writing.

The consortium has argued for rhetoric and composition's independence from English by claiming that

Although many rhetoric and composition programs are still located nominally in English degrees, or placed in English departments, most have a distinct identity and have moved toward autonomy within those structures, or even separation in independent units. (Consortium 2004, 5–6)

The consortium has also argued that it is clearly distinct from communication and creative writing, though there is fruitful intersection between these distinct fields.

The consortium's arguments are persuasive and sound. They muster claims of freestanding departments, freestanding doctoral programs within other departments, and freestanding emphases within doctoral programs in English. They claim institutional markers of disciplinary status: journals, conventions, listservs, and other apparatus of scholarly communication.

The energy that the consortium has placed into establishing the disciplinary status of rhetoric and composition need not translate into the development of undergraduate majors. It seems to me entirely unclear whether the establishment of a research agenda, and of the scholarly institutions that foster that research agenda, is justification for the construction of a freestanding undergraduate major. There are a significant number of areas of study that flourish only at the level of research and graduate or professional study. These include professions like law, medicine or, closer to home, library science. Like rhetoric and composition, library science is composed of a diversity of humanistic and social scientific research methods. Like rhetoric and composition, library science includes historical, theoretical, applied, and pedagogical research. Unlike rhetoric and composition, there is no imperative to develop freestanding undergraduate majors in library science. The establishment of the discipline has not led to the establishment of an undergraduate curriculum.

If the consortium is successful in arguing the disciplinary independence of rhetoric and composition, I believe that there will be greater impetus to create PhDs whose training is entirely within the discipline of rhetoric and composition. This, too, seems problematic to me.

The idea that graduate programs should produce PhDs with primary, even exclusive, knowledge only of rhetoric and composition is dangerous. It is dangerous, first and foremost, to the faculty trained in those programs as they step into new professional contexts. At the doctoral level, a graduate student is immersed in the discipline; their identity as a member of the discipline is their central professional and intellectual identity. After graduation, they will move into a new context. For a faculty member in the 70 percent of institutions without *any* form of doctoral study (according to the 2005 Carnegie rankings), the discipline becomes at most an important secondary identity. The department and the college become primary communities of professional identity. Given the relative scarcity of freestanding departments of writing studies, we need to train scholars who can communicate with colleagues within broader departments of English and communication.

Those colleagues are the ones whose own grasp of rhetoric, typically in terms of consumption and gnosis instead of in terms of production and praxis, set the context in which we must teach, research, design curricula, and earn tenure. They mark the circumstances that we must face as we propose courses and programs, and so their take on rhetorical practices (and/or literacy practices) must be part of our training. We need to know how to negotiate the historical realities we inherit, rather than impose expectations for departmental and disciplinary independence that we carry with us from doctoral institutions. Within those historical realities, we can negotiate new curricular and programmatic formations.

Phrased differently, the historical moment for rhetoric to manifest itself fully in a major (as both critical and productive art, as both praxis and gnosis) is lost. Rhetoric's fragmentation in the university is the reality with which we must engage, and we should be trained to do so at the graduate level. When we arrive at the undergraduate institution in which we will make our professional lives, we can do so skilled in collaboration and primed for innovation.

An example will help: A small teaching school in western Wisconsin (University of Wisconsin–River Falls [UWRF]) is home to one of the few freestanding programs in marketing communication in the United States.[8] There is no rhetoric course in that program; there is no rhetoric program within the institution. The Department of Communication Studies and Theatre Arts offers a course called "Speech in History," and the English Department offers a minor in professional writing without a single rhetoric course, but it is fair to say that UWRF typifies a small university (6,000 students) without a fully rhetorical major.

---

8. Programs in marketing and programs in advertising are common; this program is a relatively unique hybrid, pulling together courses in marketing, consumer behavior, speech communication, journalism, public relations, composition, business, and sales into a single major. The MarComm curriculum is outlined on the Web at http://www. uwrf.edu/marcomm/, but the Web is a poor vehicle for understanding the achievements of James Pratt of the Department of Speech Communication and Theatre Arts and Steve Olsen of Marketing Communication in constructing a profoundly rhetorical major without a single rhetoric class.

That said, the faculty at UWRF have created a major that typifies the best of the rhetoric majors in the freestanding departments of the past. The entire program is suffused with the finest elements of the rhetorical tradition: a hybrid of written and oral (and new media) genres of rhetorical production, a sense of the ethical and potentially civic aspects of rhetorical work in both praxis and gnosis. And perhaps most interestingly, rhetoric's sibling, in this context, in addition to communication and English, is marketing research.

In my tragic tales of two campuses of the University of Minnesota system, we saw the historical trend toward the devaluation of rhetorical praxis alongside literature and communication studies. These cautionary tales can at last be softened by an upbeat alternative. When rhetoric must negotiate a space alongside advertising and consumer behavior studies, rather than poetry or quantitative studies of communication apprehension, something new is created. In the MarComm program, students begin their curriculum conceiving of audiences as consumers as they pass through their early courses in consumer behavior and advertising. Consumers are acted upon; if the actions of marketing communication specialists are successful, consumers recall an advertising message and purchase a product. Their exposure to rhetoric in early courses is one that centers on the productive art, acting on the passive audience. Their advanced courses (in persuasion, for example) recreate a complex sense of audience as subjects to whom the students have an ethical responsibility. As the civic is restored to rhetorical praxis, the major opens itself to gnosis. The end result is more than any traditional mass communication or advertising major can constitute, precisely because of the rhetorical inflection.

This innovative reconfiguration of rhetoric cannot be replicated by faculty trained narrowly in a PhD with an emphasis solely on rhetoric and composition; it must derive from an understanding of rhetoric in dynamic tension with other disciplines (whether those disciplines are literature, communication, or consumer behavior). The faculty who designed this curriculum were not intent upon the disciplinary independence of rhetoric or the integrity of an undergraduate major in writing. They were intent upon fashioning a major within the available resources of their university. They found the vacant lot between English, communication studies, public relations, and advertising and they started to build. Their lesson is exemplary for us all.

RHETORIC AND THE ODD LOT

To summarize: In the first third of this essay, I pointed to the historical devaluation of rhetoric at many universities. Our sibling disciplines have cornered the market on rhetoric, though they may have done so in a way that diminishes its full productive power. And the historical era of rhetoric majors that embrace the full power of rhetoric may have passed, at most institutions—the second third of this essay details that transformation. We cannot make a whole of what has been fragmented across the American university. The best efforts of the Consortium of Doctoral Programs in Rhetoric and Composition to assert the disciplinary independence of rhetoric and composition studies cannot make that happen, at least at the undergraduate level.

And so the question is not, "What should a rhetoric and writing major look like?" Institutional realities militate against the possibility of such a thing. The question is, how can rhetoric majors be built in the spaces between majors in literature, writing, communication, marketing, and philosophy? The presumption seems to be, that as rhetoric and composition achieves status as a discipline, that such achievement will result in new undergraduate majors. The history of rhetoric in the twentieth century tells us that that is no longer possible; we need graduate training and just plain imagination to find our place at the dance.

REFERENCES

Benson, Thomas. 2003. The Cornell school of rhetoric: Idiom and institution. *Communication Quarterly* 51.1:1–56.

Berlin, James. 1987. *Rhetoric and reality: Writing instruction in American colleges, 1900–1985.* Carbondale: Southern Illinois University Press.

———. 1984. *Writing instruction in nineteenth-century American colleges.* Carbondale: Southern Illinois University Press.

Carpini, Dominic Delli. Spring 2007. Re-writing the humanities: The writing major's effect upon undergraduate studies in English departments. *Composition Studies* 35.1:15–36.

Crowley, Sharon. 2004. Communications skills and a brief rapprochement of rhetoricians. *Rhetoric Society Quarterly* 34.1:89–104.

The Consortium of Doctoral Programs in Rhetoric and Composition. "The case for rhetoric and composition as an emerging field." October, 2004. http://www.cws.illinois.edu/rc_consortium/rhetcompcase.pdf (accessed October 15, 2007).

Fleming, David. 1998. Rhetoric as a course of study. *College English* 61.2:169–91.

Gaonkar, Dilip. The idea of rhetoric in the rhetoric of science. In Gross, Alan, and William Keith. 1996. *Rhetorical hermeneutics: Invention and interpretation in the age of science.* Albany: SUNY Press. 25-87.

Gross, Alan, and William Keith. 1996. *Rhetorical hermeneutics: Invention and interpretation in the age of science.* Albany: SUNY Press.

Howard, Rebecca Moore. 2007. Curricular activism: The writing major as counterdiscourse. *Composition Studies* 35.1:42–52.

Jackson, Brian. 2007. Cultivating paideweyan pedagogy: Rhetoric education in English and communication studies. *Rhetoric Society Quarterly* 37:2:181–201.

Keith, William. 2007. *Democracy as discussion: Civic education and the American forum movement.* Lanham, MD: Lexington Books.

Mailloux, Stephen. 2006. *Disciplinary identities: Rhetorical paths of English, speech, and composition.* New York: Modern Language Association.

Miller, Thomas P. 2005. How rhetorical are English and communication majors? *Rhetoric Society Quarterly* 35.1:91–113.

O'Neill, Peggy, Nan Stevens LoBue, Margaret McLaughlin, Angela Crow, and Kathy S. Albertson. 1999. A comment on "Rhetoric as a course of study." *College English* 62.2: 274–75.

Scott, Tony. 2007. The cart, the horse and the road they are driving down: Thinking ecologically about a new writing major. *Composition Studies* 35.1:81–93.

Shamoon, Linda K., Rebecca Moore Howard, Sandra Jamieson, and Robert A. Schwegler, eds. 2000. *Coming of age: The advanced writing curriculum.* Portsmouth, NH: Heinemann.

University of California Berkeley. "Department of Rhetoric." http://rhetoric.berkeley. edu/rhetoric_major.html (accessed October 15, 2007).

University of Minnesota. 1905. *Bulletin of the college of science, literature and the arts, 1905–1906.* St. Paul: University of Minnesota.

———. 1914. *Bulletin of the college of science, literature and the arts, 1914–1915.* St. Paul: University of Minnesota.

———. 1920. *Bulletin of the college of science, literature and the arts, 1920–1921.* St. Paul: University of Minnesota.

_____. 1969. *Catalog of the College of Agriculture, Food and Human Ecology, 1969–1971.* St. Paul: University of Minnesota.

———. 1975. *Bulletin of the college of agriculture, 1975–1977.* St. Paul: University of Minnesota.

University of Minnesota. Department of Rhetoric. "Scientific and Technical Communication Major Requirements. 2007. http://www.rhetoric.umn.edu (accessed September, 2007; no longer available).

University of Minnesota Duluth. 1935. *Bulletin, 1935–1936.* Duluth: University of Minnesota.

———. 1936. *Bulletin, 1936-1937.* Duluth: University of Minnesota.

APPENDIX
Upper Division, Elective Courses in Rhetoric at Berkeley

History and Theory of Rhetoric	Public Discourse	Narrative and Image
Rhetorical Theory and Practice in the Historical Eras	Rhetoric of Religious Discourse	Genre in Film and Literature
Advanced Argumentative Writing	Rhetorical Approaches to Folklore	Rhetoric of Fiction: Form
Advanced Argumentative Writing for majors only	American Cultures as a Problem in Postmodernity	Rhetoric of Fiction: Content and Context
Philosophical Discourse	Rhetoric of Contemporary Politics	Rhetoric of Drama
Literary and Cultural Discourse	Rhetoric of Constitutional Discourse	Poetry Performance
Theoretical Inquiry into Law, Polity, and Society	Race and Order in the New Republic	Rhetoric of Poetry
Rhetoric and Theory of Film	American Political Rhetoric	Poetics and Poetry
Rhetoric, Culture and Society	Rhetoric of Colonialism and Postcolonialism	Rhetoric of the Realist Novel
Comparative Rhetoric	Rhetoric of the Political Novel	Novel and Society
Rhetoric and Literature Under the Roman Empire	Rhetoric of Modern Political Theory	Novel into Film
Discourse of Qualities	Rhetoric of Contemporary Political Theory	Theories of Film
Rhetoric of Historical Discourse	Advanced Problems in the Rhetoric of Political Theory	Selected Topics in Film
Rhetoric of Scientific Discourse	Great Theorists: Political and Legal Theory	National Cinema
Rhetoric of Philosophical Discourse	Great Themes: Contemporary Political and Legal Theory	Rhetoric of Narrative Genres in Non-literate Societies
Language, Truth and Dialogue	Introduction to the Rhetoric of Legal Discourse	Rhetoric of Autobiography
Theory and Practice of Reading and Interpretation	Rhetoric of American Cultures	Autobiography and American Individualism

Special Topics (if appropriate)	Law, Ethnicity and the Rhetoric of National Security	American Political Rhetoric
	Rhetoric of Legal Theory	Rhetoric of the Political Novel
	Rhetoric of Legal Philosophy	Evil and the Rhetoric of the Modern Novel
	Rhetoric, Law and Politics in Ancient Greece	Rhetoric of the Novel
	Advanced Topics in Law and Rhetoric	Rhetoric of Race and Science
	Rhetoric, Law and Political Theory, 1500-1700	Special Topics (if appropriate)
	Rhetoric of Social Science	
	Mass Culture and the Rhetoric of Social Theory	
	Rhetoric of Social Theory	
	Sexual Exchange	
	Special Topics (if appropriate)	

Summarized from http://rhetoric.berkeley.edu.

8

WRITING PROGRAM DEVELOPMENT AND DISCIPLINARY INTEGRITY
What's Rhetoric Got to Do with It?

Lori Baker
Teresa Henning

In her report on the 1993 conference for New England Writing Program Administrators, Linda Shamoon et al. cites Stephen North's call to use rhetoric as "the next formulation of our discipline," and criticizes him and other scholars like him for failing to elaborate their "bases for rebuilding contemporary writing programs as rhetoric programs" (1995, 7). She insists that we must understand what is at stake before making such a shift.

With the recent development of rhetoric and composition programs across the country and our own work to create a professional writing major in an English department with a strong creative writing major, we feel that Shamoon et al.'s concern is still apt. We, like others before us (e.g., Berlin, North, and Porter), are committed to using rhetoric for program development. We define rhetoric as the use of language for a purpose in a specific communication situation, and, as such, we acknowledge that texts are designed to bring about material effects in the world. We take a "rhetorical perspective" by embracing the theoretical consequences of this definition (i.e., reality is constructed through language, and, as such, knowledge is inherently intersubjective, social, and political). Our chapter will draw on this definition and our specific experiences with program development to give our readers a better understanding of the ways a rhetorical perspective and local practices interact in the development of a new writing major. In creating this new understanding, our chapter will make three moves. We will begin our chapter by defining what we mean by using rhetoric for program development. We will then use our own professional writing and communication major as a "case study" for exploring the ways our rhetorical definition works in a local context, and we will conclude with a discussion of the ways a rhetorical perspective is related to our concern for disciplinary integrity, a concern which is motivated by our desire to both respect the bounded nature of a discipline and create connections across disciplines and contexts.

RHETORIC AND PROGRAM DEVELOPMENT:
AN OPERATIONAL DEFINITION

In our introduction, we broadly construe rhetoric as the use of language for a purpose. While this definition is broad and certainly already accepted by our field, when developing a writing program, we are never only working with those in our field. As Shamoon et al. points out, when using rhetoric for program development, one needs a definition that works for outsiders and "helps us situate ourselves to outsiders" (1995, 14). In situating ourselves to outsiders, we believe that we need to mix practical concerns with theoretical, or as Rebecca Moore Howard tells us, we need to account for writing as a discipline in its own right while also preparing writers for careers and helping our students understand the connection between writing and participation in the public sphere (2000, xv). What we would like to explore, then, is how a definition of rhetoric can be operationalized in meaningful ways for ourselves and others, and what, if anything, this definition has to do with the disciplinary integrity of those who choose to use such a definition. Specifically, we will explore how a definition of rhetoric that focuses on using language for a purpose in a specific communication situation allows us to

- invoke all elements of the communication triangle (i.e., rhetor, interlocutor, subject, and text);

- engage with and interrogate different historical perspectives of rhetoric; and

- focus on the situational nature of writing, rhetoric, and program development.

In developing a professional writing major that includes within it courses in advanced composition, journalism, technical writing and business writing, we have born witness to impoverished notions of composition and technical writing that tend to define writing as a set of skills divorced from context. Of course, we are not alone in noticing this limited definition of writing. Scholars that write about advanced composition and/or technical communication repeatedly make this point. For instance, in *Coming of Age: The Advanced Writing Curriculum* (2000), Lynn Bloom's "Advancing Composition" and Richard Bullock's "Feathering our Nest" offer poignant descriptions of the ways advanced composition can fall prey to a "skills approach" that marginalizes what composition specialists do. For instance, Bloom cites Katherine Adams's historical overview of advanced composition courses, noting that one vision of advanced composition is as "advanced remediation for students who [need] more than freshman composition" 10), while Bullock points to the way that first-year composition often becomes conflated with the larger terms *rhetoric* and *composition* and is used to represent all a compositionist is capable of doing. Similarly, as Johndan Johnson-Eilola in "Relocating the Value of Work" shows, technical communication has routinely been reduced to a set of discrete skills (2004).

In each of these cases, this impoverished view of writing is possible because those who hold it have reduced the act of communication and writing to one piece of the communication triangle—textual constraints. Yet, in our experience, we do not believe that our colleagues are really committed to this impoverished view of writing. We often find that the very ones who reduce writing to a set of skills are often the same ones who bemoan the lack of critical thinking and logic in their student essays. In so doing, they acknowledge a wider understanding of writing as something more than a discrete skill set.

A limited definition of writing as a discrete skill set is also problematic at the programmatic level because it tends to support an uncritical and disjointed view of curricula. For instance, limiting writing to textual constraints encourages an understanding of course design as being based on paper production. As Robert Schwegler points out in his article in *Coming of Age*, such an understanding of course design is problematic because it limits us to "a curriculum of writing courses rather than a writing curriculum of courses designed to develop expertise and knowledge important to writers" (2000, 27). Limiting the conception of curriculum to that of writing courses also supports an uncritical perspective of curriculum design that Schwegler argues tends to be the norm for academics. He states:

> Many in the professoriate view curricula uncritically, simply as sets of courses, and curriculum development as the creation of a list of courses characterized by some kind of formal unity, achieved either through a theme, such as the

> study of American culture, or formal categories, such as historical periods,
> genres, and major figures. A curriculum, however, is a set of practices and
> material conditions. . . . (25)

In the end, committing oneself to a rhetorical perspective that honors
all aspects of the communication triangle allows us to resist the limited
views that Schwegler describes and honor our sense and Schwegler's that
"the things that should be studied and practiced in writing courses—the
processes of composing; discourse genres; contexts; readers; media;
links among texts, knowledge, power, and action—form clusters distinct
enough to deserve courses of their own, yet related enough to constitute
a discipline and a curriculum" (29).

In addition to committing ourselves to a rhetorical perspective that
accounts for all aspects of the communication triangle, we are also
committed to engaging with and interrogating historical perspectives
of rhetoric. Engaging with historical perspectives on rhetoric can help
us make the work we do meaningful to those outside our discipline by
allowing us to align the work we do with a broader liberal arts education (something our institution already values). It is often useful for us
to define the scope of rhetoric broadly as Sonja Foss, Karen Foss, and
Robert Trapp do in their "Perspectives on the Study of Rhetoric." They
remind readers that rhetoric is an ancient art dating back to classical
Greece that draws upon not only ancient texts but "other periods" and
"a variety of contemporary disciplines such as psychology, sociology, literary criticism, English and philosophy" (2003, 19). Similarly, we often
remind those from other disciplines of the ways our professional writing
and communication major benefits from the work of their disciplines
but also can contribute to that work in a meaningful way. Students also
benefit from conceiving of rhetoric as a broad liberal art as they are able
to take a range of courses to meet the requirements of one major. They
have the potential to develop a strong rhetorical understanding of a variety of disciplines and texts that they can later apply to a variety of unique
career and writing contexts.

In engaging with historical perspectives on rhetoric from the stand-
point of a broad liberal art, our program echoes a commitment described
by others in our field. For instance, Kathleen McCormick and Donald
Jones, in "Developing a Professional and Technical Writing Major that
Integrates Composition Theory, Literacy Theory, and Cultural Studies,"
note that while their major is "financially feasible" in the way it draws

upon existing courses, it is "intellectually viable" in the way it invokes key historical and rhetorical concepts such as "audience analysis" and "ideological analysis of discourse conventions" (2000). McCormick and Jones's approach is also appealing because while it is important to us that our program engages with historic rhetorical categories such as kairos, stasis, audience, invention, style, and arrangement, it is also important to us that students continually interrogate the usefulness of these historical perspectives. McCormick and Jones's emphasis on ideology allows us to be sensitive to John Trimbur's concern, as reported in Shamoon et al. 1995, that program development needs to do more than "import traditional ideas of rhetoric" (Shamoon et al. 1995, 15). According to Trimbur, program development also needs to "account for heterogeneous realities such as class and mass culture" (15).

We are particularly concerned with the interrogation aspect of our commitment to a historical perspective on rhetoric because we also want to allow for the possibility of a civic understanding of rhetoric. As Thomas Miller convincingly argues, too often "composition courses have valorized personal expression while doing the institutional work of teaching students how to pass by conforming to the status quo" (2000, 34). In opposition to this perspective, we, like Miller, want to allow for an understanding of rhetoric as a "political art of negotiating received beliefs against changing situations to advance shared purposes" (34).

Our commitment to engaging and interrogating historical perspectives of rhetoric is also closely aligned to our commitment to account for the situational nature of the work we do, which in turn allows us to develop a flexible curriculum. Honoring the situational nature of both writing and program development is important because as James Berlin reminds us, "A curriculum does not do this on its own, free of outside influence. Instead, it occupies a position between the conditions of the larger society it serves—the economic, political, and cultural sections—and the work of teachers-scholars with the institution" (1996, 17). Our program attempts to respect our unique context by doing, as Ruth Overman Fischer and Christopher Thaiss aptly put it, "what you can with what you have right where you are" (2000). Or as Diana Ashe and Colleen A. Reilly point out, by honoring the unique context of our program and its broader connections to the institution and community, we can capitalize on two important principles of smart growth: "take advantage of compact building design" and "mix land uses" (2007, 9). The former principle, as Ashe and Reilly note, suggests the "efficient use of space and resources," while the latter "highlights the importance of integrating the use of resources by commingling different populations" (9).

Fischer and Thaiss's pragmatic approach and Ashe and Reilly's smart growth principles resonate with us because we, too, have few professional writing faculty, but our program is housed in an English department with a strong creative writing program and specialty in journalism. Also, departments outside English such as communications and art have public relations and graphic design courses, respectively, that could benefit professional writing students. By taking a rhetorical approach to program development, we are able to see how all of these courses relate to text production and have developed an interdisciplinary major that reflects many of our institution's existing strengths.

RHETORIC AND PROGRAM DEVELOPMENT IN CONTEXT: A CASE STUDY

Southwest Minnesota State University's (SMSU's) Unique Context

So far, we have offered an operational definition of how rhetoric relates to program development. We would now like to turn our attention to considering the ways that the professional writing program in which we work reflects each aspect of our definition. However, before considering how our program relates to the three aspects of our definition, it is important to first describe the unique context in which we work. As noted in the introduction, our institution is a small, liberal arts university whose mission includes outreach and service to the region in the state system. SMSU is one of seven universities in the state's university and community college system, a system with its own mission and strategic plan governed by a chancellor and board of trustees. Thus, any new programs need to link to both the school's and system's goals. Writing courses at SMSU are housed in the English department, which offers three other majors, with creative writing as the largest and most well-known major, followed by our English licensure program, and a traditional literature major.

Our professional writing and communication (PWC) major of today has roots almost ten years old, when our school entered into a partnership program with the University of Minnesota in several degree programs which were then located in their College of Agricultural, Food, and Environmental Sciences. The scientific and technical communication (STC) degree offered by the rhetoric department was one of those programs. The rhetoric department was offering its degree via interactive television (ITV) and online classes at several sites in addition to its St. Paul campus; partnering with SMSU was the first attempt for both schools at collaborating across systems. From the beginning of the partnership, neither school envisioned more than ten to twelve students enrolled in the major at SMSU. Numbers were, in fact, lower than that with about six to eight students at the end of the program. The degree was viewed by students as very specific, and the students who did enroll tended to be transfer students or upper-level students changing their major. The University of Minnesota (U-M) was able to place all graduates in a wide variety of positions in its urban setting. Students at SMSU, however, are often committed to staying in our rural region and were worried that a specific focus on technical writing would drastically limit their opportunities for employment. The partnership lasted for several years, surviving multiple interim and new administrators at both schools, until finally U-M, citing budget reasons, ended the partnership. A two-year phase out of offering courses took place.

At SMSU, we were just beginning to develop momentum with recruiting students, and students who were coming to SMSU were just able to see the program in the catalog and could hear from graduates who had found success in it. Wanting to capitalize on that momentum, plus build something more appropriate for SMSU's student body and regional needs, Professor Suzanne Black, with the help of Professor Lori Baker, developed the PWC major using the U-M design, which incorporated a writing core, speech core, visual core, and individualized expertise area, yet which was built on existing SMSU courses (see figure 4). These SMSU courses, as listed in figure 4, came from the English department and speech, art, and business programs. Students would also be allowed to transfer online technical writing classes from Minnesota State University, Mankato, opening up the possibility of collaboration within our state university system rather than with U-M. Originally, only two new courses were developed for the English/writing core: English 460: Writing for New Media and English 492: Professional Writing Theory (which would serve as the capstone); thus, we could argue that we did not need a new hire to cover additional courses because Black's load had always included a course reassignment to oversee the partnership, and that reassignment would no longer be needed.

The new major passed through the SMSU process, receiving departmental, curriculum committee, and full faculty assembly approval in

April of 2004. The administration agreed to the new major. The next step was system approval, a finicky process entailing evidence to prove that need for such a program existed (i.e., jobs would be available) and that the program did not duplicate already existing programs in the state university system.

At this point, however, Black, one of the two lead professors, took a leave of absence for a year, effectively halting the progress of the major until the administration could be assured that it could be staffed. At the end of the year's leave, Black decided not to return, which meant a second year of delay for the program, while conducting a national search for a replacement.

While the major itself was not able to come online during those two years, Baker, who was also serving as chair of the English department, worked to retain the line dedicated to the major and to keep the major in sight, both for the department and the administration. This was not always easy, as some faculty who had been on leave or sabbatical during the original passage of the major questioned why we needed it and whether it was a wise use of resources. Students, in the meantime, were approaching Baker asking when or if the program might be finalized.

Eventually, the department was able to hire Professor Teresa Henning to replace Black. Henning was charged with reviewing the curriculum to make certain that it was built on an appropriate theoretical framework and that it fit with national standards as well as regional needs. Henning created a departmental subcommittee to take ideas to before presenting to the full department. She fortuitously received reassigned time in the spring semester when a course was cancelled for low enrollment; for her reassignment, she finalized the review of the curriculum, revised courses, enabled the passage of the revised major through the department, curriculum committee, and faculty assembly, and did all the research and writing of the twenty-page system-level proposal to gain system-level approval.

Applying an Operational Definition of Rhetoric to SMSU's Unique Contexts

While the historical context and specific decision-making processes that led to SMSU's PWC major might be unique to SMSU, the framing of the major from a rhetorical perspective and the application of our core rhetorical principles are possible by any campus. Now that readers have an overview of the unique contexts that have given rise to SMSU's PWC major, we would like to return to our original definition of rhetoric and analyze the ways the three aspects of our definition are evident in the major. We will begin by considering the ways we have relied on the communication triangle to resist impoverished definitions of writing.

Invoking the Communication Triangle to Resist Impoverished Definitions of Writing

The PWC career opportunities description in figure 1, its learning outcomes listed in figure 2, its program emphasis described in figure 3, and its course offerings noted in figure 4 all reflect traces of our commitment to account for all aspects of the communication triangle. This commitment is most obvious in the major's title: professional writing and communication. This title is purposeful and had to be argued for twice, once when Baker and Black first proposed the major and again when Henning brought the major to the department and then the faculty assembly for discussion and re-approval. The title invokes a broader spectrum of writing rather than only technical or scientific writing. It also calls upon a more popular or industry-related perspective of communication. Although the speech program at SMSU voiced concerns about what they viewed as the appropriation of a term from their discipline, we were able to argue that that is an academic perspective not shared by people and organizations outside of the academy; in addition, the curriculum we developed is interdisciplinary, drawing upon courses in speech as well as art, and so would involve discussions of communication that are beyond a traditional view of written text only. In giving the major a broader title, we are able to make space for departmental, institutional, and local needs: our department's need to find a home for journalism courses, which had become an uneasy fit with creative writing; our institution's needs to create programming that fits with a demand in the region and to find ways to increase enrollment without additional resources; and our local region's industry needs for communication professionals.

Fig 1. Career Opportunities Statement for SMSU's Professional Writing and Communication Major (SMSU 2009, "Major")

College graduates with professional writing and communication skills pursue career opportunities in a variety of fields such as journalism, periodical and book publishing; software publishing; advertising and related services; computer systems design and related services; corporate communications; corporate training; government agencies and other not-for-profit agencies.

The Professional Writing and Communication (PWC) Major prepares students for these careers by offering a balance of writing, rhetoric, and communication courses in a liberal arts context. These courses are designed to help students become flexible thinkers, writers, and communicators with the ability to write and communicate in a variety of contexts and environments, including electronic ones. The curriculum consists of core courses in writing, journalism, oral and visual communication, rhetoric, history, and electives in business, politics, ethics, public relations, computer science and psychology, all of which will prepare students to be successful communicators in a variety of contexts.

The career opportunity description and the learning outcomes for the major (see figures 1 and 2) also attempt to demonstrate how the communication triangle will be engaged in throughout the major. For instance, after listing the possible careers the major will prepare students for, the career opportunity description notes the following:

The Professional Writing and Communication (PWC) Major prepares students for these careers by offering a balance of writing, rhetoric, and communication courses in a liberal arts context. These courses are designed to help students become flexible thinkers, writers, and communicators with the ability to write and communicate in a variety of contexts and environments, including electronic ones.

Here the reader will note that the career opportunity description hints at aspects of the communication triangle related to not only text but contexts and writers. This commitment to engaging all aspects of the communication triangle is even more evident in the specific learning outcomes listed in figure 2, which explicitly refer to rhetoric, audience, and purpose.

Fig 2. Learning Outcomes for SMSU's Professional Writing and Communication Major (Henning 2007, 2)

Graduates of the Professional Writing and Communication Major will be able to:

- Understand and apply principles of rhetoric and document design to a variety of communication situations, including written, oral, and visual ones
- Apply critical thinking, reading, listening, and writing skills to specific communication tasks or problems
- Demonstrate a consideration for purpose, audience, and context in communicating
- Demonstrate an ethical sensitivity to language, including its inflammatory and persuasive aspects
- Create documents that are 'user-friendly' in content, structure, and design
- Make use of credible, reliable, and relevant source material (both primary and secondary) in a manner that is appropriate for specific communication situations
- Write documents in a variety of electronic environments
- Manage large projects effectively by allowing adequate time to write, complete research, revise, and receive feedback
- Vary levels of style and language use as appropriate for the communication situation
- Produce a variety of documents that are grammatically and technically correct

Fig 3. Program Emphasis for SMSU's Professional Writing and Communication Major (SMSU 2009, "Major")

The Professional Writing and Communication Major teaches students to become flexible and ethical writers and communicators who can be successful in a variety of contexts including, but not limited to, manufacturing, journalism, advertising, grant writing, technical writing, and software publishing. Faculty in the Professional Writing and Communication Program are committed to working together to provide students with a liberal arts education that is enhanced with practical experiences such as internships and service learning opportunities that prepare students to earn a living as writers. Through this combined liberal arts and technical emphasis, the Professional Writing Major supports SMSU's mission to help students become "engaged citizens in their local and global communities."

The curriculum that was developed for the major resists the impoverished notion of writing and causes students to examine all relationships embedded in the communication triangle. The overall curriculum, as described in figure 4, requires students to take classes not only from the English department in writing but from speech and art, with their foci on oral and visual communication, as well as classes that they choose from professional contexts and an expertise area. The courses in the writing core certainly expose students to textual expectations of the different genres but also with different audience expectations, subject matters, and writer purposes. The text, or form, is not generally the primary consideration. Objectives in the writing classes require that students apply and integrate what they are learning from their different classes. While we cannot wholly control how the students integrate material from their writing courses into the other required courses being taught outside of the English department, all students in the major will draw upon all of the knowledge they have gained across disciplines in the capstone course. The overall structure of the curriculum is in keeping with Schwegler's call to develop "a writing curriculum of courses" rather than "a curriculum of writing courses" which is formed via "clusters distinct enough to deserve courses of their own, yet related enough to constitute a discipline and a curriculum" (2000, 27). The courses demonstrate a mix of genres, theory, history, and cross-disciplinary writing concerns.

Fig 4. SMSU's Professional Writing and Communication Major List of Courses (SMSU "Academic," 2009)

Professional Writing and Communication Major   Total Credit Hours:
                                                                  at least 53

  A. Written Communication Core   Credit Hours: at least 20
          4___ENG 204: Basic Print Journalism
          3___ENG 360: Scientific and Technical Writing
          3___ENG 361: Advanced Composition
          4___ENG 460: Writing and New Media
          3___ENG 420: Copy Editing

One of the following:

4___ENG 305: Literary Non-Fiction Workshop

3___SPCH 260: Introduction to Public Relations Writing

3___ENG/BADM 317: Business Communications

B. *Oral Communication Core*   Credit Hours: 6

3___SPCH 303: Advanced Public Speaking

One of the following:

3___SPCH 310: Persuasion

3___SPCH 360: Org. Comm. and Interviewing (may not double-count here and in F)

3___SPCH 330: Mass Media and Society

3___SPCH 410: Communication Analysis

C. *Visual Communication Core*   Credit Hours: 6

3___ART 102: Foundations of Art and Design (2D)

3___ART 240: Concepts of Graphic Design

D. *Professional Context*   Credit Hours: 6

Select two classes from the list below. These two classes must come from different disciplinary perspectives. Additional classes may also be used in the expertise area.

Perspectives from Business

3___BADM 380: Management Principles

3___BADM 383: Organizational Behavior

3___BADM 390: Business Law I

3___BADM 420: Diversity Management

Perspectives from Marketing

3___MKTG 301: Marketing Principles

Perspectives from Ethics

3___ PHIL 103: Ethics

3___ PHIL 105: Ethical Issues in Business

3___ PHIL 107: Environmental Ethics

Perspectives from Politics and Public Administration

3___POL 324: Local and Rural Politics

3___POL 340: Public Policy and Administration

3___PBAD 320: Public Theory, Policy, and Organization

Perspectives from Psychology

3___PSYC 318: Group Dynamics

3___PYSC 325: Attitudes and Persuasion

E. *History and Theory*   Credit Hours: 6

3___ENG 362: History and Structure of the English Language

3___ENG 492: Theory and Practice of Professional Writing (capstone)

F. *Professional Expertise Area*   Credit Hours: 9

In consultation with their advisor and at least one faculty member from the relevant program, students will select and design a professional expertise area. An expertise area should include at least three classes, with at least six credits taken at the 300 level or above.

Possible areas may include, but are not limited to: public relations, journalism, technical writing, linguistics/composition, accounting, management, marketing, computer science, a natural science, new media, graphic design, or communication theory.

Student may also use an existing SMSU minor to fulfill the requirements in this area.

Restrictions

No courses with "D" grades will count toward the major. A GPA of 2.5 must be maintained in major courses. Majors should choose A–F grading option for major courses. Majors must earn a B- or better in SPCH 110, and English 102 and 103. Majors must also plan to take 40 credit hours at the 300 or 400 levels. Majors may meet this requirement by making careful selections within the major OR majors may meet this requirement by taking electives or upper-level Liberal Arts Core courses.

Engaging and Interrogating Different Historical Perspectives of Rhetoric

The career opportunities description and learning outcomes both make reference to history, but it is the specific courses of the PWC major that help us to see how different historical perspectives of rhetoric might be engaged or interrogated, questioned and/or applied. For example, English 460, Writing and New Media, interrogates core notions of rhetoric and how and whether those core notions are applicable, adaptable, or perhaps not relevant to different media such as Web design, podcasting, and visual text elements. In English 492, Theory and Practice of Professional Writing, the capstone course, students will be developing a portfolio that will include a reflective document in which they must describe and assess their work in the portfolio as it relates to the theories of rhetoric and professional writing that they have been interrogating all semester long. We hope to see in these reflective statements students discussing, analyzing, and negotiating among various rhetorical theories, including rhetorical theories growing out of speech communication and visual design, making sense of what they have been exposed to and what they are taking from it.

In developing the program, we ran into outdated perspectives on rhetoric held by some of our department members, those who held a form-based or current-traditional view of writing and rhetoric, who initially struggled to see how and why a professional writing degree would be of value. In seeing the full curriculum, however, those department members appeared to come to a different understanding of the scope and framework we were building. Many faculty members think that students will major in this degree in order to get a job, which is true enough; but we expect as faculty engage with the curriculum and students during the advising process that they will continue to learn more about contemporary views of rhetoric as this major presents itself.

Accounting for the Situational Nature of Rhetoric in Program Development

The situational nature of rhetoric and writing is reflected in the curriculum in several ways. The social context of writing situations is reflected in the different writing courses and approaches that students are required to take; for example, the social contexts students encounter in a journalism class and the writing assignments they will engage in might be much different that those in a traditional argument class such as our Advanced Composition class. The social contexts faced in our Scientific and Technical Writing class vary greatly from those possible in the Literary Non-Fiction choice. Different courses and tracks will highlight different social contexts, forcing students to experience writing for a wide variety of contexts and adapting to each.

The curriculum also reflects situational considerations in one obvious way: not all classes are taught by English/writing faculty. Clearly, there is an interdisciplinary approach here to delivering the major's content that is in part inscribed by our institution's locations and resources, in addition to the theoretical reasons described earlier concerning why we would want to have such an approach. Because of the academic division of disciplines, however, not all aspects of the curriculum were able to be negotiated in the same way. For example, while the business department welcomed the cross-listing of their Business Communications class with English (and invited an English department member to teach the class given that their faculty member who does so is retiring), the speech program was not willing to cross-list the public relations writing class, even though it is currently taught by an English department member with a split load.

Other curricular evidence of the situational nature of the PWC major includes allowing professional expertise areas outside of English, such as public relations. While allowing for such expertise areas indicates a reliance on other academic areas outside of the English department, it is also an acknowledgment of realistic, or real-world, possibilities: our students may well take jobs in which they focus on public relations writing. The academic divisions between writing and speech and business do not exist in the same manner in the workaday world. Thus, our curriculum allows for and encourages the same sort of situational adjusting, or niche creation, as will be validated in the job market.

RHETORIC AND PROGRAM DEVELOPMENT: OUR DISCIPLINARY INTEGRITY

Now that we have considered how our specific program reflects traces of our commitment to using rhetoric to inform program development, it is important to consider, as Shamoon et al. suggest, what is at stake in invoking rhetoric in the development of any writing program (1995, 14). For us, the stakes of using rhetoric for program development are directly related to our disciplinary integrity. The juxtaposition of the terms *discipline* and *integrity*, and their potentially agonistic relationship, seems a particularly apt way to sum up these risks. On one hand, as Lisa Ede notes, "disciplines are inherently conservative . . . they tend to discipline rather than encourage progressive practices" (Bullock 2000, 24). In other words, disciplines can be homogeneous rather than heterogeneous. They can dictate an ideology rather than interrogate ideologies. On the other hand, a disciplinary perspective can help us avoid notions of writing that are solely skills-based or driven only by what Howard calls a "lay exigence" (2000, xxii).

The concept of integrity, when coupled with discipline, can temper a homogeneous disciplinary impulse. Integrity suggests a desire for wholeness or completeness; it is also related to a desire to stick to our principles. For us, the risk of developing a program from a rhetorical perspective is that we will do so in a rigid manner that fails to account for our desire for wholeness and our desire to connect with a variety of communities and constituencies.

To maintain our disciplinary integrity, we want to use our commitment to a rhetorical perspective in a way that respects the needs, desires, and values of our students. We know that students and their parents will be attracted to our major because of the promise of a good job. In Minnesota alone, a 17 percent job growth is expected for writing jobs in general (ISEEK 2005, "Career: Writers"), and the prospect for technical writers specifically is even more optimistic, with a twenty-three percent growth in jobs expected (ISEEK 2005, "Career: Technical Writers"). While we want our students to find good jobs when they leave the program, we do not want our program to fall prey to catering solely to industry because doing so can lead to the very impoverished understanding of writing that we are trying so hard to resist. We would like to use our rhetorical perspective to create classroom experiences for our students that incorporate a variety of perspectives that may include but are not limited to business-driven concerns about writing and communication.

In addition to respecting the needs of our students, we are also committed to maintaining our integrity by using rhetoric to honor the needs of our institution and local and regional communities. Our institution is a small, comprehensive liberal arts university located in rural, southwest Minnesota. It is both a dorm- and a commuter-campus that serves a mix of international, first-generation, and non-traditional students. The active faculty union gives faculty the power to make curriculum decisions, and this union keeps adjunct faculty to a minimum. However, the commitment to full-time faculty lines as well as recent decreases in the state budget for higher education also limits economic resources for new faculty lines. As such, the institution is always seeking ways to do more with less. New programs need to consider ways of creatively responding to these limitations; we want to ensure that the design of our program retains its integrity in the face of these institutional needs and constraints.

Because we have been empowered to design new curricula, we can invoke a rhetorical perspective in that design. However, since our fellow faculty members have the power to approve that design (or veto it) and since we value creating connection with others, we have to also commit to a curricular design that is practical and sensitive to our institution's needs. By defining rhetoric as a broad liberal art with a connection to a variety of disciplines and by creating a major that draws on the expertise of various disciplines, we feel that we are able to both preserve our disciplinary integrity and serve the unique needs of our institution and students.

Creating an undergraduate program rooted in rhetoric preserves disciplinary integrity not only at the local, institutional level but at the disciplinary level as well. In recent years, as noted in the introduction, numbers of undergraduate writing majors have increased, filling the gap in writing studies between serving first-year composition and graduate programs. While the nature of what a writing major or a writing studies program should contain, what courses and themes should be included, has been debated (the collection *Coming of Age* captures many of these debates), building a program with a rhetorical framework such as we have described will allow space for a variety of writing majors, each with room to negotiate the civic, historical/theoretical, and technical aspects that *Coming of Age* emphasizes. The rhetorical framework that we outline allows for flexibility in design and, to an extent, rhetorical values, yet would maintain a disciplinary wholeness. The sheer existence of a writing major can, as Howard says, "function as an instrument of institutional activism that accomplishes what writing across the curriculum or first year composition cannot: the demonstration of writing as an intellectual discipline rather than as a means of inflicting discipline upon the bodies of students" (2007, 43); a writing major based firmly in rhetoric with a full appreciation of the communication triangle keeps that impoverished, "disciplining" approach to writing at bay while helping to establish how and why writing is worthy of disciplinary status.

As Howard argues, considering how the writing major can transform the work of the discipline and the institution is now in "the realm of ideology" (2007, 42). In "Ideology, Theory and the Genre of Writing Programs," Jeanne Gunner invokes Terry Eagleton to define ideology as points at which "cultural practices are interwoven with political power" (2002, 8). Gunner goes on to explain that ideology is analogous to the operating system on a computer in that "ideology precedes practice and theories of practice" (8). While ideology precedes practice, ideology can be best observed by a focused analysis on those cultural practices that are related to power. Howard argues that the "cultural practices" of institutionalizing a writing major open up those traditional, skills-based ideological arguments about writing: "The process of establishing a writing major can challenge the traditional normative vision of writing instruction and offer in its stead a representation of writing as a discipline and its instruction as a part of the intellectual work of the institution" (2007, 42). Creating a writing major based in the rhetorical principles we describe helps to consolidate the discipline's, the institution's, and the department's ideological definitions of writing and rhetoric while leaving room for what practices and specific curricula are appropriate given an institution's and a department's local context.

RHETORIC AND PROGRAM DEVELOPMENT: CONCLUDING REFLECTIONS

By applying an operational definition of rhetoric to our program, we have come to better appreciate the importance of resisting impoverished definitions of writing, engaging, and interrogating various historic perspectives on rhetoric and situating the work we do. As our case study illustrates, our major uses rhetoric to challenge the disjointed list of courses that Schwegler describes and instead envisions a connected curriculum that engages all aspects of the communication triangle. Our case study also demonstrates how a historical perspective of rhetoric allows us to link rhetoric to a broad liberal arts tradition, thereby allowing us to educate faculty, students, perspective employers, and others as to rhetoric's scope and relevance. Finally, our case study reveals the ways that an understanding of the situational nature of rhetoric supports the interdisciplinary nature of our professional writing program.

While we have finished developing our program, we realize that in order to honor our rhetorical approach we cannot truly view our work as finished. Lest we forget, Tony Scott reminds us, "Neither the student nor the educational institution are transhistorical givens. Each is continually recreated by the daily labors of human agents and is therefore a potential site of positive change and hopeful possibilities for writing that have yet to be conceived" (2007, 90). In short, we are seeking to use rhetoric to create an ideology of connection rather than competition because, as Lester Faigley points out in *Fragments of Rationality*, "agency resides in the power of connecting with others and building alliances"

(1992, 199). Such agency is only possible for students and faculty if we use the cultural practice of program development as an opportunity to create an ideology of connection rather than competition, while simultaneously making the best out of the constraining material conditions that are always a feature of college institutions.

REFERENCES

Ashe, Diana, and Colleen Reilly. 2010. Smart growth of professional writing programs: Controlling sprawl in departmental landscapes. In *Design discourse: Composing and revising the professional and technical writing curriculum,* eds. David Franke and Alexander Reid. West Lafayette, IN: Parlor Press and the WAC Clearinghouse. (forthcoming). 28 pages in manuscript.

Berlin, James. 1996. *Rhetorics, poetics, and cultures.* Urbana, IL: National Council of Teachers of English.

Bloom, Lynn. 2000. Advancing composition. In Shamoon et al., 2000.

Bullock, Richard. 2000. Feathering our nest? A critical view from within our discipline. In Shamoon et al., 2000.

Faigley, Lester. 1992. *Fragments of rationality.* Pittsburgh, PA: University of Pittsburgh Press.

Fischer, Ruth Overman, and Christopher J. Thaiss. 2000. Advancing writing at GMU: Responding to community needs, encouraging faculty interests. In Shamoon et al., 2000. CD-ROM.

Foss, Sonja K., Karen A. Foss, and Robert Trapp. 2003. Perspectives on the study of rhetoric. In *Professional writing and rhetoric: Readings from the field,* ed. Tim Peeples. New York: Longman.

Gunner, Jeanne. 2002. Ideology, theory, and the genre of writing programs. In *Writing program administrator as theorist: Making knowledge work,* eds. Shirley Rose and Irwin Weiser. Portsmouth, NH: Boynton/Cook.

Henning, Teresa. 2007. Minnesota State Colleges and Universities New Program Application. Marshall, MN: Southwest Minnesota State University, English Department.

Howard, Rebecca Moore. 2007. Curricular activism: The writing major as counterdiscourse. *Composition Studies* 35.1:41–52.

———. 2000. History, politics, pedagogy, and advanced writing. In Shamoon et al., 2000.

ISEEK: Minnesota's Internet System for Education and Employment Knowledge. 2005. Career: Technical writers. http://www.iseek.org/sv/13030.jsp?id=100209 (accessed May 22, 2007).

———. 2005. Career: Writers. http://www.iseek.org/sv/13030.jsp?id=100485 (accessed May 22, 2007).

Johnson-Eilola, Johndan. 2004. Relocating the value of work: Technical communication in a post-industrial age. In *Central works in technical communication,* eds. Johndan Johnson-Eilola and Stuart A. Selber. New York: Oxford University Press.

McCormick, Kathleen, and Donald Jones. 2000. Developing a professional and technical writing major that integrates composition theory, literacy theory, and cultural studies. In Shamoon et al., 2000. CD-ROM.

Miller, Thomas. 2000. Rhetoric within and without composition. In Shamoon et al., 2000.

Schwegler, Robert A. 2000. Curriculum development in composition. In Shamoon et al., 2000.

Scott, Tony. 2007. The cart, the horse, and the road they are driving down: Thinking ecologically about a new writing major. *Composition Studies* 35.1:81–93.

Shamoon, Linda K., Rebecca Moore Howard, Sandra Jamieson, and Robert A. Schwegler, eds. 2000. *Coming of age: The advanced writing curriculum.* Portsmouth, NH: Heinemann.

Shamoon, Linda, Robert A. Schwegler, John Trimbur, and Patricia Bizzell 1995. New rhetoric courses in writing programs: A report from a conference for New England writing administrators. *Writing Program Administration* 18.3:7–25.

SMSU. 2009. 2009–2010 Academic catalog. http://www.smsu.edu/Catalog/catalog_pdf/English.pdf (accessed October 9, 2009).

SMSU. 2009. Major: B.A. professional writing and communication. http://www.smsu.edu/Academics/Programs/English/Indexcfm?ID 3837 (accessed October 9, 2009).

SECTION TWO

Curricula, Locations, and Directions of Writing Majors

9

REMEMBERING THE CANONS' MIDDLE SISTERS
Style, Memory, and the Return of the Progymnasmata in the Liberal Arts Writing Major

Dominic F. Delli Carpini
Michael J. Zerbe

> *Reading maketh a full man; conference a ready man; and writing an exact man.*
> —Francis Bacon, *Essays*

INTRODUCTION

Over the past four decades, the theory and practice of writing pedagogy have not treated the five canons of classical rhetoric equally. For a number of theoretical and institutional reasons, invention, arrangement, and delivery—the first, second, and fifth canons, respectively—have received the most attention. But as rhetoric and composition has matured as a discipline, and as it has gained disciplinary security within the academy (as evidenced not only by conferences, journals, and book series but also by the growing number of tenured faculty, department chairs, and upper-level administrators with backgrounds in rhetoric and composition), we now have the opportunity to rethink the discipline's relationship with the rhetorical canons, in particular, with the canons of style and memory.

Perhaps most telling in these institutional changes is the notable number of majors and minors in writing that have been, and continue to be, established (and which provide the occasion for this book) (National Council of Teachers of English 2007). In effect, these new majors have bridged the gap which previously existed between scholarly activities and graduate education in rhetoric and composition and the delivery of undergraduate writing courses—which until recently were largely limited to first-year writing, Writing Across the Curriculum and Writing In the Disciplines (WID) initiatives, and (outside of creative writing) a small assortment of elective writing courses. The growth of writing majors, however, has changed this landscape dramatically. Programs in writing studies, professional writing, technical writing, and other similar rubrics have provided the opportunity for undergraduates to study topics which until recently were reserved for graduate school. And for those of us who teach in such programs, this new landscape might provide a catalyst for examining how we deliver writing instruction at all levels.

Our past emphasis upon delivering the "universal requirement" and the consequent "service" mission of our discipline, has largely limited our work to the practical delivery of writing "skills" needed for college, often delivered by a changing cast of full-time professors with a variety of primary interests, as well as by teaching assistants and other contingent faculty.[1] In such a world, though experimentation and scholarship have continued to theorize what we *might* do, the actual delivery of writing pedagogy has still been limited by its role within the larger institution—as direct preparation for the academic reading and writing students will perform in college. And, as David Bartholomae reminded the Conference on College Composition and Communication's (CCCC's) membership on the occasion of receiving the 2006 Exemplar Award, this is important work. But looking now over a changing landscape that includes new writing majors, we clearly would be remiss to consider only the institutional authority and the opportunities that these days provide; we are also compelled to rethink some of the assumptions and practices that have guided rhetoric and composition during the first generation of its existence—a generation based largely upon efficient delivery of a single course (or course sequence). The large question we ask is this: What facets of our disciplinary traditions might be once again available to us in these new environs? We can address only a small piece of that larger question here: How has our treatment of the rhetorical canons been truncated in the quest for an efficient delivery of the "universal requirement"? More specifically, we wonder how an increased attention to the canons of style and memory—two middle sisters of the five canons—might enrich the rhetorical education we offer to our students.

In this chapter, we detail ways that we have begun to reinvest these canons with prominence in our writing program. We focus primarily upon Advanced Composition, a required 300-level course in the professional writing major at York College of Pennsylvania that highlights the canons of style and memory. Before we discuss this course in detail, though, we explore the causes of the dominance of the other three canons in writing course design as well as the effects that the lack of attention on style and memory have had on student writers. After presenting a description of the course content and goals, we provide examples of projects from that course. We then conclude the chapter by analyzing student feedback to the course and speculating upon the ways that this course, and the growing selection of upper-division writing courses made available by majors in writing studies and professional writing, might effect writing pedagogy more generally—including the delivery of first-year writing.

THE DOMINANCE OF INVENTION, ARRANGEMENT, AND DELIVERY

The canons of invention, arrangement, and delivery have dominated writing curricula developed during the first generation of what is now called composition studies. Though that resurgence reintroduced rhetoric to English departments, it did so in a landscape dominated by the practical and under-resourced delivery of first-year writing. Those exigencies created undesired side effects, creating a somewhat impoverished and pragmatic version of the rhetorical canons, each seen as a distinct portion of a "writing process" that proceeds from pre-writing activities that generate ideas through arrangement and delivery activities that package those ideas. But the canons are not freestanding units; picking and choosing among them, and treating them as steps in a process, ignores the essential interrelatedness of the canons as a method of developing rhetorical skills. Arrangement, style, and memory, for example, are all to a degree forms of invention. (In fact, in classical schema, so is the act of oral delivery; the extemporaneous element requires the nimble rhetor to use remembered stylistic schemes to respond to the needs of kairos). But the discipline's focus upon the universal requirement, as noted by the wave of abolitionists of the 1980s and 1990s, stresses efficiency and process. This focus has occurred for several institutional and disciplinary reasons, reasons that have begun to dissipate as writing majors have allowed for a wider view of writing pedagogy.

First, the canon of invention was treated in ways that best fit the study of literature—the dominant field in English departments from which renewed interest in rhetoric grew and in which many of rhetoric's early champions had formal graduate training—in that the development and discussion of ideas is of paramount importance (Crowley 1998, Delli

Carpini 2006). Further, students were encouraged to create essays that enact the ideal of the "well-wrought urn" forwarded by literary formalism. Thus, once ideas were generated by inventional techniques (techniques that grew in popularity through the work of expressivists like Peter Elbow), students were taught to arrange (the second canon) these ideas in a way that was both clear and logical to the reader. And finally, the fifth canon of delivery—which, in its original form, was about oral performance—was adapted to the needs of academic writing, moving students toward the presentation of a (presumably revised and edited) finished text to the instructor.

Second, the canons were impoverished by the belief that invention, arrangement, and delivery can seemingly be taught with no attention to grammar. This loss of grammar as an essential element in the teaching of writing, however, stems not from the larger understanding of grammar as facility with the language's structures but in response to the notion of grammar adopted in its streamlined "skill and drill" versions—versions that several studies showed were of no benefit to students' actual writing.[1] Thus, first grammar was isolated from live writing; then, this ineffective version of grammar instruction was abandoned (and with it grammar instruction more generally), followed soon on the trash heap by the teaching of the sentence, as Robert Connors has chronicled (2000). Thus, the teaching of grammar and sentence style was out of fashion soon after the resurgence of rhetoric began, and it still is in many circles (Mulroy 2003). But, as we discovered as we worked with writing majors in our expanded curriculum, teaching prose style without some attention to grammar is difficult if not impossible; it is tough to explain, for example, how to subordinate an idea stylistically or discuss word order without a knowledge of independent and dependent clauses and various kinds of phrases. Thus, systematic instruction in style and, by extension, memory (see below for a discussion of the connection between these two canons) was lost, perhaps inadvertently, when instruction in grammar ceased; the other three canons filled the void.

Third, student writing has been expected to conform to disciplinary ideals and the ideals of standardized written English. Ironically, the loss of grammar instruction did not come with a concomitant lack of

---

1. A long line of research suggests that formal grammar exercises divorced from student writing have limited value. See, for example, Joseph M. Williams (1981), Hillocks (1986), and Mahala and Swilky (1997) as well as the recent National Commission on Writing report (2003).

attention to proper usage in student texts. Instead, the rich and complex field of grammar instruction has been reduced to a massive academic style sheet or template. In this version, writing curricula and handbooks have attempted to model for students what "correct" writing is meant to look like, divorcing it from the activities of invention, arrangement, and memory that help students to explore syntactical strategies. In such a scheme, invention becomes divorced from language play and exists only in the realm of ideas; arrangement becomes outlining; style becomes conformity; memory becomes the rote learning of rules; and delivery amounts to presenting an edited text. These are not the canons envisioned by the large program of learning envisioned by the early rhetors.

Fourth, the focus upon process-based writing, with its reliance upon multiple drafts, has (ironically) given the student text—based upon its conformity to preimagined academic and private genres—priority, as a type of infinitely refinable commodity. For all the mantras associated with the process movement, when the end product becomes a type of Platonic ideal extant in the mind of the teacher (and by extension, an ideal students seek to reproduce), process-based pedagogy becomes more like an assembly line and less like an art studio or public forum. Though techniques of brainstorming, freewriting, and looping allow for some free-play of language, those techniques are then processed through more lockstep measures that aim at conformity; arrangement envisions the construction of a model text for an ideal reader; style becomes the study of disciplinary or academic conventions; memory is focused more upon content and grammar "rules" than rhetorical tropes and appropriate stylistic patterns; and delivery becomes an act of conformity and cleanliness—a final polish.

Though all of the canons have suffered in this sterilized version, our experiences with teaching our Advanced Composition course have suggested that its effect upon canons of style and memory has had the most deleterious effect upon student writing. Those canons have suffered a type of benign neglect, coming not so much from the assumption that they are unimportant but the assumption that—given effective invention and arrangement—they essentially take care of themselves. In terms of style, effective invention and clear, logical arrangement, the assumption went, would reveal a writer's authentic voice (i.e., her style) without any additional effort on the part of the writer: in other words, the writer's style would reveal itself naturally from the ideas that the writer was exploring, and the style would change naturally and appropriately as a result of the changing content that the writer produced. This assumption, on one hand, fits nicely with the Ciceronian contention (with which we wholeheartedly agree) that style and substance cannot be divorced from one another, that changes in either potentially change both. However, the sense that developing content is the only—or even the central—task of invention assumes that the discovery of ideas is divorced from language play. It suggests that attention to the rhetorical situation would seamlessly result in appropriate stylistic decisions. What is missing from this formula is the reality that an understanding of content does not necessarily come with the language abilities to nuance those ideas in language; in fact, the rhetorical canons would insist that invention in content and invention in style are inseparable as activities. Further, the progymnasmata, a set of rudimentary stylistic exercises that asked students to play with figures and tropes, stands as testimony to the early rhetors' belief of the crucial connection of the two. If effective style is to emerge from the invention process, it can only do so in a mind that has been exercised through figures, tropes, and other forms of stylistic play. Hence, as we define the canon of style, it is intimately connected with memory—with the knowledge of linguistic techniques that can be drawn upon in rhetorically useful and appropriate ways. Eloquentia is a function of kairos and linguistic preparation—and that linguistic preparation is what we have come to mean by a pedagogy of style.

As should be clear from the above discussion, then, the related fourth canon, memory, has also suffered as a result of limited definitions of invention and the loss of the concept of the progymnasmata, where the elements of stylistic memory were developed.[2] If one believes that invention leads naturally to a style appropriate for the rhetorical situation, then there is really no need for schemes and tropes or discussions of word order or point of view—the stuff of style—to be remembered by a writer. Several generations of writers have graduated from high school and college having been taught only a few figures of speech—largely those that are taught in the context of the formalist analysis of literature and creative writing: simile, metaphor, analogy, onomatopoeia, alliteration, irony, and so forth. Other features of style, such as those related to word order (hyperbaton, epistrophe, symploce, and so forth), sentence structure (periodic and cumulative), implied sentence elements (zeugma in all its forms), and restatement (e.g., epizeusis and scesis onomaton),

---

2. See Sharon Crowley's seminal study of this canon in *The Methodical Memory* (1990).

have not been taught at all. Absent those pedagogies, the baby has been lost with the bathwater, as memory, conceived as a rhetorical storehouse developed by students through stylistic exercises and play, disappeared from our rhetorical lexicon; it has instead been treated as a not particularly useful way to remember ideas—not particularly useful because ideas can be referenced when they are needed in that they can be looked up on the Internet or in a book or journal or can be recorded by the writer for future use. And having such tools in a handbook is little help during the act of invention. Perhaps Plato's fear in *Phaedrus* that writing would destroy memory has come home to roost in our electronic environment.

CONSEQUENCES OF THE LACK OF ATTENTION TO STYLE AND MEMORY

In the development, administration, and delivery of our writing major, we have come to believe that the lack of attention to style and memory has shortchanged student writers. While content does indeed influence stylistic abilities, and vice versa, this interrelationship does not happen automatically; attention to prose in which the primary focus is on style rather than content, we have come to believe, is a necessary element of writing instruction. Borrowing from Rude, we define style as "the cumulative effect [of a writer's] choices about words, their forms, and their arrangement in sentences" (2006, 251). Borrowing from Gorrell, we expand this definition to include choices about making and breaking so-called rules of language use and about punctuation (2005). Extending the argument pertaining to the canon of style, we submit that the canon of memory also deserves renewed study because memory holds the bits of discourse—the schemes, tropes, and techniques that not only make up the stylistic repertoire of effective writers but which connect style to occasion.

It can be argued, of course, that a knowledge of building blocks of an art form is not essential for the creation of art. Indeed, we know of wonderfully talented musicians who do not read music. This ability is rare, however, and it seems as if we teach writing in a way that provides an environment for a "naturally" talented writer to flourish but fails to teach the vast majority of "typical" writers who do need grounding in words, phrases, clauses, and sentences. (Neither do we know whether natural talent comes from exposure to language variety through early childhood influences.) And learning to read musical notation certainly does not impede a play-by-ear musician's ability to perform: on the contrary, it can greatly enhance it by opening up an entire repertoire of musical theory and composition that may heretofore been unknown to the musician.

In too many ways, the teaching of writing without regard for style and memory is like teaching music without teaching notes. We have focused on larger elements—ideas that are similar to themes or melodies in music—but not on the component parts of these ideas, which are notes for themes or melodies and words, phrases, and clauses for ideas.

Just as invention leads musicians to learn about notes, chemists about atoms and molecules, and softball players how to throw, catch, and hit, writers benefit by developing skill with words, phrases and clauses, and sentences—building blocks which are best studied and manipulated within the context of style. And also like musicians, chemists, and softball players, writers must internalize those elements in ways that allow the appropriate and natural uses of the basic building blocks of their art. This connection of form and function in the memory actualizes the potential of a writer to produce fluid, clear, timely, and decorous writing—writing that even at the sentence level fits content and purpose to style. It also increases their sensitivity to style as they read, and so allows the act of reading to lend itself to subtle forms of mimesis.

Of course, there is no doubt that a system—be it of musical notes or of words, phrases, and clauses that make up prose style—can be (and has become) oppressive. That is why our Advanced Composition course includes an explicit articulation that what is being studied is, indeed, a system. We explain to students that the system of style and memory that we present has been successfully employed to teach writing over many centuries in many different (western) cultures. Students may choose to follow, resist, change, and/or obliterate the system—but not to ignore it. And they have done all of those things. What we have found is that writing majors benefit greatly by explicit attention to, and guided practice in, stylistic exercise that hearkens back to the rhetorical canons of style and memory and which reconstitutes the stylistic exercises and playful spirit that reconstitute the progymnasmata. Our Advanced Composition course is at the heart of this reinvigoration of stylistic learning.

A PROFESSIONAL WRITING CURRICULUM THAT BALANCES THE CANONS

The advent of new undergraduate programs in writing, as we have found, presents an opportunity to think more robustly about the place and teaching of style and memory. With the belief that the canons still provide a viable model for a writing pedagogy, we designed (and continue to redesign) our major in professional writing in a way that gives each canon its due (see appendix). While no course in our major focuses solely on one canon, several of our applied writing courses, such as Writing in Professional Cultures and Writing for the Web, and theory-based courses, such as Interdisciplinary Writing and Rhetorical Theory, primarily target the canons of invention and arrangement. The first two courses introduce students to print and online genres and rhetorical situations—to the ideas and spheres of inquiry—common to many of the professional contexts within which our students will eventually work. The latter two courses approach invention and arrangement more generally. In the Rhetorical Theory course, for example, we teach students that logos, ethos, and pathos appeals are invention considerations in any rhetorical situation; in the Interdisciplinary Writing course, with a nod to Cicero's insistence in *De Oratore* that writers know something about everything, we teach our students about how arguments are constructed and supported—and arranged using, for example, the introduction-methods-results-and-discussion framework—in various forms of human inquiry (i.e., humanities, social sciences, natural sciences).

Style and memory are not completely absent in these courses. For example, the Interdisciplinary Writing course involves a discussion on the use of passive voice in the sciences, and Writing for the Web includes a discussion of the types of writing styles that are effective in online environments. Concomitant with these discussions is the notion that students should internalize (remember) these stylistic expectations and the cases within which they are most appropriate or decorous. Additionally, the canon of memory is discussed in the Rhetorical Theory course, especially with respect to the rhapsodes and logographers such as Lysias who memorized enormous amounts of text and recited publicly in various combinations and recombinations.

We ask our students to think about the fifth canon of delivery primarily in two ways. First, the Writing for the Web course introduces many of our students to an entirely new form of delivery; they are of course not new to the Internet, but they *are* often new to thinking about the kinds of visual and alphabetic texts that this medium of delivery requires. Second, we require our students in many courses to "deliver" work orally as well as in writing. Thus, for example, we ask our students to make formal presentations of their work in most of the courses mentioned above, as well as in courses such as Teaching and Tutoring of Writing and Senior Seminar in Professional Writing. Our students must, as a result, think about how their work can be best delivered in various media.

It is our required course in Advanced Composition, though, that brings the canons of style and memory to the forefront. In this course, which most of our professional writing students take as sophomores or juniors and which is also required for literary studies majors and for secondary education English majors, we focus on prose almost entirely at the sentence, clause/phrase, and word levels. We ask our students to experiment extensively with their own style(s) and to learn to recognize the use of stylistic techniques (and consequent success or lack thereof) in the work of others such as student peers, well-known essayists or authors, or almost any writer. Here is how a typical semester-long Tuesday/Thursday section of the course is structured:

Table. Advanced Composition

Week 1	Introduction to Course: Style (and Content), Rhetoric, *Progymnasmata*, Features of Style
Week 2	English Grammar and Sentence Types, Coordination of Sentence Parts: Words, Phrases, Clauses. Parallelism. Semicolon as Coordinator
Week 3	Emphasis/Subordination of Sentence Parts: Words, Phrases, Clauses
Week 4	Sentence Length, Sentence Order, Periods, Pronouns: Antecedents, Agreement, Case
Week 5	Commas, Dashes, Colons, Modifiers, Concision
Week 6	Active and Passive Voice, Hyphens, Sentences: Beginnings, Fragments, Comma Splices
Week 7	Review, Exam
Week 8	Infinitives, Restrictive and Non-Restrictive Clauses, Prepositions, Point of View: First Person and Second Person
Weeks 9 and 10	Figurative Language
Weeks 11 and 12	Presentations
Week 13	Transitions: Cohesion and Coherence at the Sentence and Paragraph Levels
Week 14	Repetition/Restatement
Week 15	Wrap-up and Review

This curriculum relies on several basic assumptions. First, it assumes that style can be studied productively and successfully. To help students see style as the central topic of study, we break it down into various elements: emphasis and subordination, repetition/restatement, sentences, sentence length, clauses, phrases, parts of speech, word order, point of view (first person, second person, third person), tone, active and passive voice, parallelism, and punctuation. Each of these elements is studied individually, and then layered in ways that lead students to a more sophisticated understanding of style, an understanding that is inextricably intertwined with an ability to deliver more complex, and more nuanced, content. Additionally, we maintain that the intensive study of style leads to the development of rhetorical memory, through which students come to connect specific forms with specific and appropriate occasions.

Second, our curriculum assumes that knowledge of grammar is helpful—indeed, perhaps essential—to the study of style. And we do not take for granted that our students know grammar. Some have not been exposed at all to concepts such as parts of speech, phrases and clauses, parallelism, and the like; and very few have come to a complex understanding of how those concepts inform the construction of live sentences.[3] Thus, a significant portion of the course is devoted to these concepts, with the understanding that adherence to *conventions of standardized English* is a rhetorical decision that must be made on a case-by-case basis, whereas *grammar* describes the systems through which the language works. We want our students, for example, to understand what a sentence fragment is and to use it or not use it consciously, for specific reasons that are related to the rhetorical situation at hand—but with an understanding of its grammatical construction and reasonable functions. As such, as discussed below, we engage students in many exercises through which they are asked to reflect upon and reason through the choices that they make. Though these exercises are no doubt somewhat artificial, they constitute a type of progymnasmata that prepares them to return to their own writing processes with a fuller stylistic memory.

We typically require our students to complete five projects as part of the Advanced Composition course, including various projects that focus upon stylistic techniques and practices such as coordination and subordination, varying sentence structures, controlling long sentences, using figurative

---

3. See The National Commission on Writing report, which noted that, "There are many students capable of identifying every part of speech who are barely able to produce a piece of prose" (2003, 13).

language, writing with action verbs, and so forth. Common to all of these projects is the structure of the tasks students perform. They begin with an analysis of a text selected by the instructor and then move on to experiment with the stylistic elements they have analyzed by producing a brief piece of writing themselves—brief enough that the focus is truly on each sentence. Both of these tasks are facilitated by the use of highlighting and commenting functions in Microsoft Word: students highlight a particular passage in the text selected by the instructor, then in their own writing, and use the comment function to identify the stylistic strategy used and to explain why it is being used in this specific place/rhetorical situation. These comments thus ask students to link form to function, and so to begin to develop the memory of how specific techniques fit specific rhetorical occasions—creating synapses between kairos and eloquentia.

For example, the coordination/subordination project asks students to first locate three instances of coordination and three instances of subordination in an excerpt of a text selected by the instructor. For this project, Dominic Delli Carpini has most recently used an excerpt of John Krakauer's *Into the Wild*, while Mike Zerbe has used an excerpt of Jhumpa Lahiri's short story collection *Interpreter of Maladies*. We ask the students to identify instances as coordination or subordination of words, phrases, or clauses and to explain the selected text's role in the sentence: what it modifies and/or its relationship with other parts of the sentence and/ or its stylistic effect. Then we ask the students to write a few paragraphs on a topic of their choosing and to comment upon the choices they have made to subordinate or coordinate specific ideas. Finally, we ask students to explain what they have learned about style from reading and analyzing the text selected by the instructor and how it may have impacted (or not impacted) their own style in the part of the project in which the students write on their own.

Figure 1 provides an example of one student's analysis of the use of coordination and subordination in Lahiri's *Interpreter of Maladies* (all student writing used by permission). As shown in the comments on the right, this student identifies the use of either a coordinate or subordinate element (or both, as in the first comment) and its role within the sentence. These comments are three of the six comments we asked the students to write (three for coordination, three for subordination).

In the next part of the project, we ask students to write on their own. We suggest a topic, although we allow students to write about other topics if they wish, as long as the topic lends itself to the use of the stylistic elements

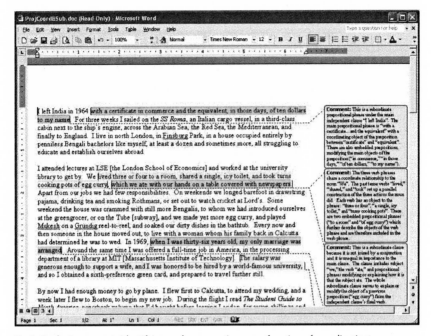

Fig 1. Student comments identifying and commenting upon function of coordination and subordination.

under consideration in the project (the students can always choose a new topic if the first one doesn't work out). We encourage the student to write as they would normally at first and then revise their text as necessary to identify and/or add examples of coordination and subordination, assuming such additions are both possible and appropriate. (If they do not seem to be, we would ask the student to choose another topic.) Figure 2 shows the work of a student who wrote a paragraph on a vacation cabin that her family used to visit. Again, we ask the students to identify and comment on examples of coordination and subordination in the text—their own, this time—and to explain the role of these examples.

In the last part of the project, we ask students to reflect on what they have learned about style (and content) by studying coordination and subordination in the prose of a noted author or essayist and in their own work. Figure 3 demonstrates such reflective comments. The comments serve two purposes. They demonstrate to us that this student is able to clearly identify examples of coordination and subordination and understand how Lahiri and the student herself are using these strategies. And they ask students to form memories of the uses of the technique studied.

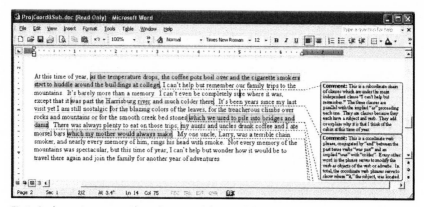

Fig 2. Student-written text with explications of rhetorical choices for use of coordination and subordination. Shown are two of the six comments we asked the students to write (three for coordination, three for subordination).

Zerbe did ask this student to spend some more time on the relationship between style and content: to explain why, for example, Lahiri or the student would choose to coordinate or subordinate elements of a particular sentence. What we seek in an explanation of this sort is a discussion of why, for instance, the student would choose, in her description of her family's vacation cabin, to coordinate the three prepositional phrases, each starting in general with "for the [adjective] [noun]," in the fourth sentence of her paragraph on the vacation cabin (perhaps because she wants to use parallelism to treat equally each of the three memories for which she yearns—"the blazing colors of the leaves," "the treacherous climbs over the rocks and mountains," and "the smooth creek bed stones" and to use "for" each time because some of the phrases are a bit long) and why these ideas are, overall, subordinate to the main idea of the sentence, that is, "It's been years" (perhaps because the student wants to emphasize the amount of time that has passed since she's been to the cabin more than the other ideas contained in the sentence).

Our goal in the Advanced Composition course with respect to memory is to devote enough attention to strategies such as coordination and subordination so that they begin to be retained in the students' minds. Thus, for example, we hope that this student will, in future writing, internalize thinking like this: "Here is a good place to use subordination, because I want to make it clear to the reader that this idea is not as important as this other one."

Other projects in the Advanced Composition course follow a process similar to that used for the coordination/subordination project.

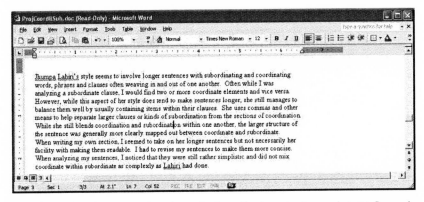

Fig 3. This student demonstrates how the study of specific elements of a sample text influenced the student's own stylistic decisions.

The varying-sentence-structure project, for example, asks students to identify and discuss different structural types of sentences (simple, compound, complex, compound-complex, inverted, interrogative). Zerbe has most recently used an excerpt from Mary Shelley's *Frankenstein* for this project; Delli Carpini has used an excerpt from Wallace Stegner's "A Wilderness Letter." Both of these texts contain long, complex sentence structures. The students then once again write their own prose, this time focusing upon the use of a wide variety of sentence structures—long and short, complex and simple, direct and inverted, periodic and cumulative—as an architectonic to analyze both the style and grammar of the sentences. The next project, focused on the use of figurative language, asks students to identify and discuss schemes and tropes in a selected text and in their own prose; we first spend about two to three weeks in class learning everything from anadisplosis to zeugma and ask students to consider the various uses of these figures. We have found that the students especially enjoy this section of the course, primarily because we ask them to take ownership of several figures of speech and present them to the class in oral presentations accompanied by handouts or PowerPoint slides. (It gives English majors a chance to use specialized vocabulary that makes them feel like professionals who work in the many fields that have their own language.)

Figure 4 provides an example of a student's work, demonstrating her use of figurative language in her own writing. This excerpt exemplifies what we are trying to accomplish in the Advanced Composition course. The student not only identifies the schemes and tropes that she chooses to employ, but she also explains why their use is appropriate given the

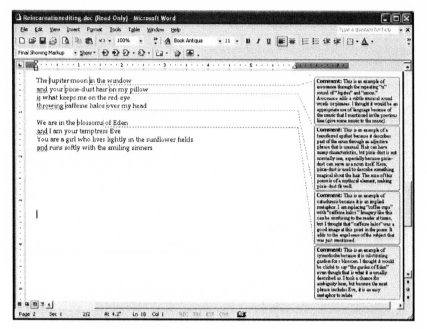

Fig 4. This student has incorporated several figures of speech into this text and described its intended function; though this example uses poetry, most students use prose for the exercise, with equal success.

content—and, more generally, the rhetorical situation—that the student wants to explore. The student has, we think, spent enough time on her text and on her self-analysis of it to retain in her memory some of the stylistic strategies she used. On future writing occasions, she will, we hope, think to herself something like, "Ah ha! Here is a good place for catachresis."

There are a variety of other similar projects as the course proceeds. For example, Delli Carpini asks students to complete a sentence-combining project. This project begins by asking students to write several paragraphs on a suggested topic using only simple sentences—itself a stylistic challenge, and one that reinforces their knowledge of sentence grammar. Then, students are asked to combine sentences using the various strategies that we have been discussing—coordination/subordination, appositives, absolute phrases, parentheticals, relative clauses, semicolons and dashes, and so forth. They are also asked to explain those choices in their marginalia. Figure 5 demonstrates one student's ability to demonstrate his careful choices. In his sentence combining, this student is beginning to show not only the ability to successfully manipulate specific stylistic strategies but also to name those strategies

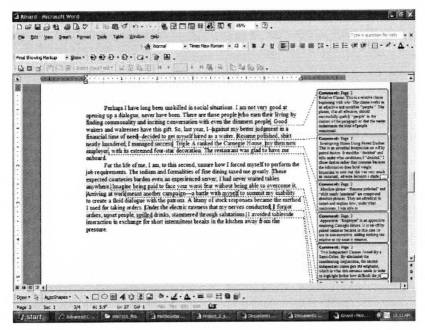

Fig 5. This student has chosen a wide array of sentence-combining techniques based upon rhetorical goals that are explained in the margin comments.

(demonstrating a growing knowledge of sentence grammar) and to articulate the reasoning behind his stylistic choices—choices he has made by remembering past exercises in the techniques chosen such as the uses of the dash, the effect of appositives, and the uses of restrictive and nonrestrictive clauses.

Zerbe asks students to complete an action-verb project in which the students must write a 500-word essay on a topic of their choice and use no forms of the verb "to be" in their prose. This project helps the students to think about the use of action verbs as an indicator of a lively, concise style that is often highly valued in our society, and we have interesting discussions about why this is so. As a result of the prohibition of the verb "to be," students must write in active voice and in either present or future tense. The project departs from the highlighting methodology used for other projects, but, similar to these other projects, the students are asked to describe the effects (if any) of this exercise on their own style.

Both Delli Carpini and Zerbe ask students to complete a style-synthesis project as a culmination for the course. This project does not involve any text selected by the instructor; students are asked to write an essay or some other kind of text on a topic of their choice, to identify the rhetorical situation for which the essay or text is intended to exist, to revise the essay or text, and to identify and explain a number of stylistic choices—which may include any of the style topics that have been discussed as part of the course—that they make in the essay and discuss why these choices are, in the student's view, rhetorically effective.

In addition to the projects for the Advanced Composition course, we ask students to keep a style journal, which has become one of the favorite parts of the course. For the style journal, students write down an excerpt (i.e., a word, phrase, clause, sentence, or small group of sentences) of prose or poetry that they read or hear and that strikes them as stylistically notable. The students then explain in more detail exactly what the reasons are for the stylistic notability (which can be positive, negative, or both): the use of an unusual word order, a striking figure of speech, a breach of a traditional rule of grammar, an example of nonstandard vocabulary or unusual dialect, a curious use of tone or point of view, or some other peculiarity. We ask students to pay attention to memorable or effective phrases that they read and hear in their everyday lives, to consider the ways that the writers or speakers are making conscious stylistic choices, and to articulate the technique and effect of those choices. The students explain the stylistic choice and judge whether or not the use of the stylistic device contributes to the writer's fulfillment of his or her rhetorical objective. As with the projects, we hope that the students internalize some of the stylistic strategies that capture their attention so that they can use them (or not) in appropriate rhetorical situations. Figures 6–8 demonstrate typical student style journal entries:

Fig 6. Journal Entry

"Landis's defense—based primarily on public relations—took a serious, if not severe, if not deadly hit." (From an analysis of the Tour de France)

- Interrupter, enclosed in dashes give more information about the subject but could be removed from the sentence without changing its meaning

- a climactic series and the end reflects the severity of the event's effect upon Landis' defense, and is made more effective by asyndeton—leaving out the coordinating conjunction

- Coordination of phrases in a parallel structure, and using anaphora ("if not") creates emphasis, balance, and rhythm

- Delay of "hit" to the end of the sentence with the use of the coordinated subordinate phrases puts the word in the point of most emphasis.

Harris [the author of one of our textbooks] says that anaphora can imply ignorance or lack of knowledge about a subject. Possibly this analyst's delivery also hints at his disbelief about how stupid the defense was to let this happen? I was only half listening to the news, but this sentence caught my ear. The interruption and the repetitive phrasing were effective.

Fig 7. Journal Entry

"Demeter, Goddess of Grain and Fertility, the Great Earth Mother, searched for nine days for her lost daughter Persephone, who had been carried off by Hades, God of the Underworld."

—from *The China Garden* by Liz Berry

What sticks out the most in this sentence is the use of many appositives to describe Demeter and Hades. They add more information to the names so that the reader has an idea of who they are. This is an intro sentence to the story of Demeter and Persephone and the changing of the seasons. This story is an interesting way to start off the book, because the ties to the story aren't evident until the reader is almost finished reading. It acts as a memorable bit of foreshadowing.

Fig 8. Journal Entry

"Where is your car at?" (asked by my roommate)
While ending sentences in prepositions is a taboo, I have never really figured out why this is. Yesterday, when my roommate asked me the whereabouts of my car, I began to wonder why it is at all necessary to add the "at." I came to the conclusion that prepositional phrases act as modifiers, and when they are placed at the end of sentences, they modify nothing. In essence, ending sentences with a preposition is like a dangling modifier.

Fig 6, 7, and 8: Student style journal entries demonstrate the ability to analyze texts in everyday reading and listening.

These style journal entries are typical of the work of our students as they grow in their knowledge of style and illustrate several things about the pedagogical utility of this assignment and the teaching of style more generally. First, they show that students are now more sensitive to the language around them; they are paying attention to language in new ways and hearing that which otherwise might have passed unnoticed: figure 6 comes from a television broadcast, figure 7 from a novel, figure 8 from everyday discourse. In all cases, and for each of the three students, reading or hearing these language uses caused them to consider both the stylistic choices and their effects upon the audience. In figure 6, the student used a strong understanding of stylistic structures to demonstrate the careful stylistic choices of the copy read by a sports commentator. In figure 7, the student mused about how the novelist used the technique of apposition to include a great deal of information in the sentence—and how that sentence was used in the larger context of the book. And figure 8 shows how students who have style and grammar on their minds come to analyze all that they hear and read; in this case, we can see the student puzzling through the grammatical rule about prepositions that she had long been taught but only now was coming to understand in her own terms. Though not a textbook explanation of the grammar, her analysis certainly illustrates how having these stylistic issues in her memory helped her exercise key grammatical logic.

Finally, we should reiterate that though style is our focus, we do not dismiss the canons of invention, arrangement, and delivery in the Advanced Composition course. In fact, it is the interaction among the canons that makes the course function. We ask students why particular styles are effective or not effective in specific rhetorical situations given the content to be covered and its potential organization, and we ask students to invent and deliver work both written and orally. Style is foregrounded as a feature of the other canons. In this way, we seek to reinforce the idea that the canons are inseparable from one another and that, while we may select one or two on which to focus primarily, they cannot be excised from the set of five canons as a whole.

ADVANCED COMPOSITION: STUDENT FEEDBACK

Aside from the primary evidence of student learning in the course—the assignments that they complete—we also have received written feedback on the learning that has occurred there as conceptualized by the students. Asked to describe the ways that their writing and writing processes have changed as a result of the course, students responded in ways that suggest that we have indeed affected their perception of style and have begun to help them use memory to develop a repertoire of techniques for varied occasions.

On the matter of style, students reported a new consciousness of the ways that stylistic techniques affect their ability to fulfill their goals as writers. Interestingly, the barrage of grammatical and stylistic information did not constrict students but liberated them. As one typical student wrote, "Now that I know the techniques that make writing more effective, I find that I am able to stylize my own work more by going above and beyond straightforward sentences and making them my own," adding that, "I feel like my writing is more mature because it has more depth and style." Another wrote, "Now that I am aware of the tools available to me and how to properly use them, I am not afraid to work with them. Imagine what the Egyptians or Greeks could have done with power tools." A third student noted, "I now write with a goal to *reveal* important information in my piece of work, through the clarity and emphasis of the techniques." Clarity was, in fact, a common theme in student comments, suggesting that the new array of stylistic possibilities allowed them to write more precisely what they had in mind—and so enacting Francis Bacon's "exact man" (or woman).

Perhaps even more interesting are the ways that the learning of stylistic and grammatical structures has changed students' writing processes. Though some might suggest that a focus upon *product* would diminish attention to *process,* students came to understand the progymnasmata-like course as a methodology as well as a storehouse. A typical student noted that, "while writing, I think about different techniques that will improve the quality and tone of the piece I am working on. I do not sit down and think 'I am going to add zeugma and polysyndeton to this essay,' per say [*sic*], but I am aware of adding more stylized techniques to my writing." The development of rhetorical memory also seems to have given students a stronger sense of what revision means, as one student reported: "I've been through so many courses that I've had to write papers in and each professor or teacher would tell us to revise or work and not hand in the original copy—but I've never really known what to revise. I'd go through and make sure things made sense and were spelled and punctuated correctly." Another student noted that, "when revising, I now read my piece out loud and listen to the rhythm and listen for sentences that don't 'sound' right. If sentences start to sound dull or repetitive, I will work in some more stylistic techniques for variation."

Most encouraging, and a bit surprising, was how quickly rhetorical memory began to develop. Not only was this evident in student projects and style journals, in which they were quite capable of identifying techniques and their function, but also in their approach to composing. One student reported not only "a greater awareness of the specific techniques I've written, read, or potentially could apply to my writing" but also that he has gone beyond revision for content to a stronger sense of stylistic revision: "I still do look for places to change content—either adding or cutting, but now I am more conscious of how techniques support content and add power and thrust to a piece. Zeugma, dashes, parallelism are a few techniques that have left a lasting impression on me." In fact, as noted in the discussion of the figurative language project above, many students reported affection for specific stylistic techniques, one reporting that "my most common are zeugma, anaphora, parenthesis, and auxesis" and another that "I like anaphora and anadiplosis" and varying between "periodic and cumulative sentences for emphasis." Students seem, then, not only to be developing a repertoire via memory but already using those stored memories as they write. "I find that when I am writing, I am thinking to myself, 'What figure of speech can I use to say this,' or after I write, I try to figure out what figure of speech I just used." In these ways, we have begun to see that the development and use of a rhetorical memory in students, many of who noted that no doubt because of their more analytical practices of reading and revision, would continue to expand.

Students also report having developed a new understanding of grammar beyond its rules-based definition. As one student wrote that "rather than conforming to one style, learning about 'standardized' writing techniques has shown me a variety of styles that I never realized existed. Another noted that, "This class has definitely broadened my scope on the use of grammar. I now realize that grammar provides a structure, but . . . I see reasons to sometimes use non-standard English to prove necessary points of emphasis." And a third reported that, "I went from simply putting words on paper and then revising to ensure my grammar and punctuation were o.k. to being able to consciously think about HOW I want to write each sentence and paragraph."

In the end, both student projects and student observations on their own learning have encouraged us to think more widely about the role of style and memory as key elements of not only our writing major but our first-year sequence as well.

INFLUENCE OF ATTENTION TO STYLE AND MEMORY
ON FIRST-YEAR WRITING

The emphasis on the canons of style and memory in our new Advanced Composition course has influenced how we teach first-year writing. In a recent revision to our first-year writing curriculum, we thought about ways in which we could make our students more conscious of style and its appropriateness to rhetorical occasion. This year, we are teaching two new first-year writing courses. In the first course, Analytical Reading and Writing, our goal was to overcome weaknesses in students' abilities to negotiate the difficult reading materials that they encounter in college, given that most of their reading in secondary school came from either textbooks or literary texts. In that course, one of the ways that we help students to find efficient and effective ways to understand difficult texts is through a better understanding of syntactical patterns. Though our approach to syntax is not as complex in the first-year writing course, the ability to find the cadence of sentences and to understand the implicit meaning in various sentence structures (subordination and coordination, for example) does seem, in our early observations, to have helped them to become more mature readers—and so to suggest that the study of style may have implications for reading-based courses as well. The second course, Academic Writing, highlights features of formal academic and professional style that students need to master to communicate credibly and effectively in educational and professional contexts. Building upon their experience of reading the style of academic texts in the first course—reading academic style as a series of purposeful choices, not merely pomposity—we attempt to help students to find real maturity in their academic writing without resorting to the feigned complexity Joseph Williams has dubbed "academese" (a style that is all too familiar to teachers of first-year writing (1981). Additionally, we ask students to adapt their work to contexts in which a different style may be far more useful. To help make students aware of the need for stylistic code-switching, after students have completed a formal research paper, they are then asked to use that project as the basis for a piece of applied writing. Our students might thus adapt their work to a wiki, a basic Web site, a blog, a letter to the editor of the campus or community newspaper, a letter to a campus or government official, a brochure, or some other occasion. Part of the work that the student must do to adapt their writing to this alternative context is to specifically address stylistic differences between the alternative context and a more traditional, formal academic or professional context.

CONCLUSION

When our students tell us that they can no longer even read a billboard or restaurant menu without thinking about its stylistic implications, we react with a measure of barely contained glee. (One student questioned, for example, a line from a newspaper: "He died of an apparent heart attack." He went on to ask, "Can one die of an apparent heart attack? Shouldn't it be 'he apparently died of a heart attack'? Can a heart attack be apparent, as the adjective version suggests?") We believe that our Advanced Composition course enables our students to become more exacting, precise writers. This precision is manifested as a result of the attention given to issues at the word, phrase, clause, and sentence level of the writing of noted essayists and authors and of students' own writing. This attention enables students to not only recognize stylistic techniques used by other writers as well as use these techniques in their own writing, it provides them with an ability to understand and produce writing that is more complex and/or subtle in terms of its content. And though we have only begun to transfer these findings to our first-year writing program, we have already found adaptations that have benefited our students in those courses as well. In short, the study of style has the potential to raise the level of discourse and to do so in an artful way.

REFERENCES

Bartholomae, David. "4Cs Exemplar Award Acceptance." CCCC, Chicago. 23 March 2006.

Connors, Robert. 2000. Erasure of the sentence. *CCC* 52:96–128.

Crowley, Sharon. 1998. *Composition in the university*. Pittsburgh, PA: University of Pittsburgh Press.

———. 1990. *The methodical memory: Invention in current-traditional rhetoric*. Carbondale: Southern Illinois University Press.

Delli Carpini, Dominic. 2006. Composition, literacy studies, and the end(s) of civic education. In *Composition and/or literature: The ends of education*, eds. Linda S. Bergmann and Edith M. Baker. Urbana, IL: National Council of Teachers of English.

Gorrell, Donna. 2005. *Style and difference: A guide for writers*. Boston, MA: Houghton Mifflin.

Hillocks, George. (1986). Research in written composition: New directions for teaching. Urbana, IL: Clearinghouse on Reading and Communication Skills and the National Conference on Research in English.

Mahala, Daniel, and Jody Swilky. 1997. Remapping the geography of service in English. *College English* 59: 625–46.

Mulroy, David. 2003. *The war Against grammar*. Portsmouth, NH: Boynton/Cook.

National Commission on Writing. 2003. The neglected "R": The need for a writing revolution. http://www.writingcommission.org. (accessed November 15, 2007).

National Council of Teachers of English. 2007. Writing majors at a glance. http://www.
ncte.org/cccc (accessed November 15, 2007).

Plato. [360 BCE] 1956. *Phaedrus.* Trans. W. C. Helmbold and W. G. Rabinowitz. New York:
Liberal Arts Press.

Rude, Carolyn D. 2006. *Technical editing.* 4th ed. New York: Pearson Longman.

Williams, Joseph M. 1981. The phenomenology of error. *CCC* 32:152–68.

APPENDIX
York College of Pennsylvania Professional Writing Major

Courses in the professional writing major are divided into five areas as shown below. An asterisk (*) indicates that the course is required for the major; other courses are electives. Each student must complete at least two professional writing electives.

Writing Applications Courses

> WRT 210: Writing in Professional Cultures*
>
> WRT 275: Playwriting
>
> WRT 310: Creative Writing
>
> WRT 315: Advanced Composition*
>
> WRT 320: Writing for the Web*
>
> WRT 371: Advanced Creative Writing
>
> WRT 373: Advanced Nonfiction
>
> WRT 374: Writing Children's Literature
>
> WRT 380: Freelance Writing for the Marketplace
>
> WRT 410: Professional Editing*
>
> WRT 360–370; WRT 460–69: Special Topics in Professional and Creative Writing (e.g., Nature Writing, Medical Writing, The Personal Essay, Document Design)

Language History and Theory Courses

> WRT 225: Interdisciplinary Writing*
>
> WRT 290: Teaching and Tutoring of Writing
>
> WRT 305: Rhetorical Theory*
>
> LIT 310: Language and Linguistics*

Capstone Courses

> WRT 450: Experiential Learning* (i.e., an internship)

WRT 480: Senior Seminar in Professional Writing*

Students may complete a second internship, WRT 451, to fulfill one of the professional writing elective requirements.

Minor

In addition to the above required courses and professional writing electives, students are required to complete a minor as part of the professional writing major.

English and Humanities Departmental Electives

Finally, students must complete four English and humanities departmental electives.

10

CIVIC RHETORIC AND THE UNDERGRADUATE MAJOR IN RHETORIC AND WRITING

Thomas A. Moriarty
Greg A. Giberson

It's an exciting time to be a rhetoric and writing specialist. (As we write this, we realize it's *always* exciting to be a rhetoric and writing specialist, but these days, it seems particularly so.) Our job markets are strong, our graduate programs are thriving, and there's a growing movement in writing programs across the country to develop undergraduate majors in rhetoric and writing. This third development is particularly exciting—and important—because it represents a milestone in our field's development. We finally have a place in the undergraduate catalog, on the department Web site, a prominent place that puts us on equal footing with other disciplines. We're no longer just a set of service courses, or a vague concentration within a literature degree, or an exotic-sounding emphasis in a PhD program. We're a degree—just like physics, just like business, just like literature (better than literature, actually).

But as we stake our claim and secure our place in the curriculum, we need to be careful. We need to build undergraduate degree programs that will last, degree programs that will grow and evolve as the years go by and not fade away as the times and academic fashions change. We need to be careful, then, here at the start, careful as we lay the foundations for what will hopefully become a long line of noteworthy programs. We need to find a focus for our programs, one that will provide us with an ever-evolving, dynamic set of concerns that will motivate, animate, and invigorate our work for years to come.

That focus is civic rhetoric.

That answer, despite its sermonic crescendo on the page, is nothing new. We all seem to agree, at least in our journals, that training in writing and rhetoric prepares one for public life, for working together in a democratic society to make decisions and guide the course of our collective actions. But when it comes time to make our case for undergraduate degree programs, to convince our colleagues in our departments, our administrators in their distant offices, and, most importantly, our students in our classrooms and online in our program descriptions, we lose our nerve. Instead of embracing our pivotal role in civic education and "reclaiming our birthright," as Gerard Hauser eloquently puts it, we fall back on old and tired lines of persuasion, linking the value of our programs to preparation for academic or professional success (2004, 52).

That is a mistake. And in this chapter, we argue that these justifications may have negative long-term consequences for our programs, consequences that will severely hamper our efforts to establish undergraduate majors in rhetoric and writing and reinvigorate the study of rhetoric for the twenty-first century.

THE CASE FOR CIVIC RHETORIC

The case for undergraduate degree programs in general, and civic rhetoric in particular, was first made in the late 1990s, in the pages of *College English*. There, David Fleming argued that rhetoric had indeed made quite a comeback. After centuries of marginalization, the word "rhetoric" was enjoying "considerable intellectual prestige" in the academy, appearing in journals and books all across the humanities. According to Fleming, rhetoric had been transformed "from a pejorative to an honorific term" (1998, 169). Rhetoric's recent ascent was most notable in North American English departments, where "rhetoric is featured prominently at the two extremes of higher education," Fleming wrote. "At one end, a fifteen-week course on writing for incoming freshman; at the other, a multi-year program of advanced study for PhD students. Between the two, there is little or nothing" (173).

This gaping hole in the curriculum worried Fleming and raised doubts about the true state of rhetoric's revival in the modern university. "A better test for the revival of rhetoric in English departments would be the flourishing of an undergraduate *major*," he wrote. "In the past, this is what rhetoric *was*: three to four years of intense study and practice, sometime between the ages of (about) fifteen and twenty, organized to develop the discursive competencies and sensibilities needed for effective and responsible participation in public life" (173; emphasis in original).

Rhetoric education as training for public life was key to Fleming. His proposed curriculum for a "contemporary rhetoric education" included theory, practice, and inquiry, all with the goal of forming "the good rhetor, the person who has mastered the 'knowledge' of speaking and writing well, and who is conceived first and foremost as a free and equal member of a self-governing community." This curriculum would be in line with rhetoric's deepest roots, Fleming wrote, noting that the word "rhetoric," in its earliest usage, denoted "the art of the public or political [i.e., *civic*] speaker" (184). To revitalize rhetorical education, Fleming concluded, "we need to recapture this focus on the language user as citizen" (184). We need to make civic rhetoric the focus of our undergraduate majors.

Five years later, at a conference of the Alliance of Rhetoric Societies (ARS) in Evanston, Illinois, rhetoricians from both communications and English departments resoundingly embraced this emphasis on civic rhetoric. The working group tasked with discussing the teaching of rhetoric urged the alliance to issue a manifesto, one that would call for "recovering the value of rhetoric education as central to civic education" (Hauser 2004, 39). As reported by Gerard Hauser, "the relationship between civic education and rhetoric instruction was a *leitmotiv*" of the working group's discussions (40). The working group acknowledged a long-standing tension in rhetoric studies between the classical Athenian ideal of "capacitating" students for active and engaged citizenship and the nineteenth-century German research institute ideal of orderly and disciplined research and, as a secondary concern, professional education. While Athens stressed paideia and the education of the whole person for civic life, Berlin stressed the discovery of new knowledge and the training of students to conduct research on their own. Hauser noted: "One might construct this as the story of rhetoric education in twentieth- and twenty-first-century America, in which rhetoric has commitments to two models of what the ideal education ought to be: commitments to Athens and to Berlin" (40).

In order to secure a place for themselves in the modern research university, rhetoricians chose Berlin. "Rhetoricians are aware that Rhetoric Studies presents itself as a scholarly discipline through its critical and theoretical work as that enterprise is understood in the German model of the research university," Hauser wrote. But subordinating Athens to Berlin came at a price. "When Athenian commitments to *paideia* are subordinated or even cleansed from rhetoric, its centrality to society's ongoing negotiation over how we shall act and interact—to politics—is either lost or ignored" (41).

Rhetoric's loss of a role in public life motivated the working group to call for a manifesto. "To recover the value of rhetoric education as central to civic education we must reassert the role of rhetoric in our lives as citizens and social actors," Hauser wrote. "We must reassert the importance of capacitating students by focusing on their powers of performance (*dunamis*) rather than focusing exclusively on their service to discovering knowledge. Rhetoric Studies may be the best, and quite possibly the only place from which this assertion may be voiced" (2004, 41–42). The working group argued that rhetoric plays a central role in guiding and governing society. Drawing on Isocrates, the group argued that rhetoric "offered humans the possibility of living in a community whereby they might distinguish themselves from animals and one another." Furthermore, they argued that what we teach as rhetoricians "contributes to an engaged and informed citizenry and to the quality of public decision-making" (42–43).

Ultimately, the working group concluded that teachers of rhetoric must reclaim rhetoric's role in civic education. Rhetoricians must not only participate in political discourse but also in "the education of young minds" to prepare them for active and involved citizenship:

> Free societies require rhetorically competent citizens. Without rhetorical competence, citizens are disabled in the public arenas of citizen exchange—the marketplace, the representative assembly, the court, and public institutions—and democracy turns into a ruse disguising the reality of oligarchic power. Capacitating students to be competent citizens is our birthright. It has been ours since antiquity. Modern education has stripped us of it. We need to reclaim it. (52)

And reclaim it we did. Sort of. If not in our programs, then at least in our journals.

RECLAIMING OUR BIRTHRIGHT—SORT OF

The ARS's call did not go unheeded, and it did echo in our journals, at least to a certain extent. Brian Jackson summarized the call's resonance in the introduction to a 2007 article in *Rhetoric Society Quarterly*, part of that journal's Rhetorical Paths in English and Communication Studies series. Jackson cited Hauser's contribution to the discussion, as well as contributions from others like Steven Mailloux and Thomas Miller and wrote, "With the success of the ARS Conference and the construction

of these pathways across disciplines, it may seem that rhetoric education for civic engagement is almost certain to follow, for it is the very
sort of mission that the Rhetoric Society of America itself was founded
to advance" (182).

Jackson then sketched an outline of what rhetoric education for civic
engagement might look like, again drawing upon a wide number of writers. Drawing on Hauser, he argued that rhetoric education "must attend
to endowing students with a capacity to speak and write in multiple situations and 'risk the unpredictable outcomes of public expression,' rather
than deposit in their minds the content of a discipline." Drawing on
Anthony Fleury, Martin Medhurst, and Kathleen Turner, he argued that
developing a "capacity" for public and civic engagement "is not simply
a biography of the discipline," not simply "a compendium of key terms,
a body of works starting with a Greek figure, and/or a reading list of
theorists who use the word." It is, rather, a "*training of a capacity* in the
students that can be, and according to this model of education, *ought* to
be used in public life" (2007, 184–85; emphasis in original).

As Jackson saw it, there was a "growing consensus in the field" that
the focus of rhetoric education should be on civic rhetoric. To prove his
point, he looked beyond the scholarship already mentioned and reeled
off another list of writers who shared his commitment. Carol Jablonski
argues, he wrote, that rhetoric education's goal is "to encourage 'shared,
practical wisdom' and 'critical reflexivity' for 'situated' and 'transac-
tional' public advocacy." Raymie McKerrow suggests that rhetoric education "creates a deliberative community 'of engaged, rhetorically conscious, and consciously rhetorical, citizens.'" And Kathleen Turner says
rhetoric education's "mission is 'to educate citizens for an active and
productive life of participation in the *polis*'" (2007, 185).

Jackson's purpose in his article was to make a case for rhetorical performance and analysis classes in the undergraduate curriculum. After surveying the general agreement in the field on the goals of rhetoric education,
he argued that such courses would help us reclaim our birthright. "If we
can develop a stronger undergraduate rhetoric education, with courses in
performance and critical analysis that capture the political-ethical vision
that is the heritage of civic rhetoric," he argued in the conclusion, "we will
increase the likelihood that students of rhetoric will leave the university
ready to practice the rhetoric of making a difference" (2007, 199).

Not all writers, however, picked up on the ARS's call to reclaim rhetoric's place in civic education, to make civic rhetoric the focus of our

undergraduate majors in rhetoric and writing. Instead, many writers argued for the value of majors in terms of more practical concerns, in terms of what they would do for our profession and the institutions we work in, and in terms of what they would do for our students' professional aspirations.

Rebecca Moore Howard, writing in a 2007 special issue of *Composition Studies* devoted to the undergraduate major in rhetoric and writing, argued that writing majors have the potential to do a world of good, and not just for the job security of rhetoricians. "The process of establishing a writing major can challenge the traditional normative vision of writing instruction and offer in its stead a representation of writing as a discipline and its instruction as part of the intellectual work of the institution," she argued. Writing majors can function as "an instrument of institutional activism" and change the perception of our colleagues across the university. Writing majors help us to be seen as an "intellectual discipline," not just "a means of inflicting discipline upon the bodies of students" (42–43). In addition, she wrote, undergraduate degree programs offer us a number of other opportunities:

> At every institution there is an array of opportunities for the writing program to use its major to deliberately advance a rhetorically sophisticated vision of writing, student writers, and writing instruction. Those opportunities are a benefit of establishing a writing major, and seizing them will benefit not only the major but FYC, too, which will more readily be seen as part of an open-ended course of instruction rather than as a dumping-ground for the grammatically challenged. (2007, 49).

Dominic Delli Carpini, writing in the same special issue, argued that writing majors have the potential "to influence the disciplines with which we share institutional homes and to introduce students to areas of research that, until recently, were reserved for graduate studies" (2007, 15). The Writing Major at York College, where Delli Carpini works, was originally conceived as a pre-professional program, but after only four years, it "has begun to assert itself as a site of humanistic inquiry as well as a site of career development." The success of the writing major within a broader Department of English and Humanities at York elicited mixed reactions from colleagues. Delli Carpini wrote that while many faculty colleagues "acknowledge that the 'career focus' of the writing major was a positive draw," many of them felt ambivalent about it. One English colleague worried about the writing major's effect on literary studies enrollments in particular, while another said, "I'm a little worried, in general, about the erosion of literary studies programs by the far more marketable and 'useful' field of professional writing." This colleague went on to say, however, that the "PW program seems much fresher and better organized and more theoretically sophisticated than the Literary Studies major" (2007,17).

Despite these mixed reactions, the writing major had a positive influence on teaching and learning in the department. Delli Carpini wrote that one faculty colleague in philosophy acknowledged that, thanks to the writing major, philosophy students "probably pay more attention to rhetorical issues, especially when studying popular culture, film, and advertising." Another philosophy colleague noted, "Students appear more capable of reading primary religious texts and separating style from content as well as demonstrating the ability to see how style informs content." In addition, students now "recognize how important writing is in the workplace and how it is exactly those skills that the study of the liberal arts can develop" (2007, 24).

Students also found that the lessons learned in the writing major were useful in their other classes as well. Delli Carpini wrote that students in his early modern literature class used rhetorical concepts and theories to write about Shakespeare and Milton, while others applied their knowledge of rhetorical theory to better understand the philosophical works of Derrida, Locke, and Descartes. All of this was made possible by the return of rhetoric to the undergraduate curriculum, Delli Carpini concluded, "both through specific courses and through faculty and majors whose research interests lie there" (2007, 25).

Delli Carpini's article was full of good news about the writing major and its positive contributions to the academic and professional lives of our students. But hidden among all the good news was something more worrisome. As almost an aside, Delli Carpini began his article with a quick discussion of how we describe our undergraduate degree programs to colleagues and potential students. He surveyed the public presentations of rhetoric and writing programs on university Web sites and found that they tend to fall into one of three categories. They feature a practical focus, a liberal arts focus, or a hybrid of the two. Delli Carpini argued that while many writing majors start out with a practical or professional focus, they have the potential, mostly driven by student interest, to eventually include a liberal arts focus as they grow, the potential, in short, to include our "back story" and our "shoptalk"—"the scholarly and theoretical bases of our discipline" (2007, 15).

Notice, however, what these programs did not feature. They did not feature a focus on civic rhetoric. In fact, they didn't even mention civic rhetoric.

Take, for example, the programs Delli Carpini classified as having a practical focus. Millikin University's writing major, according to its Web site, "emphasizes experiences in a variety of writing contexts including journalism, professional writing, academic writing, literary writing, editing, publishing, and personal creativity. By learning to shift between these multiple contexts, Millikin's writing majors are prepared for a wide range of professional and lifelong writing, editing and publishing opportunities" (Millikin University English Department). And the University of Florida's advanced writing track tells potential students that in "our current information-rich economy, an unprecedented demand now exists for college graduates with excellent communication skills. The Advanced Writing Model [track] provides students with extensive preparation for the variety of writing tasks required of professionals in business, law, government, and administration, as well as of graduate students and educators in all disciplines" (University of Florida English Department).

The programs with a liberal arts or hybrid focus didn't focus on civic rhetoric either. Indiana Wesleyan University, for example, emphasized how their program "is designed to prepare students to become outstanding communicators with a high level of proficiency in the use of the written word. The major stresses both the artistic joy of composition and the practical application of writing skills to communication problems in everyday life" (Indiana Wesleyan University Modern Language, Literature, and Communication Department). And York College's proudly hybrid program, which, Delli Carpini wrote, explicitly keeps "one foot in each world, showing how the liberal arts and practical focuses can co-exist," (2007, 16) advertised itself this way:

> A major in Professional Writing provides an education firmly grounded in the liberal arts, while preparing students for a wide range of careers as writers or communications specialists in fields such as publishing, government and non-governmental organization (NGOs), corporate communications, information technology, social service organizations, healthcare, finance, and the arts. A Professional Writing major is also excellent preparation for students who wish to pursue law school or graduate work in professional or technical writing, creative writing, rhetoric and composition, media studies, communication, and other fields. (York College of Pennsylvania English and Humanities Department)

There are many good reasons to turn away from civic rhetoric as we develop our undergraduate majors. What sounds good in theory is not always good in practice, and what sounds good in our journals is not always applicable in our home institutions. Peggy O'Neill, Nan Stevens LoBue, Margaret McLaughlin, Angela Crow, and Kathy S. Albertson, all from the newly formed (at the time) writing and linguistics department at Georgia Southern University, succinctly outlined the main problem with focusing our programs on civic rhetoric. In a short response to David Fleming's "Rhetoric as a Course of Study," published a year after the original article, the Georgia Southern professors criticized Fleming's article on the grounds that its ideas were not applicable to the vast majority of students in the vast majority of universities. They reported that they were initially excited to see Fleming's article because "we expected to find arguments that we could adapt as we construct our proposal for a new undergraduate major" (O'Neill et al., 1999, 274).

But they were, unfortunately, "very disappointed" as they read and discussed the piece "because his arguments did not seem applicable to our situation as a public institution educating the general populace, including many first-generation college students" (274). The professors were also "frustrated by his refusal to connect the 'study of speaking and writing well' to careers and jobs." They wrote:

> In our experience, upper administrators and governing boards demand that departments proposing new majors make these connections—and make them explicitly, with more than theoretical arguments. In short, we need to prove that students who graduate with a major in rhetoric are employable. (274)

The real problem with Fleming's proposal, they concluded, was its elitism. Fleming, they wrote, "seems to direct his arguments at those at more elite institutions whose students may not have to worry about what kind of jobs they can get once they graduate or whose faculty do not need to demonstrate the practical value of a major course of study." They did, of course, believe that "rhetorical education is a viable route to success," and they wrote that they were in the midst of developing their own argument "to demonstrate that rhetorical study is not just for the elite who are obligated to serve the polis but for all citizens regardless of class, race, gender, or ethnicity" (275).

The Georgia Southern professors made an important point. We do need to be careful when crafting arguments for our programs, and we do need to develop majors that are as inclusive as possible. Their objections were also ominous and prescient, as it turns out, laying out an alternative justification for the development of undergraduate majors, a justification that has flourished in public descriptions of our programs. Their objections may have been the first hint that, somewhere along the way, somewhere between the ARS's call for a manifesto and our public descriptions of our programs, we'd lose our nerve. Somewhere between reclaiming our birthright and staking a claim in the undergraduate curriculum, we'd trade in civic rhetoric for something a little more practical, something a little more marketable to potential majors. We'd trade it in for a job.

FORM, FUNCTION, AND THE UNDERGRADUATE MAJOR IN WRITING AND RHETORIC

And that is a mistake. As we make our arguments to colleagues and administrators, potential students, and the public at large, we need to be careful to not inadvertently diminish the prospects for rhetoric education in the twenty-first century by focusing our undergraduate degree programs exclusively on practical, career-related concerns. These are dire predictions, sure, but our history suggests that our field's focus has a profound influence on the form, or shape, of our programs. Much like the modernist architectural dictum that "form follows function," the history of our field suggests that our programs grow and prosper along the lines drawn by our guiding focus.

We have heard many calls over the years for our field to move in one direction or the other, to focus on one set of concerns or another. But two broadly defined focuses in particular seem to have endured: a focus on academic writing and a focus on professional or workplace writing. These focuses grow out of a concern for empowering people in different spheres of human activity, different spheres in which training in the arts of rhetoric and writing will prepare a person to use language to participate effectively in one endeavor or another, to participate in different aspects of their lives. The focus on academic writing, arguably the founding focus of our field, empowers people in their academic lives, while the focus on professional writing empowers people in their professional lives. Civic rhetoric, the focus we are advocating here, empowers people in their public lives.

Over the years, different subspecialties of our field have become associated with these different focuses. Rhetoric and composition, though it is also the umbrella term for our field as a whole, is focused primarily on academic writing. Professional writing is focused primarily on writing for the workplace, and civic rhetoric is focused primarily on public or political writing. Our field's three subspecialties, their primary focuses, and the areas of human activity in which they empower people, can be seen in the figure below.

Discipline/Field of Study	Focus	Empowers People to Participate in their . . .
rhetoric and composition	academic writing	academic lives
professional writing	professional/technical/work-place writing	professional lives
civic rhetoric	public/political writing	public lives

Fig 1. Our field's subspecialties empower people to participate in different spheres of human activity.

Rhetoric and composition and professional writing have developed unique programs to train people to participate in different aspects of their lives, programs that have been radically shaped and influenced by their guiding focus. Rhetoric and composition developed what most of us would recognize as the modern writing program. It consists of first-year composition, supported by a writing center, and, at many places, basic writing courses and a writing-across-the-curriculum program. It also includes, at many schools, additional upper-level writing courses, such as advanced composition or tutor-training courses.

Professional writing developed professional, technical, and work-place writing programs offering courses that often fulfill a service function, as well as courses for majors and minors. These programs include service courses such as business and technical writing, which are often required courses for students in business, engineering, and science degree programs, and also more specialized courses for majors and minors like writing for the Web, grant writing, desktop publishing, and, occasionally, theory courses.

These two subspecialties have created different kinds of programs, programs that have been shaped and influenced by their guiding focus. Rhetoric and composition's focus on academic writing led to the development of programs at the two extremes: first-year composition programs to teach students the ways of writing in the academy and graduate programs to study and fully understand writing in all of its complexity. (And to train instructors to teach in those first-year composition programs, though, ironically, most rhetoric and composition PhDs teach very little first-year composition). What it did not lead to was the development of undergraduate degree programs.

This is not surprising, however, given the fact that rhetoric and composition is focused on empowering people to participate in their academic lives. There is an inherent contradiction in offering a degree—and an even greater contradiction in seeking a degree—in a field that trains one to write for the academy. If the focus of a field's training is on academic writing, a terminal degree, which implies the end of academic training and the beginning of something else, makes no sense. A student would be getting a degree in a subject designed to help her get a degree.

Professional writing as a field is not affected by the same internal contradiction and, as a result, has developed programs in many parts of the curriculum that have proven to be resistant to rhetoric and composition. Many PhD programs offer specializations in professional writing, fulfilling the same research and instructor-training goals as graduate programs in rhetoric and composition. In addition, a number of graduate programs offer professionally focused MA degrees and post-graduate certificates in professional writing. At the undergraduate level, many schools offer minors or certificates in professional writing, and a growing number of schools offer full-fledged BA degrees.

What we see in professional writing is a proliferation of programs that offer training "around the edges" of other degrees. MAs and post-graduate certificates, as well as minors and undergraduate sequences, make sense because training in professional writing empowers people in their professional lives, a sphere of human activity outside the academy. But full undergraduate degree programs are only relatively successful because these programs are unable to make a strong enough claim on empowering students in their professional lives. Sure, training in professional writing will help a business person succeed in business, or an engineer succeed on the job, but a degree in business or a degree in engineering will help even more, and may even be a prerequisite for entry into those professions. Professional writing programs, then, are pushed into a supporting role and, over the long-term, may be unable to support vibrant undergraduate degree programs.

Civic rhetoric, however, has the potential to support vibrant undergraduate degree programs in rhetoric and writing. A bachelor's degree in rhetoric and writing, with a focus on civic rhetoric, makes sense to both students and administrators, instructors and the public at large, because such a degree will empower people in their public lives, a sphere of human activity only tangentially affected by degree programs in other disciplines. Civic rhetoric has the potential to send a simple yet powerful message to potential students. If you want to be effective in business or medicine, two potential professional lives, get a degree in finance or biology. But if you want to be effective in your public life, get a degree in writing and rhetoric.

Unlike professional writing, which plays a supporting role to training in other fields that prepares people for their professional lives, civic rhetoric has the potential to play a leading role in preparing people for their public lives. And unlike rhetoric and composition, which primarily prepares people for success in the academy and has found a home at its two extremes, civic rhetoric has the potential to prepare people for success outside of school and will be at home throughout the curriculum. Focusing our undergraduate degree programs on civic rhetoric will help us not only reclaim our birthright, our leading role in civic education but also secure a place for rhetoric in the academy in the twenty-first century and beyond.

REFERENCES

Delli Carpini, Dominic. 2007. Re-writing the humanities: The writing major's effect upon undergraduate studies in English departments. *Composition Studies* 35.1:15–36.

Fleming, David. 1998. Rhetoric as a course of study. *College English* 61.2:169–91.

Hauser, Gerard. 2004. Teaching rhetoric: Or why rhetoric isn't just another kind of philosophy or literary criticism. *Rhetoric Society Quarterly* 34.3:39–53.

Howard, Rebecca Moore. 2007. Curricular activism: The writing major as counterdiscourse. *Composition Studies* 35.1:41–52.

Indiana Wesleyan University Modern Language, Literature, and Communication Department. Writing. Indiana Wesleyan University. http://cas.indwes.edu/Academic-Divisions/Modern-Languages-Literature/writing/ (accessed December 1, 2007).

Jackson, Brian. 2007. Cultivating paideweyan pedagogy: Rhetoric education in English and communication studies. *Rhetoric Society Quarterly* 37.2:181–201.

Millikin University English Department. Writing major. Millikin University. http://www.millikin.edu/english/majors.html#writingmajor (accessed December 1, 2007).

O'Neill, Peggy, Nan Stevens LoBue, Margaret McLaughlin, Angela Crow, Kathy S. Albertson. 1999. A comment on "Rhetoric as a course of study." *College English* 62.2:274–75.

University of Florida English Department. Advanced writing. University of Florida. http://www.english.ufl.edu/programs/undergrad/tracks/adv_writing.html (accessed December 1, 2007).

York College of Pennsylvania English and Humanities Department. Professional writing. York College of Pennsylvania. http://www.ycp.edu/academics/5667.htm (accessed December 1, 2007).

11

COMPOSING MULTILITERACIES AND IMAGE
Multimodal Writing Majors for a Creative Economy

Joddy Murray

At one point while students were working on their in-class projects for the Multimedia Authoring class I was teaching, it occurred to me just how much these students were juggling: They had been researching community events and organizations for Web sites they were constructing; story-boarding and working in groups to determine who was going to film interviews for the mini-documentaries on student life they were producing; and reflecting on and writing about how they were going to integrate the still photography they shot and edited into arguments for campus involvement—arguments that would eventually become large-format posters distributed in common-use areas. These students were undergoing a composing process that demanded constant production of image *as a means* to refine their process (not the other way around). As these students worked, I realized that what they were producing wasn't really the Web page, the short film, or the collage; these students were learning to create innovation itself. As a learning laboratory, they came to terms as to what it means to compose with images of both sight and sound, and, as they did so, they came closer to what it means to be a producer within a creative economy—an economy that relies less on producing a manufactured product or producing a service and more on producing innovation itself. Said differently, these students were using their knowledge and skills of multimedia to create rhetorically constructed images, and, at the same time, learning to become innovators for a new creative economy as they composed multimodal texts.

What many of these students did not realize at the time was that as they became multiliterate they also became better prepared for a changing economy. Richard Florida's book, *The Rise of the Creative Class: And How It's*

Transforming Work, Leisure, Community and Everyday Life (2002), defines the creative economy as the next "large-scale economic transformation" (66):

> Many say that we now live in an "information" economy or a "knowledge" economy. But what's more fundamentally true is that we now have an economy powered by human creativity. Creativity—"the ability to create meaningful new forms," . . . —is now the *decisive* source of competitive advantage. In virtually every industry, from automobiles to fashion, food products, and information technology itself, the winners in the long run are those who can create and keep creating. This has always been true, from the days of the Agricultural Revolution to the Industrial Revolution. But in the past few decades we've come to recognize it clearly and act upon it systematically. (5)

Undergraduate majors today must take into account this reality, and one good way for students to learn that innovation itself is the key to their professional and economic futures is to stress what Florida calls the "three Ts" of economic development: technology, talent, and tolerance (266). For my purposes here, these three Ts serve more as a set of values (with talent referring specifically to the degree to which students are multiliterate). In order for students to be comfortable in being able to handle so many literacies—sometimes at once, sometimes in rapid succession—they must first understand how to compose non-discursive images as well as discursive images. Just as the creative economy puts a value on technology, talent, and tolerance, so must multiliterate students value multimodal composing.

Composing a variety of texts—from traditional print to less traditional hypertext and cinematic texts—requires a set of courses that redefines traditional paths to literacy because anything else has the effect of stifling innovation and multimodal rigor. If a typical path to literacy in higher education can be described as learning what it takes to write the traditional, academic essay (i.e., print mechanics, print research, print rhetorics and disciplinarity), then new undergraduate majors must develop the necessary scaffolding and preparation required to become multiliterate and accustomed to multimodal textual production technologies. Many students in that Multimedia Authoring class were struggling not just with unfamiliar technology (though that was certainly part of it) but with finding the inventional tools needed to innovate with image. Clearly, a course such as this one is less effective if it not sufficiently built into a sequence of courses within a major that demands they compose with image from very early on. Though texts may vary considerably in means of production, consumption, and distribution (all of which necessarily alters the nature of both the text and its composition), the one element that remains central to printed text, hypertext, and filmic text is image. In order to build an undergraduate major that can accommodate the variety of texts students must ably navigate—in order for students to become multiliterate *composers*—we need to develop courses within the major that put image at the center of the "spiral" so students can gain experiences in the classroom that leads to rhetorical proficiency for any textual mode.

Becoming able to operate technology, however, is not sufficient nor even necessarily relevant to English studies, but learning to integrate technology into compositional practice is. Literacy is bigger than whether or not a student can use Flash, Word, or Final Cut. What I teach students is how to compose for any mode: how to create rhetorically suitable texts, no matter what kind of text it is. In order to be digitally literate, students must learn more than technical proficiency in software and hardware. In *Multiliteracies for a Digital Age* (2004), Stuart A. Selber rightly observes that "too few teachers today are prepared to organize learning environments that integrate technology meaningfully and appropriately" and, instead, have the "mistaken" view that to become digitally literate, students merely need to learn about computers at the operational level (1). Perhaps a close analogy to this line of thinking would be to assume that once a student understands the operational functionality of a pen and paper our obligations to their learning how to compose is complete. Clearly the technology, though important, is only part of what a student must learn to practice composition—in the end, perhaps even only a small part. Selber notes three important aspects of multiliteracies for digital texts (though these three categories seem applicable to many other types of literacy as well):

My view is that teachers should emphasize different kinds of computer literacies and help students become skilled at moving among them in strategic ways. The three literacy categories that organize my discussion—functional, critical, and rhetorical—are meant to be suggestive rather than restrictive, and more complimentary than in competition with each other. . . . Students who are not adequately exposed to all three literacy categories will find it difficult to participate fully and meaningfully in technological activities. . . . Likewise, there are three subject positions connected to the literacy landscape: students as users of technology, students as questioners of technology, and students as producers of technology. (24–25)

It should not go unnoticed that this is not such an unfamiliar set of metaphors, as Selber calls them. If we view the codex as a technology (which it so obviously is), then we can see these three literacies at work in a more traditional English studies classroom: the mechanics of reading challenging texts (functional literacy), the ability to develop a critical stance and become familiar with previous critical viewpoints (critical literacy), and the reflective praxis necessary to produce printed documents and codices of their own (rhetorical literacy). As such, one way to view Selber's three literacies is to see them as an extrapolation of what faculty in English studies already unceremoniously do with codex technologies, only applied to digital technologies. Regardless, Selber emphasizes the important contribution of an entire set of courses focused on these literacies, not just one class or one specialty: "one of the larger questions for teachers will be how to scaffold instructional activities that illuminate the relationships and interdependencies between these multiple literacies" (25). The interdependencies not withstanding, the challenge to designing these types of courses for the undergraduate major is less about how to "illuminate" between these three literacies than it is about how to find what they hold in common.

Selber is not alone in wishing to broaden digital literacy beyond the functional: Laura J. Gurak's *Cyberliteracy: Navigating the Internet with Awareness* (2001) also calls for a more critical understanding of digital technologies, especially as it relates to the way we teach our students multiliteracy. It is not enough that students learn to read, research, and compose about and for the Internet, they must "recognize that technologies have consequences, and that we can decide how we allow the Internet to be part of our lives" in order to be what she terms "cyberliterate" (7):

Technologies are invented by people and imbued with design choices that give these devices (software included) certain trajectories. . . . The choices built into the Internet, and the choices we then make about how to use it, require a far more critical framework than we currently have. . . . The ubiquity of the Internet has brought with it an acceptance of certain social conditions that are linked to the technology. (2–3)

Nowhere are these "trajectories" more evident than in classrooms in which teachers are frustrated because their students use Internet sources that are not credible, or in which students assume a certain informality in their writing because of their everyday experience with e-mail and social networking pages. Like Florida's emphasis on "tolerance," students have to learn not only about the social and cultural assumptions that are programmed into software and their interfaces but also about the assumptions behind their own actions (and their rhetorical effect). It is precisely because technology has thus far been dominated by a lack of diversity that it is problematic for many today. The value of diversity in a creative economy is that "greater and more diverse concentrations of creative capital in turn lead to higher rates of innovation, high-technology business formation, job generation and economic growth" (Florida 2002, 249). It is also the case that the opposite—increased specialization within and among disciplines, increased monoculturalism, and/or increased social privilege—works to decrease diversity and, as a likely consequence, decrease innovation. Courses that work to unmask both the technologies and the historical development of those technologies would help students become more culturally aware, especially if these students set out to investigate these technologies themselves. Another possibility, however, is to address diversity in terms of technology: to unveil and critique the "imbued" design choices, interface assumptions, and "certain social conditions" behind digital technologies as a way of addressing diversity and, possibly, spark even further innovation.

For such an undergraduate major to survive, however, it must be a dynamic one. Just as we are having to come to terms with the changing nature of texts and authors, we must also come to terms with a concept of a major that is malleable, free to self-adjust, and ready to adapt to changing technologies. I often emphasize to students that though they may be struggling with compositional strategies for print, hypertext, and film, changes are already imminent that will likely change those strategies: digital paper, 3-D printers, holographic time-based media, etc. The number and frequency of these changes in media are only going to increase, and there will be less and less time to create courses that take advantage of these textual technologies: "The main problem with so many formalized programs is that they put forward a universal approach to computer literacy that disregards the continuous and contingent interplay between context and technology" (Selber 2004, 26). It is the nature of a vibrant and healthy major to change, but as long as the major is centered on the printed text such as that found in the traditional codex, it will always be developing supposedly new courses for new technologies—a relationship that seems backwards at the very least.

What, then, could replace the notion of *printed text* as the center of our composition major? What centralizing concept might provide an aid to composers, no matter what mode or type of text they may endeavor to create—past, present, and future? The answer is *image*.

Students asked to compose multimodal text inevitably must come to terms with the use and impact of image as language. One consequence of the centrality of image to language is that image must be of a fundamental consequence to both discursive and non-discursive text. Specifically, inasmuch as language may be limited by discursive forms, language has within it the ability to overcome its own limitation through the use of non-discursive forms.[1] One potential consequence of such a view is that invention, no longer limited to the "chain of reasoning" or to discursive thought as a whole, has an entirely different realm to explore: the networks and interactions between non-discursive images and emotions. Non-discursive text has the ability to literally "be in the world"—to experience, to live, to feel—because it does not require linearity or a hierarchy. In short, image as a centralizing concept in composition becomes complex and adaptive: it thrives through change, and it generates text from "the bottom up." Text is no longer the province of the "single genius" or the "paradigm shift"; rather, invention takes advantage of the distribution made possible through networks. Steven Johnson makes a similar point regarding the history of intellectual development in his book *Emergence: The Connected Lives of Ants, Brains, Cities, and Software* (2001):

> Both theories are inadequate: the great-man story ignores the distributed, communal effort that goes into any important intellectual advance, and the paradigm-shift model has a hard time explaining [itself]. . . . But plug more minds into the system and give their work a longer, more durable trail—by publishing their ideas in best-selling books, or founding research centers to explore those ideas—and before long the system arrives at a phase transition: isolated hunches and private obsessions coalesce into a new way of looking at the world, shared by thousands of individuals. (64)

An undergraduate major based first on image as a central compositional force in textual production separates the issue of technology long

---

1. See Susan Langer's *Feeling and Form: A Theory of Art* (1953) for an exhaustive explanation of the terms "discursive" and "non-discursive."

enough to focus on rhetoric: to whom will this text appeal, why, and how? Digital technologies (or whatever technology is next) remain in the service of the rhetor, opening up questions of critical awareness, tolerance, and the "power and problems" of technology for further investigation:

> Unless people become familiar with the social, rhetorical, and political features of digital communication, they will be led into cyberspace with only a limited understanding of both the power and the problems of this technology. To become cyberliterate, people need to . . . not only become more efficient computer users but also to become more sophisticated about critiquing, challenging, and anticipating how these technologies are designed, implemented, and used." (Gurak 2001, 11)

This, in other words, is a two-pronged approach: one that simultaneously encourages students to become more literate in technology (functional, critical, and rhetorical), as well as one that is always independent of technology by keeping at its core image, not the codex.

Both Plato and Aristotle emphasize that the success of the rhetor may in large part be measured by the images he or she can evoke in the audience. In fact, the marriage between writing pedagogy and the use of images has a long history. Discursive invention—that is, the formulaic, procedural-bound inventional schemes so often discussed in writing pedagogy—has always been the first choice of teachers and students because, like discursive image-making, it seems the most directly transferable into a sender-message-receiver format. It is time, however, to alter our view of the undergraduate major in such a way that does not attempt to make it simpler, clearer, or more rigidly defined. A major that values non-discursive textual production thrives to the degree that it is complex and adaptive, and it does so without a specific rubric for invention. Such a major allows students to learn the value of image and the many ways it can be composed (using many different technologies—old and new); the result is a student who values non-discursive text at least as much as discursive text.

Both rhetors and poets have long known the centrality of image to writing, but few compositionists view what they are doing when they write as composing images. Writers, even writers for an academic audience, are encouraged to be clear, to explicate through explicit details, to elucidate and illuminate through example, and then to revise—all words that are evocative of associations with the term "image." It might not be a huge cognitive leap to propose that as writers mature, in general, they become more proficient at both creating images as they read, as well as depending on images (of all the senses) as they write.

Creating an undergraduate major that simultaneously emphasizes multiliteracy *and* the central role of image to composing has the dual benefit of being adaptable to changing technologies while encouraging students to practice becoming innovators for a new, creative economy. Compositionists will continue to do what they do best by helping students befriend the process of writing—no matter what media or mode it takes. As a force for student empowerment, as a means to become critically aware of both technology itself and its sociocultural milieu, as a way to practice both analyzing and creating rhetorical texts: composing through image has the potential to become the centralizing concept that allows undergraduate majors to have a dynamic, authorial relationship to the many modes of text experienced every day.

REFERENCES

Bruner, Jerome S. 1960. The process of education. Cambridge: Harvard University Press.

Florida, Richard. 2002. The rise of the creative class: And how it's transforming work, leisure, community and everyday life. New York: Basic Books.

Gurak, Laura J. 2001. Cyberliteracy: Navigating the Internet with awareness. New Haven, CT: Yale University Press.

Johnson, Steven. 2001. Emergence: The connected lives of ants, brains, cities, and software. New York: Simon & Schuster.

Selber, Stuart A. 2004. Multiliteracies for a digital age. Carbondale: Southern Illinois University Press.

Langer, Susanne K. 1953. Feeling and form: A theory of art. New York: Schribner.

12

NOT JUST ANOTHER PRETTY CLASSROOM GENRE
The Uses of Creative Nonfiction in the Writing Major

Celest Martin

> *Having a major, of course, dramatically changes a field's standing in the academy.*
>> —Downs and Wardle, "Teaching about Writing, Righting Misconceptions"

A HOME FOR THE HYBRID: WELCOMING CREATIVE NONFICTION TO THE WRITING MAJOR

As late as 2003, theoretical concerns prevented composition studies and creative writing from engaging in productive dialogue. One result of this scholarly cold war was to leave creative nonfiction an orphan (Hesse 2003). However, many from the academy in both of these writing disciplines have been calling for a union of the two, realizing that the theories and pedagogies of each inform and strengthen the other. (See, for example, Mayers 2005; Eldred 2005; Couture and Kent 2004; Kamler 2001; Bloom 1998; and, to some extent, Bizzell 1999). The reluctance of both disciplines to claim creative nonfiction is easing, and indeed, as this essay will demonstrate, some compositionists see creative nonfiction as a way of releasing its instructors and students alike from working in "classroom genres." (Bloom 2004; Eldred 2005). For our writing majors, such a shift is a healthy one. As Wendy Bishop notes, it doesn't do us any harm either:

> Write a successful memoir like Susanna Kaysen's *Girl, Interrupted* as an English Department member in the 1980's and this seemingly "minor accomplishment" would have been mentioned patronizingly, if at all, during tenuring discussions. Do the same and be optioned for a film in the 2000s, and you'll accrue praise, cash, envy, and a promotion (2003, 264).

More theoretically, Douglas Hesse expresses why creative writing and composition are so important to each other and why academic snobbery between them is counterproductive, and hints that creative nonfiction may be a bridge between them:

> It is just as debilitating for compositionists to snub creative writing for holding undertheorized views of writing as it is for creative writers to snub composition for merely transmitting rudiments. The genres of creative nonfiction, at least for now, inhabit a kind of middle ground between composition and creative writing programs. . . .

The challenge for creative writing programs is to understand why rhetoric and composition has a continued stake in these fields (rhetoric and belles-lettres) one important not only for historical and conceptual reasons but also for the ways large numbers of students understand the terrain of writing and their own possibilities as writers. The even bigger challenge is for composition programs to understand this stake too (Hesse 2003, 264).

Even though I would hesitate to call creative nonfiction part of the mainstream culture of the 4 Cs (Conference on College Composition and Communication), it does merit a special interest group at our national convention, and every year there are more sessions dedicated to its place in the profession. In 2007, when Robert Root and Michael Steinberg were on a panel together with two others in creative nonfiction, there was standing room only in a large ballroom in New York. Certainly, we cannot say it is no longer a contested site, but in looking through "Writing Majors at a Glance," (National Council of Teachers of English 2007), which announces up front it does not include *creative* writing majors, most writing majors include some form of creative nonfiction. Some clearly give it more weight than others, recognizing that it goes far beyond memoir, that it has many subgenres, and that students may profit from reading nonfiction and analyzing it rhetorically as well as from writing it.

Perhaps the most certain sign that creative nonfiction has arrived in the discipline is its appearance in that sacrosanct region—our textbooks. According to one compositionist:

> "Process" has been perhaps the most influential concept in late twentieth-century Composition scholarship and practice. Who of the initiated new generation of Composition instructors doesn't teach through drafting and

revision long after Flower and Hayes's protocols have faded in the discipline's collective memory?

Despite this shift to process, the last four decades are most marked by changes in its antithesis: product. The years have seen a series of critical camps enlarging our concept of what writing instruction should comprise. While the focus has been on first-year composition's purposes—to introduce students to the academy; to help them to understand their own lives, to express their own voices, to do the civic work of fighting injustice or enacting citizenship—the most concrete results have been the shifts in the kind of products students compose, most of which are recognizable *only as classroom genres*. A glance at the last few decades of textbooks reveals the shift from personal experience and research papers, to academic discourse, to forms of formal argument, and to public fieldwork, and now, if interest holds, to creative nonfiction (Eldred 2005; emphasis added).

All this being the case, I find it more productive in this essay to discuss the ways in which creative nonfiction serves our writing majors, and why it should be considered a legitimate form of professional writing, as practical as business communications or legal writing but with an *aesthetique* all its own. More productive, that is, than arguing about whether it has a place in composition studies—that has already been established. In other words, I will devote the rest of this essay to arguing for the *uses* of creative nonfiction: How does it serve our writing majors? What possibilities does it hold for rounding out our students' portfolios as we send them forth into the writing world and the world of work? What can it teach them about rhetoric? About genre?

I posit the following uses of creative nonfiction for our majors, uses that will serve to divide this essay into sections:

- To learn about and practice craft, craft that can be applied as much to a persuasive business proposal as to a personal memoir

- To provide students who choose to write in the personal genres with a way of doing so that is crafted and audience-oriented

- To teach our writing majors the conventions of a "literary genre"(through both reading and writing) that belongs as much in the province of rhetoric as it does in literary studies, and to sensitize their awareness of rhetorical choices when writing in a creative genre, as well as the consequences of those choices for their audience

- To give our double majors, those students who are scientists, environmentalists, nurses, or engineers, a way of communicating in prose about their work that is accessible to nonspecialists, prose that we hope may take its place alongside that of Richard Selzer, Lewis Thomas, Rachel Carson, Annie Dillard, and Carl Sagan, to name a few.

- To provide our majors with the marketable skill of freelance writing or the possibility of becoming a staff writer for a magazine in their interest area. Creative nonfiction, at the very least, is *not* a "classroom genre." *And*, it can be taught in our first-year courses, those courses perhaps most prone to spawning writing that will not be used outside of the classroom. We might begin to reconfigure these courses into something akin to Introduction to Writing Studies. While such a reconfiguration might use some of what Downs and Wardle suggest in their much-talked-about article (2007), it also might incorporate some of Robert Root's pedagogical suggestions (2003).

CRAFT

> *I should also note briefly here why I choose the term craft criticism to denote this particular type of work. I do so partly because craft, by virtue of its seeming ubiquity, is one of the most important words in the discourse about creative writing in America.*
>
> —Tim Mayers, *(Re)Writing Craft*

I love to write. I have been involved in our faculty senate now for several years, and it's become a kind of joke that if legislation is wordy or poorly written, "Celest will fix it." Although I'd prefer to be doing something creative, I try to rewrite these senate documents with the same attention to language, to audience, and to ease of processing that I would a poem or a personal essay (forms in which I might actually wish to complicate the processing). I am of the philosophical belief that if one calls herself a writer, she should be able to pen a poem or a public pamphlet with equal ease. But I'm aware that this belief is not shared by all in composition studies, and that it was perhaps fostered by my own undergraduate mentor. Below is the story of how I came to craft.

I introduce to you Steven Darian, a creative writer with a degree in applied linguistics, who approached all language from its structural underpinnings. Much of my writing life, as well as my chosen discipline, has been shaped by this man. Indeed, it was he who pointed me in the direction of Ross Winterowd's doctoral program in rhetoric, linguistics, and literary studies. In 1969, he was bold enough to use the Christenson Rhetoric Program to teach freshman composition. Daily, he braved the sneers and whispers of his literary colleagues in the English department as he indefatigably wheeled his overhead projector through Armitage Hall. He'd bought the projector himself—the height of classroom technology in that era. Our first revelatory composition lesson was this: *the modifier is the essential part of any sentence.* On the transparency would go the examples of this radical concept. (Until then, I'd thought it was the subject and verb!) Suddenly, words hung together in beautiful ways. Because I'd had twelve years of Catholic school training in grammar, I was likely the only one in the class nerdy enough to know things like "the absolute construction," "the infinitive phrase," and "parallelism." I loved it. Steven Darian was my hero, and the day he praised my extended, well-modified sentence was the day I learned what craft was. Of course, knowing what it was and being able to exercise it in my writing all the time were, and are, two different things. Craft mastery can only get better with time. But we can teach it. And creative nonfiction is an excellent vehicle for doing so—and for teaching its extension to all forms of writing to our majors. If one can write well, then there is no excuse for not doing so all the time, no matter what the genre.

But in our desire of late to emphasize writing as a response to a rhetorical situation—rhetorical in the sense that there is a distinct and ever-changing variety of audiences or a particular exigency—compositionists have moved away from craft and toward "the public," as though somehow the two are mutually exclusive. Doug Hesse has this to say about the relative lack of emphasis on "craft" in composition studies and how creative nonfiction might enrich the field.

> The crucial question is whether composition now much claims genres other than those that live mainly in the academy. I think mostly not. Composition studies are more concerned with writing rather than with writers. It supports identities of "students as writers" or "biologists as writers," subject positions that subordinate "writer" to some prior and primary identity. Composition studies does not generally support the complementary subject positions of "writer as student" or "writer as biologist," in which the subject position of writer is foregrounded. One quality occluded in composition's very political and social turns is that of writing as craft, as the making of textual artifacts

whose maker is important *as* maker. Articulating a relationship between creative nonfiction and composition studies would help to inscribe that position,
not as an exclusive one, but certainly as a vital one (2003, 263).

Tim Mayers, in *(Re)Writing Craft: Composition, Creative Writing, and the
Future of English Studies* (2005), offers in his very readable and cogently
presented arguments, an area of study for compositionists and their
students alike who may also be engaged in the study of creative nonfiction. Although he speaks here primarily of poetry and fiction, elsewhere
in the text, he includes creative nonfiction under the same umbrella.
Craft criticism attempts to situate the writing of poetry and fiction, and
the teaching of poetry and fiction writing, within institutional, political,
social, and economic contexts. As such, many of the concerns of craft
critics might be called rhetorical. Some craft critics are concerned, for
instance, with audiences for poetry, with the ways in which these audiences might receive poems, and the ways in which these audiences
might be expanded. . . .

> Yet many creative writers publish, and present at conferences, other kinds of
> work (than their poems, stories, and novels). Some—having divided profes-
> sional duties—publish and present academic literary criticism or composition
> scholarship as well. And many produce critical prose that focuses squarely on
> issues of contemporary "creative" text production in academic settings. This
> kind of critical prose is craft criticism (2005, 35).

Here, Mayers presents an area of study visited by Chris Anderson (1987,
1989), and Winterowd (1990), one that has received little attention in
composition studies outside of classroom genres, yet one that can lead
to fruitful scholarship as well as areas of inquiry for our majors. Root
and Steinberg's textbook, *The Fourth Genre* (2007), includes many craft
criticism essays. I can say from my own experience in using this text that
students have found these essays invaluable in understanding the *making*
of creative nonfiction, a genre that few have had prior experience with.
Perhaps one of the most insightful essays for newcomers to the genre
is "Collage, Montage, Mosaic, Vignette, Episode, Segment," Root's own
essay (2007). This piece of craft criticism provides options for writers
learning to manipulate one of the trickiest elements of crafting fact:
chronology. Mastering chronological strategies can make the difference
between a well-written personal narrative that remains a text created
to fulfill an assignment or one that moves into the realm of a powerful

thematic statement, potentially publishable in the many venues now available for essays and other forms of creative nonfiction. For those of our majors who aspire to travel writing, and have been locked into the trip that begins with the alarm clock going off and ends with the plane landing, this essay, and others like it, is a boon both for them and for the writing instructors who have to read those "vacation" essays.

Although the uses of creative nonfiction are far from limited to personal writing, as I will demonstrate later in this essay, memoir does seem to be the preferred subgenre of many of the students who fill at least the first-level course in creative nonfiction, if in fact the department offers more than one level. Perhaps it is because of their age—perhaps it is because of the very human tendency to want to tell our stories. Much has been written about the value of personal writing in books devoted to writing theory and pedagogy (Paley 2001; Elbow 2000; Kamler 2001; Couture and Kent 2004), as well as in countless articles in our professional journals and the professional journals of sociologists, medical professionals, psychologists—the list goes on. But what creative nonfiction offers students is a way to craft the personal if they choose to make the personal public, a way to reach the universal. As Lynn Z. Bloom posits in her exploratory piece, "The Essayist in—and behind—the Essay: Vested Writers, Invested Readers," indeed, personal essays that successfully reach audiences year after year, generation after generation, demonstrate that a writer's private presence in the essay is most effectively transmitted through a public persona (2004, 95).

Bloom's work explores the personae presented by the canonical essayists—she calls them "superstars" who appear in our anthologies: E. B. White, Joan Didion, George Orwell, Martin Luther King, Virginia Woolf, Lewis Thomas, Annie Dillard, and so on. A meticulous empirical study, it is also a call to transform our pedagogy and our own writing practices—an invitation, in fact, for writing teachers who consider themselves compositionists to engage in creative nonfiction. I quote from her conclusion below, and although it is a lengthy quote, I think it is one well worth including here:

> If more teachers wrote essays or academic articles with presence that acknowledged their authorial investment, they would be better able to teach students not only the craft but the art. Until recently, composition studies scholars took the ideas—and indeed the personae—of academic essayists with presence, such as Peter Elbow, Donald Murray, Mike Rose, and Nancy Sommers—to heart but

dismissed or trivialized the genre in which they wrote as too obvious, too easy, too confessional: "U.S. composition teachers have created a school genre that can exist only in an expressivist composition classroom" (Dixon 257). However, now that more academics have begun to try such writing themselves, they have realized how hard it is, in the absence of a predictable form and conventional academic language, to present profound ideas simply, with elegance and apparent ease. It is even harder to create a credible persona of the sort that appears with regularity in such publications as the *American Scholar, Creative Nonfiction, Writing on the Edge, Fourth Genre*, and the serial volumes of *Best American Essays*, among others. Yet they are also experiencing the rewards; while conventional academic articles engender citations, personal essays inspire fan mail, dissertation chapters, invitations to parties—and republication.

As writers of the genre, teachers and other essayists can with greater authority show students ways to convey the presence that can transform their own worlds and their relationship to their readers from distance and abstraction to immediacy and engagement. As writers of personal sounding essays, teachers could speak with authority about the inevitable disparity between the private person behind the work and ways to translate salient elements of self-characterization to the public document. *They could have students try to consciously control features such as motive, voice, degree and nature of investment in the subject, with an awareness that what beats on the page is the vitality of the writer's vision, not the bleeding heart of the writer behind the work.* (2004, 107; emphasis added)
Well said, Professor Bloom! There could be no better final sentence with which to end a discussion of craft.

THE RHETORICAL GENRE

> *Genre, as many students of the subject have observed, functions much like a code of behavior established between the author and his reader.*
> —Heather Dubrow, *Genre*

> *Genre both organizes and generates the conditions of social and rhetorical production*
> —Anis Bawarshi, *Genre and the Invention of the Writer*

I would have to claim creative nonfiction as the most rhetorical of the nonpublic (literary) genres. The adjective "creative" signals to readers that they may expect "story-like" features such as the following:

- Dramatic scene

- Full recording of dialogue

- Status details

- Narrative points of view

- Composite characterization (Winterowd 1990)

On the other hand, the noun "nonfiction" suggests to them that what they are about to read is, for the most part, true. A plethora of literature attempting to legislate the line between fact and fiction exists: Wolfe (1973), Zavarzadeh (1976), Hollowell (1977), Hellman (1981), Fishkin (1985), Smart (1985), and Foley (1986), to name a few. Hence, the sacredness of the reader-writer contract in nonfiction and hence the multiple levels of rhetoricality it spawns. Here I would like to demonstrate what creative nonfiction can teach our students about basic rhetorical concepts like ethos, pathos, and logos, as well as about genre and style.

While it is not my purpose to delineate the line between fact and fiction, this demarcation *is* a critical generic concern for students to wrestle with. The debate is never-ending, and while there will not be a definitive answer, it is important for each of our writing majors to decide where that line is for him. Included in students' course packets should be essays like Bloom's "Living to Tell the Tale: The Complicated Ethics of Creative Nonfiction" (2003), Williams' "Never Let the Truth Stand in the Way of a Good Story: A Work for Three Voices" (2003), and Mimi Schwartz's "Memoir? Fiction? Where's the Line?" (2007). Each of these pieces raises compelling genre issues. Each forces writers to examine their *ethos*. And each relates in some way to Dubrow's discussion of genre as social code (1982), another area of lively debate in a time when *social code* is increasingly difficult to define, often flouted even when definitions are agreed upon, yet rigidly adhered to by certain cultural subgroups (adolescents, for example, flout some social codes while adhering rigidly to those of their own making). In a generation where one's word is not the sacred bond of our grandparents' era, what does a writer owe to her readers when she claims that her work is "nonfiction"?

Another work important for students to absorb is Chris Anderson's *Style as Argument* (1987). Although Anderson claims in his introduction that his "intention in this book is not to establish an epistemological framework for considering the genre of nonfiction," he later states his purpose:

As my analysis unfolds I want not only to explain the central strategies and forms of contemporary American nonfiction but also to demonstrate how its rhetorical self-consciousness prepares us to regard style itself as argument, a tacit but powerful statement about the value of form as form, style as style. (1987, 5-6)

It seems to me that "rhetorical self-consciousness" *is* a generic marker, and that the use of style as argument is a concept unique to works of creative nonfiction. Anderson draws on Wolfe, Mailer, Didion, and Capote to make his case, authors (except for the oft-anthologized Didion) that many students are unfamiliar with. An assignment I found valuable in helping students to intuit the genre was this: I asked them to read Anderson's work (quite accessible to upper-level students), then to read one of the primary texts he uses to demonstrate his theory. (Most chose *In Cold Blood*—no doubt the availability of two movies about Capote and the making of this work influenced their choice). Then I asked them to compose their own original nonfiction work demonstrating Anderson's theory—using their style as argument. One student wrote a prize-winning essay about her parents' divorce using Didion's technique of authorial silence. Though it could be argued that the real feature here is style, I would argue that the sheer rhetoricality of that style is one of the hallmarks of the genre.

So it is that discussions of style raise still more genre issues for students to explore:

- How is creative nonfiction different from fiction?

- How is it different from journalism/from very good feature articles?

- How is it different from the modern in-depth magazine article in, for example, *Science, Psychology Today,* or *National Geographic?* Are they close cousins?

- What are its subgenres? How does one define a subgenre? Create a new one?

Winterowd, in his 1990 text *The Rhetoric of the "Other" Literature,* views the nonfiction genre through speech act theory, cognition, reading theory, and his own inimitable lens. He, too, is responsible for defining the genre and for examining closely what constitutes ethos, pathos, and logos in literary nonfiction. He does this in ways that will push our majors to try foregrounding these terms when they encounter and create texts other than those overtly marked as persuasive.

In *Literary Nonfiction: Theory, Criticism, and Pedagogy,* Chris Anderson cites the qualities of creative nonfiction, qualities that I believe mark it as a genre, as a way to unite it with composition.

> This is the argument of the essays in *Literary Nonfiction* taken as a whole: that literary nonfiction, by its nature reveals to us the complexity and power and rhetorical possibilities of language—and that the complexity and power and possibility of language ought to be the unifying concern of rhetoric and composition as a discipline. (1989, xxiv).

Finally, Root defines nonfiction thusly:

> Nonfiction n.
>
> 1. The written expression of, reflection upon and/or interpretation of observed, perceived, or recollected experiences.
>
> 2. A genre of literature made up of such writing which includes such sub-genres as the personal essay, the memoir, narrative reportage, and expressive critical writing and whose borders with other reality-based genres and forms (such as journalism, criticism, history, etc.) are fluid and malleable;
>
> 3. The expressive, transactional, and poetic prose texts generated by students in college composition courses.
>
> 4. (obsolete) not fiction (2007, Nonfiction)

Of this definition, I can only say that it would be a wonderful exercise for students to see themselves defined in a genre, (number 3, above) and then play with the parameters a bit, stretching them here and there, arguing about what constitutes a "poetic prose text," and involving themselves with the language that will mark them as rhetoricians when they leave our care.

BEYOND THE PERSONAL: CREATIVE NONFICTION ACROSS THE CURRICULUM

> *When you write, you lay out a line of words. The line of words is a miner's pick, a wood carver's gouge, a surgeon's probe. You wield it, and it digs a path you follow. Soon you find yourself deep in new territory. Is it a dead end, or have you located the real subject? You will know tomorrow, or this time next year.*
>
> — Annie Dillard, *The Writing Life*

Not all of our majors want to write memoir. And creative nonfiction is so much more. It is Diane Ackerman, Lee Ann Schreiber, Rachel Carson, Patricia Tichnor, Annie Dillard, Lewis Thomas, Richard Selzer, Carl Sagan, John McPhee, and Scott Russell Sanders, to name a few. Many of our majors are double majors—wildlife conservationists, marine explorers, resource economists, civil engineers, pre-med students, musicians and artists. They also want to write—about their passion. At the 2007 CCCC conference, Robert Root explained this drive in his own words:

> Nonfiction is a perspective on the world. Its texts are composed by writers animated by the nonfiction motive, the need to know or to comprehend a specific, limited topic. The writer chooses nonfiction as a medium because of a desire or a need or a drive to understand a portion of the world and to record and respond to that understanding. (2007, Nonfiction)

One year after Steven Darian's Freshman Composition course, I was enrolled in Magazine Article Writing. It wasn't creative nonfiction (the term had not been coined yet), but in many ways, Frank McQuilken taught it as though it were. For one thing, he spoke of being *compelled* to know about a topic, of becoming a mini-expert, much the way Root does. He valued the power of language and had a shrewd sense of audience. McQuilken was an elfin Irishman, and our course met at 8:00 a.m. Monday/Wednesday/Friday. If he'd been on a Thursday night toot, we didn't have Friday class. We missed a lot of Friday classes, but he made up for it the other two days. Blue eyes gleaming under unkempt light brown hair, he'd take his students to lunch, ask about our lives, and when we'd willingly pour our misunderstood hearts out, he'd query unsympathetically, "What do you see in that?"

Most of us would look a little wounded at his lack of empathy, a few would give pithy answers, and still others attempted what passed for matter-of-fact hippie-cool-shock in the early '70s. But McQuilken wasn't looking for any of that. "I see an article!" he'd exclaim. "You love your Dad—but when he tells you you're just going to wind up an educated housewife, it rankles! Write about it! Query *New Woman!*" Most of McQuilken's sentences ended in exclamation points. He reminded us over and over again, as Root does above, that when we'd researched an article, we'd be an expert on that topic—and that there were many ways to market that specific, limited topic. He introduced us to Max Gunther's *Writing the Modern Magazine Article* (1968), and that Christmas, hearing nightly how enamored I was with the course, my father presented me with Hayes B. Jacobs's *A Complete Guide to Writing and Selling Nonfiction* (1967). From then on, I wanted to be a full-time writer. Sadly, I've never had the guts to quit my day job. But I never lost that "nonfiction motive," or the excitement of possibly selling my work. (Although *New Woman* expressed interest in my query, they did not end up buying my article on the history of women's education—but I earned what McQuilken called "a premium rejection letter," a handwritten note from the editor explaining why they couldn't buy it.)

So when, in the early '80s, I began to hear about creative nonfiction, I got excited again. Here was a genre somewhere between magazine article writing and creative writing. What might its possibilities be? And could I teach it without treading on journalism's toes? I'd been hauled over to the journalism chair's office once as a new faculty member when I'd made the mistake of telling my advanced comp section that what I was teaching them was really magazine article writing. It was an exciting class, with majors from all disciplines, my most gifted writer a young woman from geosciences. But I didn't have the name for what I wanted to teach, so innocently, I gave the class the only one I knew. And academia, being the territorial place that it is, journalism didn't take kindly to it. I had some explaining to do.

For those who wish to write about their passion in a way that goes beyond being merely accessible—is also artful and aesthetically pleasing—they must first be exposed to the writers I named at the beginning of this section. For this reason, it becomes imperative that courses in the reading of creative nonfiction literature (or literary nonfiction or the literature of fact—whichever title suits the department) are offered to our majors, as well as courses in the writing of the genre. Certainly, writing assignments can be created in the reading course that model the reading, but because our majors are unlikely to have read creative nonfiction of any length prior to their arrival at college, they do need to be steeped in the genre to begin to understand all of the ways in which it may be used. The problem with a first-year writing course that employed fictional literary models was simply that *they were the wrong models*, not that this time-honored, multidisciplinary pedagogical tool of modeling is flawed.

The student reading John McPhee's *The Pine Barrens* for the first time has an epiphany: he has a unique geographical area or culture in his state that he's always wanted to know more about. But he never knew he could turn it into anything more than a research paper.

The young woman reading Diane Ackerman's *A Natural History of the Senses* is delighted and intrigued by the writing style she finds there. She never knew she could use her vast knowledge of anatomy for anything outside of exams or the surgery she is planning to do in the future. She may go on to read Richard Selzer in the same course and find that yes, surgeons do write!

Compositionists have been calling for work that will move students beyond the classroom genres in all disciplines: In the foreword to *The End of Composition Studies,* Doug Hesse writes:

> One prospect for composition, then, is to become writing. By this I mean discarding composition's narrow mission of serving academic discourse, with all of the practices that have thereby accreted. Chief among them is a clutch of forms, formulae, and rump genres specially adapted to and convenient for composition classrooms. Instead of focusing on *students as students* learning to write as students for situations in which students supposedly write, we might better focus on *students as writers* learning to write for extra-disciplinary, extra-academic situations, in the genres practiced there. The recent interest in creative nonfiction—in genres from the memoir, new journalism, the profile, and nature writing to the essay (in the historical tradition of Montaigne and not the school catch-all)—suggests one turn toward writing, away from composition. (2004, [xii])

There is even recognition that young students can begin to learn the pleasures of nonfiction inquiry while they are still in elementary school, exposed to all disciplines at once. Stephanie Harvey has written an important book for elementary and middle school teachers called *Nonfiction Matters: Reading, Writing, and Research in Grades 3–8* (1998) full of practical suggestions for involving students in writing about all kinds of topics with what Root calls above "the nonfiction motive." It's time, then, for departments of writing and rhetoric to include creative nonfiction, both reading and writing, that goes beyond the personal and imbues our majors with the skills to write about any topic creatively . . . and with passion.

REAPING THE REWARDS

> *No man but a blockhead ever wrote, except for money.*
> —Samuel Johnson *The Life of Samuel Johnson*

The students I have had who have won national writing contests, or even our local, but well-funded, "Writing about the Sea" essay contest, have writing lives that are forever changed by this first exposure to recognition for their work. A few of my travel writers have sold their pieces to small, online publications, and some to larger, print publications. The combination of writing, seeing one's name in print, and receiving a paycheck for it is addictive. These are the kids who keep in touch with me for years afterward, whose successes I rejoice in, who while they may have other careers, never stop writing. When I first start talking about venues for publishing their writing in the travel writing class or in Writing in the Expressivity Tradition, some of my students get a bit nervous. After class, they slither up to my desk, head hung low, checking to make sure no other students can hear them, and whisper, "Is publishing a *requirement* for this course?" I look them in the eye and say, "Absolutely not. What's a requirement is that you try."

After so many years of classroom genres (our writing major is only two years old), and exposure to professional writing that will be useful in the workplace, students are a little shocked to find that writing and rhetoric also offers a genre that is marketable, that can be freelanced. Some of them, of course, have taken creative writing in the English department and have been encouraged to market their fiction, poetry, or screenplays, but they think of compositionists as "the practical writers." So it comes as a pleasant surprise to some of our students that a writing major can prepare them for more than the workplace, for technical writing, or even, exciting though it may be, for designing gaming software (though this is certainly a highly lucrative field).

And what about us, the writing instructors? Must we have been published in *The New Yorker*, or in one of the prestigious nonfiction journals like *Creative Nonfiction, River Teeth*, or *Fourth Genre* to begin teaching students in this genre? Can we incorporate creative nonfiction into the first-year writing course and build on it from there for our majors? In the concluding chapter of *Sentimental Attachments*, Janet Eldred makes a wonderful analogy with what Oprah Winfrey has done for reading and what we could do for writing—our own and our students'. Far from vilifying Oprah for "popularizing" literature, Eldred speaks of appropriating her strategies when she writes, "We can lament that our professional literature lacks the written spark we try to teach, or we can, Oprah-like, begin to transform our disciplinary publications" (2005, 101). And then she offers us this reason to write:

> We should write not because we want to compete with our colleagues in creative writing and not because we're bored by our own academic publications.

> We should write essays and compositions because we have a long tradition of teaching them, we have studied them deeply and have admired them, and because of this academic and creative work, we have a distinctive perspective to offer and a beautiful form through which to explore our deep-seated, dappled, disciplinary thoughts. (104)

Such words ease the doubts of those of us who may not have heretofore published in creative nonfiction and wonder if we should have the temerity to encourage our students to do so, wonder if indeed we even know quite what creative nonfiction is and how best to teach it. Eldred's words remind us that we are more familiar with the genre than we think. Her words and sentiments are echoed by Root, from the student side:

> Students who write personal essays in composition class are writing literary nonfiction, particularly if they push their pieces away from the mere recording of personal experience or the mere expression of egocentrism into some territory that connects with readers. "Once More to the Lake," no matter what else it is, is also a "How I Spent My Summer Vacation" essay with significant modifications and considerably greater reach.

If this is the kind of writing that's out there, that people write now, why aren't we encouraging our students not simply to read it but to write it—to be apprentice nonfictionists, preparing to join the conversation? Why can't they be writing in a viable genre instead of training in a "non-genre" and trying to excel in forms they won't use after college? (2003, 254–55)

Earlier, in the genre section, I suggested that one of the areas students should discover for themselves is the difference between creative nonfiction and magazine article writing. I suppose some would argue that depending upon the magazine, there is none. In other words, an article for a how-to magazine (how to use that extra space under your stairs; how to make cheese) would certainly not qualify as creative nonfiction. On the other hand, an article for *National Geographic* might. The best way for our majors to learn the vagaries of the market is to have on hand a copy of *Writer's Market* for the appropriate year and a good trade handbook. I would recommend Lee Gutkind's *The Art of Creative Nonfiction: Writing and Selling the Literature of Reality* (1997). Since Gutkind is the editor of the journal *Creative Nonfiction*, he is indeed an expert in the field. Another recommendation I would make is that we take creative nonfiction seriously enough that we offer an entire course devoted to helping our students publish their work in it, work they have completed in previous courses. In other words, this might be one choice for a capstone course, or simply a 400-level course with prerequisites. The problem with trying to fit the publishing into the same course where one is teaching the art and craft is simply this: there's never enough time to do more than familiarize students with the venues and to help a handful of the most persistent and most talented get their work out there. Our majors deserve better. And since the subject area can and should be broad-based, an instructor needs a whole semester (or quarter) in order to facilitate placing as many first-time authors as possible.

I end this essay with a quote from Gutkind himself. I chose this quote because it illustrates, once again, the rhetorical nature of creative nonfiction—its emphasis on audience, on reader/writer identification, on logos, on pathos. Moreover, it also illustrates once again why the mastery of this genre is a skill we should be offering to our writing majors:

> This is the basic objective of creative nonfiction: Capturing and describing a subject so that the most resistant reader will be interested in learning more about it. The writer establishes a certain humanistic expertise, becoming a reader's filter so that the reader will gain intellectual substance (about baseball, politics, science, or any other subject) while focusing on the drama and intensity of ordinary people living unusual, stressful, and compelling lives. (1997, 2)

What a rhetorical challenge!

REFERENCES

Anderson, Chris. 1989. Literary nonfiction and composition . In *Literary nonfiction: Theory, criticism, and pedagogy*, ed. Chris Anderson. Carbondale: Southern Illinois University Press.

———. 1987. *Style as argument*. Carbondale: Southern Illinois University Press.

Bawarshi, Anis. 2003. *Genre and the invention of the writer*. Logan: Utah State University Press.

Bishop, Wendy. 2003. Suddenly sexy: Creative nonfiction rear-ends composition. *College English* 65:257–75.

Bizzell, Patricia. 1999. Hybrid academic discourses: What, why, how. *Composition Studies* 27:7–22.

Bloom, Lynn Z. 1998. *Composition studies as a creative art*. Logan: Utah State University Press.

———. 2004. The essayist in—and behind—the essay: Vested writers, invested readers. In Couture and Kent 2004.

———. 2003. Living to tell the tale: The complicated ethics of creative nonfiction. *College English* 65:276–89

Boswell, James. (2008). *The Life of Samuel Johnson*. New York: Penguin Classics.

Couture, Barbara, and Thomas Kent. 2004. *The private, the public and the published: Reconciling private lives and public rhetoric*. Logan: Utah State University Press.

Downs, Douglas, and Elizabeth Wardle. 2007. Teaching about writing, righting misconceptions: (Re) envisioning "first year composition" as "introduction to writing studies.'" *College Composition and Communication* 58:552–84.

Dillard. Annie. (1989). *The Writing Life.* New York: Harper and Row.

Dubrow, Heather. 1982. *Genre: The critical idiom.* London: Methuen.

Elbow, Peter. 2000. *Everyone can write: Essays toward a hopeful theory of writing and teaching writing.* New York: Oxford University Press.

Eldred, Janet Carey. 2005. *Sentimental attachments: Essays, creative nonfiction and other experiments in composition.* Portsmouth, NH: Boynton/Cook

Fishkin, Shelly Fisher. 1985. *From fact to fiction: Journalism and imaginative writing in America.* Baltimore, MD: Johns Hopkins University Press.

Foley, Barbara. 1986. *Telling the truth: The theory and practice of documentary fiction.* Ithaca, NY: Cornell University Press.

Gunther, Max. 1968. *Writing the modern magazine article.* Boston, MA: The Writer.

Gutkind, Lee. 1997. *The art of creative nonfiction: Writing and selling the literature of reality.* New York: John Wiley & Sons.

Harvey, Stephanie. 1998. *Nonfiction matters: Reading, writing, and research in grades 3–8.* Portland, ME: Stenhouse.

Hellman, John. 1981. *Fables of fact: The new journalism as new fiction.* Urbana: University of Illinois Press.

Hesse, Douglas. 2004. Foreword. In *The end of composition studies,* ed. David Smit 2004, [ix-xiii]. Carbondale: Southern Illinois University Press.

———. 2003. Who owns creative nonfiction? In *Beyond postprocess and postmodernism: Essays on the spaciousness of rhetoric,* eds. Theresa Enos and Keith Miller. Mahwah, NJ: Lawrence Erlbaum.

Hollowell, John. 1977. *Fact and fiction: The new journalism and the nonfiction novel.* Chapel Hill: University of North Carolina Press.

Jacobs, Hayes B. 1967. *A complete guide to writing and selling non-fiction.* Cincinnati, OH: Writer's Digest.

Kamler, Barbara. 2001. *Relocating the personal: A critical writing pedagogy.* Albany: SUNY Press.

Mayers, Tim. 2005. *(Re)writing craft: Composition, creative writing, and the future of English studies.* Pittsburgh, PA: University of Pittsburgh Press.

National Council of Teachers of English. *Writing Majors at a Glance.* 2009. http://www.ncte.org/library/NCTEFiles/Groups/CCCC/Committees/Writing_Majors_Final.pdf (accessed October 15, 2009).

Paley, Karen. 2001. *The politics and practice of teaching first-person writing.* Carbondale: Southern Illinois University Press.

Root, Robert L., Jr. 2003. Naming nonfiction: a polytych. College English 65:242–55.

Root, Robert L., Jr. 2007. Collage, montage, mosaic, vignette, episode, segment. In Root and Steinberg 2007.

Root, Robert L., Jr. 2007. The Nonfiction Motive. Paper presented at the Conference on College Composition and Communication, March 21-24, in New York, U.S.A.

Root, Robert L. Jr., and Michael Steinberg. 2007. *The fourth genre.* 4th ed. New York: Pearson Longman.

Schwartz, Mimi. 2007. Memoir? Fiction? Where's the line? In Root and Steinberg 2007.

Smart, Robert Augustin. 1985. *The nonfiction novel.* Lanham, MD: University Press of America.

Williams, Bronwyn. 2003. Never let the truth stand in the way of a good story. *College English*:65:290–303.

Winterowd, W. Ross. 1990. *The rhetoric of the "other" literature.* Carbondale: Southern Illinois University Press.

Wolfe, Tom. 1973. The new journalism. In *The new journalism,* eds. Tom Wolfe and E. W. Johnson. New York: Harper & Row.

Zavarzadeh, Mas'ud. 1976. *The mythopoeic reality: The postwar American nonfiction novel.* Urbana: University of Illinois Press.

13

THE WRITING ARTS MAJOR
A Work in Process

Jennifer Courtney
Deb Martin
Diane Penrod

*Revision . . . tests our ability to be honest with ourselves about our
strengths and our weaknesses. Who enjoys that sort of honesty, anyway?*
—Jan Burke (quoted in Jim Fisher's *The Writer's Quote Book:
500 Authors on Creativity, Craft, and the Writing Life*)

As writers and teachers of writing, many of us can empathize with
Burke's characterization of revision: sometimes uncomfortable, almost
always revealing, and, we hope, ultimately useful. In this chapter we, as
faculty in Rowan University's Department of Writing Arts, discuss how
key aspects of revision—self-reflection, openness to feedback and new
information, and flexibility—serve as a productive framework for keeping our ten-year-old program relevant. As stand-alone writing departments and programs have grown significantly in the last few years,
accounts of their histories have flourished: for example, in a recent special issue of *Composition Studies*, in *A Field of Dreams: Independent Writing
Programs and the Future of Composition Studies* (2002), a collection of articles each describing stand-alone writing programs or majors, and in
Coming of Age: The Advanced Writing Curriculum (2000). As these recent
publications suggest, there are competing perspectives about what constitutes the discipline of writing studies and what a major in such a field
might entail. Kurt Spellmeyer points out, for example, that in our tech-
nology- and information-saturated culture, "what we refer to as 'reading'
and 'writing' have never been more varied or more complex" (2002,
278). As knowledge in the academy is increasingly segregated into more
and more specialized niches, Spellmeyer calls for a discipline that helps
students to synthesize information and connect with real-world issues,

rather than to merely analyze isolated texts. Reading and writing, then, become activities bound up with literacy, technology, and ever-changing knowledge. Simultaneously, Thomas Peele reminds us that even as we refine and revise our disciplinary definitions of writing, we also contend with a slow-moving academy that does not always reflect the most current disciplinary thinking (2007, 96).

Against this complex backdrop of disciplinary innovations and institutional constraints, in this article we share the process by which our ten-year-old stand-alone writing department works to establish, reflect upon, and revise our mission and our disciplinary identity. We observe that though institutional and disciplinary changes often feel exceedingly slow, in fact departments are always in flux; a new hire, a retirement, a course that unexpectedly does not fill, or a mandate from administration all signal constant, ongoing shifts. While much of the recent discussion has been on designing and establishing the writing major, we advocate a process that enables departments to continually redefine and revise even well-established programs. To model—or to suggest one version—of this process, we first provide an institutional history and describe a recent departmental values clarification exercise. Next, we move to an overview of our current program—with an eye toward future shifts in direction—and finally, to a portrait of our students, who will be hugely influential in how we reshape our department in the future. Based on our experience with the clarification exercise and our ongoing surveys of student satisfaction, we argue that new writing departments need to establish a clear mission and develop a set of specific values to guide them through inevitable changes. Formalizing key beliefs and goals into a coherent framework will enable departments to welcome and even initiate change within disciplinary and local contexts.

OUR INSTITUTIONAL HISTORY

Rowan University is a public, regional university in southern New Jersey, serving just over 10,000 students at the undergraduate and graduate levels. Admission has grown increasingly competitive, with students entering in 2006 ranked in the top 21 percent of their high school classes (Rowan University 2006). Our department, part of the College of Communication, houses the first-year writing program and the writing arts major. We are one of the largest departments on campus, serving approximately 1,400 students in our first-year writing program and over 300 in our major.

Our development as a department began in 1966, when a group of faculty on our campus, then Glassboro State College, separated from the English Department to teach journalistic and public relations writing in the Department of Communications. Fast-forward to the 1990s, when significant changes occurred on our campus, which in turn affected our department. In 1992, Glassboro State College received a $100 million gift from Henry Rowan, and the college's name was changed to Rowan College of New Jersey. In 1996, Rowan College became Rowan University, consisting of six colleges—Business, Communication, Education, Engineering, Fine & Performing Arts, and Liberal Arts & Sciences—and a graduate school. Under the aegis of the dean and other department chairs within the College of Communication, each program became stand-alone; the College of Communication consisted of five departments: Communication Studies, Journalism, Public Relations/Advertising, Radio/Television/Film, and our department, then called College Writing, which at the time represented what we primarily taught—first-year writing.

After becoming a freestanding department in 1996, we launched several initiatives to ensure our place in the university's changing landscape. Our first act was simple, yet, in retrospect, quite bold: we formed a well-received interdisciplinary course with our College of Engineering. This course, College Composition II—a research and argument course—which fulfills the requirement for engineering students, is a four-credit, project-based course in which writing and engineering design are fully integrated; currently, three Writing Arts faculty teach the course in conjunction with five to six engineering faculty each fall. The success of this initiative has lead to other linked courses across campus, notably with the Art, Biology, Business, Computer Science, and History departments, establishing our presence on campus as a collaborative, interdisciplinary faculty.

In 1998, our department was granted state approval to offer an undergraduate dual major with elementary education as well as a stand-alone specialization in composition and rhetoric, which became our new department name in 1999. Also in 1998, we received state approval to offer an interdisciplinary master's degree in writing, which was co-sponsored with the department of professional writing, which, at the time, consisted of journalism and creative writing. In 2003, our department expanded again. This time, the creative writing faculty joined the composition and rhetoric faculty. The expansion required a suitable name change—to the Department of Writing Arts. In 2005, the dean of the College of Communication proposed another important milestone in our department's growth. Beginning fall 2006, all of the departments in the College of Communication, including Writing Arts, began offering bachelor of arts degrees. On our campus, the Department of Writing Arts is considered to be a "signature program," one of distinction and excellence that is held up for other campus initiatives to follow; in 2004, we were awarded the Conference on College Composition and Communication (CCCC) Writing Program Certificate of Excellence.

OUR DISCIPLINARY FRAMEWORK

As the institutional history suggests, our work as writing instructors has evolved significantly over the years, at times parallel to disciplinary evolutions, at times in response to specific changes at Rowan. And as we mention above, the writing major—in the broad, disciplinary sense—is clearly evolving; at the 2007 CCCC conference, for example, numerous panels described writing majors in various states of proposal with different emphases—from civic rhetoric to professional writing. While many programs show the intellectual heritage of rhetoric/composition that their faculty have (and as our former departmental name illustrates), the field of rhetoric/composition has extended its vision to encompass a wider, richer construction of the discipline of writing. When our department expanded to include creative writing, for example, we went from a department of composition/rhetoric to one of writing arts, a more inclusive, but less well-defined, disciplinary department encompassing the values not only of rhetoric/composition but also of creative writing, as well as our electives courses from journalism and communication studies. Redefining our disciplinarity in a local sense, by considering who we are, what we look like, and what we do, has become paramount. The self-reflective process we describe below, while grounded in our own unique position, is one we urge all departments consider.

Our Department of Writing Arts recently worked to formalize our process. After a 2004 departmental self-study and site visit from consultant-evaluators from the Council of Writing Program Administrators, an ad hoc committee, called the discipline committee, was formed. The name of the committee alludes to its overarching purpose: to explore and articulate how the department functions as an entity grounded in an evolving notion of writing-as-discipline.[1] To this end, the committee

---

1. Along the same lines, Aronson and Hansen, writing about the program at Metropolitan State University, write that, "As a department that offers majors and advanced study in writing in addition to composition, we believe we are better positioned to meet disciplin-

worked for nearly two years to articulate key programmatic values. While necessarily locally grounded, this type of self-definition is a powerful mechanism for establishing departmental identity, particularly for new departments or those in flux, and enables departments to respond to changes and develop new directions within a clear guiding framework.

Because all the heady possibilities for exciting and innovative courses can lead to impulsive or "patchwork" curricula, we believe that writing departments and programs need to explicitly articulate their conceptual frameworks to create cohesive curricula and prioritize departmental initiatives. To that end, we see ourselves as a department-in-process. Articulating what we aspire to do, as well as what we actually do, enables us to consciously chart our own course and continually compare our desired goals to our actual outcomes. Tim Peeples, Paula Rosinski, and Michael Strickland, in a discussion of their own department's evolution, use a similar process, one also grounded in revision: "What we find most powerful about this framework is the way it emphasizes the rhetorical, productive, compositional nature of program development: we write and re-write our programs" (2007, 57–58). As we exhort our students to revise—to seek out and reflect on new information and new shapes for writing—and perhaps model it in our own writing, we should also enact the same principles as we design our curriculum.

The discipline committee's resulting document, a core values statement, structured our extensive review of our major's required and elective courses, in which we identified how the values should or do impact our course offerings (see appendix A for sample advising sheet). The core values statement declares:

Because writing is a powerful mechanism for creating meaning, implicit within this mechanism are power, responsibility, and deliberate choice. Therefore, the Writing Arts Department values the following for students in the Writing Arts Program:

1. Writing Arts students will understand and be able to apply the conventions of a variety of writing genres and rhetorical concepts.

2. Writing Arts students will understand writing and reading within both a theoretical framework and through practical application.

---

ary goals than programs that focus on first-year composition only. We have identified a disciplinary core to our department, driven by questions that are familiar to most writing professionals" (2002, 59).

3. Writing Arts students will demonstrate the ability to critically read complex and sophisticated texts in a variety of subjects.

4. Writing Arts students will demonstrate self-critical awareness of their writing.

5. Writing Arts students will understand the impact evolving technologies have on the creation of written texts.

6. Writing Arts students will both grasp and appreciate the value of the written word and that such power requires ethical responsibilities in its application.

7. Writing Arts students will be familiar with the current standards and dynamic nature of the grammar, mechanics, and usage and be able to apply them appropriately.

8. Writing Arts students will be able to discover, evaluate, and investigate information in the creation of text.

9. Writing Arts students will have knowledge of the post-graduate options available to them in professions and/or graduate studies.

The values statement makes clear that we value writing as a discipline or as a unified area of study. We are not, for example, a department of rhetoric, nor are we a department that identifies itself as service-oriented. The emphases on reading, genre, ethics, information literacy, self-aware-ness, and professional development are meant to encompass all types of writing and to prepare our students not only for literary writing but for writing for public audiences on current topics. We also explicitly value reading. The capacity to engage flexibly with writing that is diverse in purpose, audience, and genre is a distinguishing feature of our writ-ing arts graduates. To provide this range of experience with texts, our department draws upon numerous print and electronic sources for course material. Within the major's required courses, for example, stu-dents read a variety of fiction and nonfiction texts, ranging from Stephen King's *On Writing* to chapters from Charles Cooper and Lee Odell's *Evaluating Writing* to Michael Ondaatje's *The Collected Works of Billy the Kid* to Leonard Shedletsky and Joan Aitken's *Human Communication on the Internet* to Edward Tufte's *Beautiful Evidence*. The department also expects students to become comfortable writing in electronic environments, so students learn how to build and maintain blogs, Web sites, and wikis. Additionally, throughout their coursework, students develop a multipur-pose electronic portfolio, as we discuss below.

While the work of the *faculty* on the discipline committee has lead to a clearer programmatic vision, that vision has also been shaped by our *students*.[2] For example, during the 2004–2005 academic year, we conducted an alumni survey, asking former students about their experiences in the program, the most useful and most disappointing aspects of their experience, and their current employment status. Further, we talk informally with our students during advising sessions and during classes; these discussions have lead to some significant changes. Specifically, we kept hearing that students were not sure what to do with a writing arts degree. Dual majors, particularly those in education, did not identify as writing arts majors; instead, they identified as pre-service teachers. Some students did not see how the courses related to one another; for example, some students focusing on creative writing chafed at having to take courses that examined writing in education contexts or that involved academic reading. We see this as a fairly predictable source of confusion for students; Thomas Peele also notes this problem in his discussion of his program: "Many of the students in the writing emphasis are interested in becoming creative writers; some of them express frustration at having to study genres of writing that seem to require a different mindset" (2007, 95). Additionally, student feedback indicated that we could do a better job of advising. In response to these student concerns, we developed an Introduction to Writing Arts course (see chapter 14) that presents students with an overview of the major and an explicit rationale for the disciplinarity of the program. As part of this course, we implemented a survey of our incoming students that seeks to assess their understanding of our core values during their first semester; when they graduate, students will fill out the same survey. Results will be compared to determine how well students perceive departmental values are integrated into their coursework. To ensure that we continue to respond to our students' experiences and concerns, we began, in fall of 2007, to implement an exit survey that students will complete, anonymously, as part of their final portfolio (discussed below).

---

2. A less visible but extremely important element of the committee's work relates to faculty development. The committee has eight members; when we began our work in the fall of 2004, two members were new hires and one member was in his second year on the faculty. In the fall of 2006, our newest faculty member joined the committee. For junior faculty, the committee's discussions helped to orient them to department culture and values. The committee also gave a voice to these faculty members, allowing them to shape the direction of the department in a context-rich group where questions about department and institutional history could be answered.

CORE COURSES

We have developed a core of five courses and a portfolio seminar. Four of the courses, Introduction to Writing Arts; The Writer's Mind; Writing, Research and Technology; and Evaluating Writing are offered in our department. The fifth course, Communication Theory, is offered by Communication Studies. Many of the related electives are housed in other departments mainly within the College of Communication (see appendix A). The requirement that students take several related courses from departments other than ours is a reality born of our institution's staffing, scheduling, and curricular needs. Historically, when the curriculum was designed, the department had limited resources, and allowing students to take courses outside of the department was necessary. The discipline committee has recently evaluated the range and configuration of approved electives to ensure that students are taking courses pertinent to the core requirements. In reassessing our core requirements, however, we have tried to configure our key courses in a way that provides students with a body of disciplinary courses that create coherence among elective choices. For new departments with limited staffing, this approach to curriculum design helps to assure full content coverage and enough credit hours to satisfy student graduation requirements. The curriculum also encourages discussions between faculty members teaching the courses to provide consistency (but not uniformity) across sections and facilitates an in-progress review of each core course's content to ensure that content and departmental values align.

Introduction to Writing Arts

Our Introduction to Writing Arts course, offered for the first time in fall of 2007, and described in this volume (see chapter 14), aims not only to define for our students what "writing" is but also to introduce students to writing as a discipline, defining it as a social and technological practice that can be understood in theoretical as well as practical terms. It previews the "big three" courses that anchor our major. These classes, The Writer's Mind, Writing, Research and Technology, and Evaluating Writing, follow a trajectory that addresses cognition and invention, praxis, and evaluation.

The Writer's Mind

The Writer's Mind investigates the variety of possible approaches and processes that writers use. Through an examination of readings

generated by professional writers, coupled with material by noted compositionists, students study the relationship of writing to thinking, as well
as how writers learn to write intelligently and creatively. In this course,
students experience writing first and foremost as revision, since we
believe that real writing begins once a writer puts an idea to paper. This
academic focus takes place within the recursive setting of crafting a portfolio of their own works—drafting, conferencing, revising, and reflecting
on the successes and failures of their prior approaches and processes.
The audience for each piece is contained to the class—the writer's
response group, the instructor, and anyone else from whom the writer
seeks feedback. The goal in focusing on writing in this way is threefold:
to make students more competent writers, to make them more aware of
what happens as writers write for an audience, and to demonstrate how
soliciting and managing feedback makes writing more effective.

Writing, Research and Technology

The second course in the sequence, Writing, Research and Technology,
guides students on an exploration of new media and the relationship
between these ubiquitous and ever-changing technologies and the
new rhetorical contexts they create. Like The Writer's Mind, Writing,
Research and Technology represents a blend of theory and praxis, particularly as it pertains to nascent configurations of writing. In part, the
course includes the study of theories, assumptions, and conventions
characterizing electronic communication, and, in part, the course is a
practical confrontation with tools of the technology, including search
engines, Web logs, Web pages, e-mail, listservs, and wikis. Students create, collaborate, and critique writing in electronic environments as well
as analyze multimodal discourse from a diverse range of contexts using
various and available rhetorical tools.

Evaluating Writing

Our current capstone course, Evaluating Writing, centers on how students who have interdisciplinary training in writing arts come to know
the criteria for writing produced in both professional and school-based
contexts. Grounding this course is the recognition that regardless of the
context, all writing is evaluated in some manner. Consequently, for any
writer or writing teacher to succeed, it becomes critical to explore how,
why, and under what conditions written texts are reviewed. Our course
is necessarily a blending of theory and practice and is presented to

students as a place to identify and examine the criteria writers use when measuring or judging a written text. Depending upon the discourse community, criteria change. For these reasons, it is important for students in this class to think of themselves as writers first.

Portfolio Seminar

In the Portfolio Seminar, each student completes an electronic portfolio consisting of pieces from each of the core courses, as well as two pieces of their choosing. The portfolio, which students begin compiling during the introductory course, includes a reflective essay in which students specifically address how their work reflects (or does not reflect) the department's core values. The seminar functions not as a traditional classroom course but more as extended advising or as independent study. The student's faculty adviser, with whom they will have met throughout their coursework, reads each portfolio.

We see this course as functioning in valuable ways: as we noted earlier, some students requested more advisement. Though all students are assigned a faculty adviser, few students regularly meet with them, and the course ensures regular contact. Further, the course gives students a tangible record of their work as writing arts majors—they can then use that body of work as they apply for jobs or graduate school. In composing the reflective letter specifically in response to the department's values, students make the connections between their courses and their learning. As a component of the portfolio seminar, students complete an anonymous survey about their perceptions of the major. They include a receipt in their portfolio as evidence of having completed the survey. We use the survey results for programmatic assessment, thus continuing the self-reflection process.

Creative Writing Concentration

In addition to the writing arts core courses, students may pursue a creative writing concentration, in which they select six courses from options including poetry, fiction, plays, television and film scenarios, and children's stories. Students begin the concentration by taking the introductory courses, Creative Writing I and Creative Writing II, which provide a basic knowledge of the techniques involved in crafting poems, short stories, and plays. Students complete four additional courses (see appendix B) working with their advisers to design the rest of the concentration. Recently, after a curricular review, The Writer's Mind was incorporated into the concentration, providing, we believe, more cohesion among the "big three" and the creative writing courses. The concentration is available to all students, not only writing arts majors, and is especially attractive to English and journalism majors.

OUR STUDENTS

The reasons how and why students come to be writing arts majors are as complicated and shifting as the definitions of writing itself. Individual orientations, experiences, and expectations affect how students view writing and the major. Pre-service teachers are most likely to define writing within the context of other literacies including speaking and reading. They view the major as a value added to their education degree. For example, in response to an anonymous 2007 departmental survey question asking, "Why did you decide to become a writing arts major?" one pre-service teacher captures a common view: "I liked the diversity in the program. Also, I thought it would be a nice complement to my education degree." Stand-alone majors, however, are more varied in that they more often see writing as an art, emphasizing its intrinsic rather than pragmatic value. They are varied in their reasons for being a major as well as in their future plans.

The following are composite profiles of students intended to demonstrate the range of values and perspectives students bring to the major. The portrayed students are fictitious in that they do not represent individuals but rather the range of students we have as Writing Arts majors. In understanding our students' orientations and motivations, we are more effective in shaping the program. In sharing these profiles with a wider audience of professionals, we hope to demonstrate the problems and potential such a wide mix of competing interests brings to the program. Of course, there are students who at the end of their degrees do not see themselves as writers, but who value their undergraduate degrees and who have become, ideally, better readers, more adept communicators, and savvier information users.

Kerry

Kerry declared the writing arts major as a freshman. He had identified himself as a writer while still in high school. His initial concern in college was discovering where his talents and training in writing could lead. The courses he liked best were in creative writing, and Kerry took every creative writing course we had to offer. He started thinking of ways he could support his love for creative writing and still make a living. He took a technical writing course and found he liked collaborating on projects, solving problems, and finding creative ways to present information using both text and visual elements. His creative writing background fostered an understanding for the value of words and increased his flexibility as a thinker. A concentration of courses in the biological sciences and two internships defined him as a burgeoning technical science writer.

Joe

Like Kerry, Joe entered the program as a freshman, identifying himself as a writer seeking entrée into a yet unidentified professional position. Joe was determined not to prepare himself for a job that required little creative or personal investment. For him, that meant public relations, medical writing, and technical writing were beyond consideration. Joe focused early on careers in writing for radio, film, and television. "I can write, and I can write about RTF" was his mantra. Through his radio, television, and film studies, Joe developed a technical as well as a critical understanding of the business. He also learned both sides of the camera—production and script writing—and gained the expertise that enabled him to write with insight about the profession. During his studies, Joe completed several internships. Upon graduation, a contact Joe made during a semester-long internship in New York resulted in a job offer.

Asheika

Asheika is an elementary education student with a dual major in writing arts. Originally, she chose English as her dual major, but after taking the first-year composition sequence and several education courses, Asheika realized that learning is fundamentally about literacy not primarily about literature. She recognized that teaching elementary students how to be literate beings would require a strong emphasis on writing. Becoming a better writer and building a theoretical grounding for writing practices made sense to her. Another important consideration for Asheika in deciding on writing arts is her uncertainty about teaching. She is not completely convinced teaching is the right fit for her, but she thinks her writing background will afford further opportunities should she desire them in the business world. Besides the practical implications, Asheika loves to write and has found a home in the writing arts program. She'll try teaching for a few years, and we would not be surprised to see her back for an MA in writing, either to further her teaching career or just because she loves to write.

FINAL REFLECTIONS

Like any productive revision process, the process we have used to create new visions and affect change throughout the last decade has been guided by a deep and evolving understanding of the field, our discipline, and our students. This progression has necessitated our developing a perception of who we are as a department, what writing is, and what our students want and need from a major in writing arts. As illustrated in this chapter, this process is essentially ongoing and grounded in reflection, deliberation, and revision. As the landscape that is writing studies changes, all programs have to be willing to change, be ready to debate and define their values, rewrite curriculum guides and course descriptions, propose innovative pedagogy, solicit and respond to student feedback, and in general, actively seek problems and find solutions. The result of this process for our program has been relevance, longevity, and growth. The process we have shared in this chapter may serve others as they move from the stages of developing to sustaining their undergraduate writing major.

REFERENCES

Aronson, Anne, and Craig Hansen. 2002. Writing identity: The independent writing program as a disciplinary center. In O'Neill, Crow, and Burton 2002.

Fisher, Jim, ed. 2006. *The writer's quote book: 500 authors on creativity, craft, and the writing life.* New Brunswick, NJ: Rutgers University Press.

O'Neill, Peggy, Angela Crow, and Larry R. Burton, eds. 2002. *A field of dreams: Independent writing programs and the future of composition studies.* Logan: Utah State University Press.

Peele, Thomas. 2007. What do we mean when we say 'writing'? *Composition Studies* 35:95–96.

Peeples, Timothy, Paula Rosinski, and Michael Strickland. 2007. Chronos and kairos, strategies and tactics: The case of constructing Elon university's professional writing and rhetoric concentration. *Composition Studies* 35:56–76.

Rowan University. 2006. *Rowan university fact sheet, 2006–2007* http://www.rowan.edu/pdf/factsheet20062007.pdf (accessed July 10, 2007).

Spellmeyer, Kurt. 2002. Bigger than a discipline? In O'Neill, Crow, and Burton 2002.

APPENDIX A
Recommended Course Sequences

Year 1, Semester 1	Year 1, Semester 2
College Composition I 4 Gen Eds	College Composition II 4 Gen Eds
Year 2, Semester 1	Year 2, Semester 2
Public Speaking *Introduction to Writing Arts* (offered *only* fall semester) 3 Gen Eds	*Communication Theory* 1 Related Elective 1 Free Elective 2 Gen Eds
Year 3, Semester 1	Year 3, Semester 2
The Writer's Mind 1 Related Elective 1 Free Elective 2 Gen Eds	2 Related Electives 2Free Electives
Year 4, Semester 1	Year 4, Semester 2
Evaluating Writing 1 Related Elective 2 Free Electives 1 Gen Ed	*Portfolio Seminar* 1 Related Elective 3 Free Electives 1 Gen Ed

1. It is important that those courses that are italicized be completed in the suggested order. However, it is possible to take the following courses concurrently:

    *   *Introduction to Writing Arts* and *Communication Theory* OR *The Writer's Mind*
    *   *The Writer's Mind* and *Writing, Research and Technology*
    *   *Writing, Research and Technology* and *Evaluating Writing*
    *   *Evaluating Writing* and *Portfolio Seminar*

2. Be sure to spread your schedule out so that you are not forced to take too many courses that require a lot of writing at the same time.

3. Stand-alone majors are strongly encouraged to complete an internship during their final year.

4. The Writer's Mind; Writing, Research and Technology; and Evaluating Writing are usually offered during summer sessions.

SAMPLE COURSE SEQUENCE FOR ELEMENTARY EDUCATION WITH WRITING ARTS (COMMUNICATIONS) DUAL MAJOR

FIRST SEMESTER		SECOND SEMESTER		FRESHMEN
Teaching: An Introduction to the Profession	3	Characteristics of Knowledge Acquisition	3	
Health and Wellness	3	Economics or Political Science	3	
College Composition I	3	College Composition II	3	
West Civilization or World History	3	Non-Lab Science (1 biological and 1 physical science required)	3	
Contemporary Math	3	Literacies in Today's World	3	
	15		15	30
THIRD SEMESTER		FOURTH SEMESTER		SOPHOMORE
Teaching in Learning Communities I	2	Teaching in Learning Communities II	2	
Human Exceptionality	3	Educational Technology	1	
Introduction to Writing Arts	3	Teaching Literacy	3	
Structures of Math	3	Lab Science (1 biological and 1 physical science required)	4	
Public Speaking	3	Communication Theory	3	
English Literature Elective	3	Child Development	3	
	17		16	33

FIFTH SEMESTER			SIXTH SEMESTER			JUNIOR
Inquiry and Discovery in Elem Class	3		*Math Pedagogy for Elem Teachers*	2		
Practicum Assessment in Elementary Class	1		Practicum in Math and Literacy	1		
Differentiated Instruction in the Inclusive Classroom	2		Differentiated Literacy Instruction	2		
The Writer's Mind	3		Writing, Research andTechnology	3		
Related Elective-Writing Arts	3		Related Elective-Writing Arts	3		
US History to 1865 or Since 1865	3		Related Elective-Writing Arts	3		
Artistic/Creative Experience Elective	3		History of American Education	3		
	18			17	35	
SEVENTH SEMESTER			EIGHTH SEMESTER			SENIOR
Evaluating Writing	3		*Clinical Practice in Elementary Education*	10		
Related Elective-Writing Arts	3		Clinical Practice Seminar in Elementary Education	1		
Related Elective-Writing Arts	3		Teaching Students of Linguistic and Cultural Diversity	1		
Geography of U.S. and Canada	3		*Portfolio Seminar-Writing Arts*	1		
Sociology of Education	3					
	15			13	28	
					126	

Courses may be taken during the summer to lighten the course load during any semester noting 17 semester hours or more. If you choose to do this, courses must be taken at least a summer before the semester in which they are listed and must be approved by both advisors.

APPENDIX B
Creative Writing Concentration

1507.290	*CRCR 07.290*	*Creative Writing I*
1507.291	*CRCR 07.291*	*Creative Writing II*
1507.309	*CRCR 07.309*	*Writing Children's Stories*
1507.391	*CRCR 07.391*	*Writing Fiction*
1507.393		Film Scenario Writing
1507.395	*CRCR 07.395*	*Writing Poetry*
0699.363	WA 0001320	Field Experience in Communication I
0699.364	New number unknown	Field Experience in Communication II
0602.313	JRN 02.313	Magazine Article Writing
1501.401	*CRCR 01.401*	*The Writer's Mind*

14

"WHAT EXACTLY IS THIS MAJOR?"
Creating Disciplinary Identity through an Introductory Course

Sanford Tweedie
Jennifer Courtney
William I. Wolff

BORROWING, IMAGINING, AND CLAIMING

As members of a discipline that has often been accused of borrowing from others, we wish to begin by doing so.

Imagine the following statement: "The writing-studies curriculum is perhaps better defined by what it's not than what it is. It's not tidy. It has no clear boundaries. Unlike, say, economics or chemistry, there is no obvious progression of knowledge. . . . There's a reason 30 years after the discipline developed that people still wonder whether the writing-studies curriculum represents a coherent subject or a smorgasbord. For all the programs and scholarship, writing-studies professors still haven't reached a consensus about what to teach or how to teach it." We ask you to imagine this statement because we substituted "writing studies" for "black studies" in Alison Schneider's "Black Studies 101: Introductory Courses Reflect a Field Still Defining Itself," in which she considers the multiple approaches to the black studies introductory course in universities (2000, [A20]). Part of a *Chronicle of Higher Education* report, "A Revival in Black Studies," Schneider's observations came at a critical time in the history of black studies in higher education—a time when "activism, collaboration, and scholarship for and from diverse black communities" (Sharlet 2000) were beginning to unite within the discipline. Writing studies finds itself at a parallel critical point of self-definition. Recent scholarship both discusses and reflects the diversity of approaches in writing studies (Shamoon et al. 2000; O'Neill, Crow, and Burton 2002; Delli Carpini 2007). However, none focus on the role of introductory courses. In this chapter, we, like Schneider, concentrate on the introductory course because we see it as providing a locus for defining our discipline.

In "Re-Writing the Humanities: The Writing Major's Effect Upon Undergraduate Studies in English Departments," Dominic Delli Carpini sounds much like Schneider when he observes that the "undergraduate writing major has no single shape; it is, rather, an amorphous and still-developing construction that has varied missions, purposes and requirements" (2007, 16). To better understand this variety, Delli Carpini describes a "continuum moving from *praxis* to *gnosis* to delineate approaches to writing majors" (16). For taxonomic purposes, he divides approaches to the writing major into three categories: those that are practical and professionally oriented (praxis), those that favor a liberal arts approach (gnosis), and hybrids. Such diversity is not surprising. The creation and maintenance of a writing major is affected by multiple factors, including university, college, and department missions; expertise and interest of faculty; administrative support; programmatic overlap and curricular processes; funding; student interest, goals, and demographics; and location in relationship to workplace potential.

Certainly, creating and implementing the major should take into consideration local situations and exigencies. This focus on the local as the driving force behind writing majors has dominated the literature in this area. For instance, Part IV of *Coming of Age: The Advanced Writing Curriculum*, "Designing and Protecting the Advanced Writing Program," features five chapters that provide examples of writing concentrations and majors (Shamoon et al. 2000), and *A Field of Dreams: Independent Writing Programs and the Future of Composition Studies* highlights twelve different institutions' writing programs (O'Neill, Crow, and Burton 2002). One of the contributors, Jessica Yood, points out that "most writing on the state of the field [tends] to begin with institutionalized histories" (173). Localized discussions, however, are not enough. The *Field of Dreams* co-editors recognize that these stories must be relevant to others by speaking to both local and global issues, "not only to document various institutional changes related to composition but also to provide information to others who many find themselves in similar circumstances" (2002, 1–2). And while we discuss Rowan University's implementation of an introductory writing course below, we argue that regardless of whether the course's title contains *principles*, *essentials*, *foundations*, or *introductory*, it provides "a portrait in miniature of the intellectual debates and ideological divisions that dominate the field" (Schneider 2000, A20).

THE NEED FOR AN INTRODUCTORY COURSE TO THE MAJOR

According to Janice Lauer,

> a discipline has a special set of phenomenon to study, a characteristic mode
> or modes of inquiry, its own history of development, its theoretical ancestors
> and assumptions, its evolving body of knowledge, and its own epistemic courts
> by which knowledge gains that status. Its surface features include a particular
> departmental home, a characteristic ritual of academic preparation, and its
> own scholarly organizations and journals. Finally, permeating these features is
> a discipline's tone, the result of its evolution and the ways its scholars interact
> with one another and outsiders. We recognize a discipline not by each of these
> features taken singly but rather by their presence as a cluster. (1984, 20)

The introductory course can serve as the focal point for all of these features. When Lauer's article appeared in 1984, the number of undergraduate majors in writing was still small. The rising number of graduate
programs in composition studies, however, was prompting calls to question: "Is this study a genuine discipline? What are its origins, its domain
of investigation, its modes of inquiry and methods of evaluation?" (Lauer,
20). Lauer's inquiry into composition studies' disciplinary status is
instructive here because we are beginning to ask similar questions about
the nature of writing studies (or, as our department is named, Writing
Arts). Lauer attempts to answer the question by adopting what she calls a
"dynamic perspective," highlights the field's multimodality, and observes
that the "distinctive features of composition studies—its problem domain,
its theoretical assumptions and ancestry, its modes of inquiry, its epistemic
processes—have inherent advantages and risks" (25). The advantages and
risks of the discipline are manifested in the difficulty in determining a
clear research arena, which has resulted in the discipline being defined
"on an ad hoc basis by the establishment of model programs" (27).

While composition studies has established markers of disciplinarity
since Lauer's discussion, the more inclusive discipline of writing studies finds itself at the exciting and daunting stage of self-definition and
differentiation, defining itself based on model programs, as can be seen
in *Coming of Age* and *A Field of Dreams*. As more writing programs are
established, each program will identify how writing as a discipline will
be conceived based on local exigencies. Yet establishing an introductory
writing course that introduces students to "the discipline" can provide
what Robert Connors calls "a coherent vision of a center" (2002, 148).
Faculty planning such a course have an opportunity to consider what

the discipline is—in both national and local terms—and coordinate it with the curricula.

Without an introductory course, writing studies curricula fail to take into consideration that: 1) departmental majors—no matter what the subject matter—should have some sense of shared objectives and goals with similarly named majors across universities; and 2) there exists in any discipline—writing studies included—foundational information that students should understand—the "knowledge" and "heritage" of the discipline (Crowley 1998, 3). A look at writing majors, however, reveals not only a lack of foundational focus in introductory courses but a lack of introductory courses at all.[1] The most extensive database of writing majors, "Writing Majors at a Glance" (compiled by the Conference on College Composition and Communication's Committee on the Major in Rhetoric and Composition) lists sixty-four majors in writing, including both those housed within English and those in separate departments.

Curricular approaches fall into two categories: those that require a core of courses (ranging from one to ten or more) and those that allow choice within categories—or a combination of core requirements and choices. Obviously, a curriculum that includes only choices does not require an introductory course. Of those that do have required courses, very few have any sort of introductory course, and of these, many introductory courses are either literature-based—Introduction to English Studies or Writing About Literature—or when they are not, tend to be specialization-, discourse-, or genre-specific, with titles such as General Principles of Multimedia, Introduction to Professional Writing, or Introduction to Creative Writing. None offers an introductory course that envisions non-specialized writing within a disciplinary context, as we forward here.[2]

---

1. This stands in stark contradiction to other majors. For example, students at our university of ten thousand can choose from among forty-two majors, including writing arts. A look at the requirements of each college shows that in almost every case, students are required to take some sort of course that provides an initial foray into the discipline. All students in the College of Business must take four "principles" courses in accounting, finance and marketing. Education students must take Teaching: An Introduction to the Profession. While the colleges of Fine and Performing Arts and Engineering do not require courses that carry the labels of "Introduction to . . . ," "Principles of . . . ," or "Foundations of . . . ," each has a strict and extensive set of required courses that are meant as practical introductions to the field. In engineering, for example, this consists of Engineering Clinic, the first four of which focus on "the practice of engineering." (Rowan 2009, 345). All students in the College of Communication—where our department is situated—take Communication Theory. In the College of Liberal Arts and Sciences, the types of introductory courses are varied but pervasive.

2. In *Coming of Age*, part 2 of the book is titled "Considering Options for Core Courses

Despite the variety of manifestations of majors, disciplinarity of the writing major assumes commonality among these physical iterations. The beast may be amorphous, but we still recognize it. Though each major will have a different focus, Robert Connors, in his afterword to *Coming of Age*, discusses the radicalness of the advanced writing curriculum, arguing that the book "proposes and provides a program for an entirely new conception of undergraduate literacy education, one based on the centrality of writing rather than literature. This conception will be, in fact, the alternative English major for the twenty-first century" (2002, 147). This centrality of writing is found not merely in the consumption but also in the creation of texts: "an interest in the *production* of texts has been the lynchpin of writing studies for many years. The phenomenology of writing experience has been the elusive aim of a whole generation of scholars in writing studies. And such concerns are predicated on the idea that the question 'what happens when we write' is worth investigating" (Royer and Gilles 2002, 34). Yet Sharon Crowley observes that the scholarship of composition and rhetoric "typically focuses on the processes of learning rather than on the acquisition of knowledge, and composition pedagogy focuses on change and development in students rather than on transmission of a heritage" (1998, 3). Kathleen Blake Yancey concurs: "composition in the school context . . . remains chiefly focused on the writer qua writer, sequestered from the means of production" (2004, 309). We argue that the introductory course can serve as a melding of these positions, not only as a means to introduce students to the production of writing they will accomplish in the major but also for them to study the production of writing in its various modes, media, and contexts. Thus, the course we advocate is vital to reconceptualizing writing studies within the major and offers a meaningful way "to re-create and reorganize undergraduate writing offerings so that they are more than a fugitive scattering of separate enthusiasms" (Connors 2002, 149).

---

in Advanced Writing," and the first section of essays within that is called "Preparing Students for Participation in the Discipline of Writing Studies." This subsection includes Andrea Lunsford's "Histories of Writing and Contemporary Authorship" (55–58) and Sandra Jamieson's "Theories of Composing" (59–65). While we have independently arrived at similar subject matter, these authors present their courses as required but not introductory. As Lunsford states, "I advise students in all wings of English study to take this course, for it seems to me to be crucial to understanding our place in the history of textuality" (58). So while we agree on the necessity of students' exposure to this subject matter, we differ in that we believe this information is foundational to the major, not just another part of it, and that students need to be exposed to it early in their studies.

Because writing studies conceives of writing in its broadest terms, inclusive of multiple subdisciplines (rhetoric, composition, technical and scientific writing, business and professional writing, creative writing, and genre studies, to name a few) and because writing studies is concerned with many forms of writing, highly reliant on communication technology, and situated within historical periods, we suggest that departments and programs offering writing majors develop a course that *posits writing as a discipline in and of itself by establishing the sociohistorical, technological, and theoretical concerns common to all writing.* We recognize that this makes for an ambitious curriculum. Yet, because our writing studies major finds itself at a nascent stage in its development, our students, excited about the opportunity to study writing but unsure of how it relates to other, more established, disciplines, benefit from an ambitious introduction to the major that helps them to define what it is, what they can expect of it, and what they can do with it upon graduation.

THE CONTEXT FOR THE INTRODUCTORY WRITING MAJOR COURSE AT ROWAN UNIVERSITY

Background

An early iteration of the Department of Writing Arts at Rowan University broke away from the English department forty years ago. For nearly a decade, we have offered a writing major (see chapter 13). The number of majors has grown more quickly than we could have imagined, beginning with approximately 30 students in 1999, moving up to 88 in 2004, and exploding to over 350 in 2007. Alongside this, several events led us to rethink our requirements for the major: a series of new hires, a Writing Program Administrators site visit, and an extensive values clarification exercise that allowed us to better formulate our understanding of the major. As part of this extensive revision to the content of the major, we found that our students needed a course that provided an introduction to our curriculum and to writing studies. (See Chapter 13 for a complete listing of the values we established for our undergraduate major. And see appendix A at the end of Chapter 13 for the requirements of the major.)

In addition, anecdotal evidence from students reinforced this. Several of our dual majors in education—who constitute well over half of our program—did not list writing arts as one of their majors on resumés. Many early childhood and elementary education students did not realize that their writing arts degree gave them a much more specialized and informed perspective on writing and writing instruction than their future colleagues. Advisors reported students asking, "What exactly is this major anyway?" and "What can I do with it?" And many students were stumped by the question, "What will you tell an employer who asks you what a writing arts major is?" Because these were similar to the issues we, as a department, had been addressing, we felt that we needed to better articulate the issues. The introductory course provided the best setting for this.

Objectives

With these issues in mind, we devised a course to:

1. address common student concerns, including the questions: "What exactly is this major?" and "What can I do with it?"

2. address and give a context for understanding of the values of the discipline

3. provide a framework to writing studies via a course that posits writing as a discipline in and of itself by establishing the sociocultural, technological, and theoretical concerns common to all writing.

To offer a foundation for and complement our existing core courses, we devised Introduction to Writing Arts to:

- Provide an introduction to the goals, objectives and curricular content of the major

- Introduce students to potential careers based on the major

- Expose students to some of the characteristics foundational to all writing, which we have defined as:

- History and materiality of writing

- Issues in writing

- Technologies and the future of writing

Delivery

Randall McClure points out that the "formats for instruction [and] methods of delivery" will differ with each major (2007, 39). Not surprisingly, then, our introductory course is unique to our department in terms of its shape. Our delivery system is distinct yet quite possibly portable to other departments. Because of the large number of majors, we are able to deliver the following curriculum during our fifteen-week semester:

First week

Students begin the course as a large group (60–75), learning about the major and the department's expectations for its majors. At this time we introduce what it means to be a writing studies major in general and a writing arts major at Rowan in particular, and what it means to be a writer in the twenty-first century. In addition, we outline the major and introduce the one-credit, senior-level Portfolio Seminar, a new course that has students collect and reflect on writing they have completed as part of the major. This course provides several advantages: students have the opportunity to look back on the major and reflect on how well they achieved its goals; students create an electronic showcase portfolio for potential employers or graduate schools; the department has an instrument to assess student learning, which we then use to reassess the program; and a survey students fill out about the major gives us another assessment measure of the major's effectiveness.

Middle twelve weeks

Students divide into three modules of 20–25 students. Each four-week module is taught by a different faculty member, who covers one of three content areas: History and Materiality of Writing, Issues in Writing, and Technologies and the Future of Writing. See below for rationales discussions of these modules.

Last two weeks

Large group meets again. This portion of the course is devoted to practical, career-oriented concerns: what types of jobs are available to writing arts majors and what writers actually do in their careers. Speakers are brought in to discuss their experiences so that students can hear and ask questions about the working world of writers.[3]

---

3. We invite several writers each semester, and in recent years, these have included an educator who uses writing extensively in the classroom, a professional writer, a freelancer, an editor, and a creative writer.

HISTORY AND MATERIALITY OF WRITING MODULE

While the field of writing studies remains nascent, writing itself defines, for many, the shift from pre-historical to historical time. This, in a sense, is writing's greatest contribution: it creates a record whereby one person can communicate with another person(s) across time and space. By situating the sociohistorical contexts for writing and the material means for doing so, this module gives students a sense of writing's roles and possibilities through time and thus a better appreciation for where writing comes from and what sort of assumptions and perspectives today's writers operate under and within. By defamiliarizing the familiar, this module shows students that the way they write now is very different from the ways people wrote previously and that the means they use to write influence not just *how* but *what* they write.

In order to understand the way writing functions, students must understand the difference between orality and literacy, concepts that also demarcate the difference between more natural versus learned environments. Because writing is not a natural process, one must be taught to write rather than it being naturally acquired. We examine how this teaching/learning requirement has given those who can read and write power over those who cannot—slaves and women being the two most prominent examples of this—thus keeping these groups from acquiring knowledge, power, and wealth.

Among the ways to defamiliarize the technologies of writing, this module focuses on two. One is to examine our own alphabetic system in relation to others. Comparing ideographic (concept- or idea-based) and phonetic (sound-based) systems of writing shows how each promotes different means of thinking and conceptualizing, thus affecting how we perceive and interact with the world.

The second method defamiliarizes the current writing situation by showing how technologies functioned in the past. We do this through several hands-on activities, including writing on clay and using manual typewriters. Students experience how material writing conditions affect what they write (when working in clay, they produce less than they normally would and often choose to use pictures rather than words) and how they write (they see the difficulties of revising, the increased time requirement, how manually taxing these methods are, how the message can be less easily understood by others). As part of this discussion, we also look at examples of how the introduction of a technology is usually decried for ruining the established, and presumed better, way of doing things.

In addition, we discuss how current technologies have failed to adapt, the primary example being the purposefully inefficient QWERTY keyboard. To contrast this, students sample alternative technologies, specifically the Dvorak keyboard layout, keyless keyboards, and voice-recognition software. Doing so shows how our current technological moment has not reached its potential, portending changes to come. We also consider how not everything about the current moment is new, by examining, for instance, how the ascendancy of the word in print was preceded by a visual rhetoric more similar to our own current emphasis on the visual.

These shifts in technologies find parallels in reading. Just as we write differently today than we once did, we also read differently. Thus, we look at how the move from reading aloud to reading silently reflected society's change from a more communal to a more individualized concept of the person and how this paralleled changing concepts of intellectual property.

For the many Introduction to Writing Arts students who are dual majors in early childhood or elementary education, this module increases understanding of their role in the teaching of writing when they see it extending as far back as writing itself. By examining phenomena whose histories are visible in their current iterations, students see that conventions of writing are often driven by technology. For example, the emphasis on standardized spelling resulted from the development of the printing press, which allowed for dictionaries, those arbiters of standardization, to be the created cheaply and distributed widely. We also look at how the idiosyncrasies of spelling, with its tangled web of linguistic influences, will lead to inordinate amounts of energy being spent teaching students to spell, and how alternate, simplified versions of words could alleviate this problem. And we look at the role of handwriting, especially cursive, and its potential role in the classroom of these future teachers by debating the merits of continuing this practice.

The goal throughout this module is to have students understand they are part of a technological moment not of their making but that they can better understand and write within it through exposure to writing's history and materiality.

ISSUES IN WRITING

Initially, we envisioned this module as an introduction to theories of writings—social, cognitive, genre, and activity—similar to the course Sandra Jamieson describes in "Theories of Composing" (Shamoon et al. 2002); however, finding accessible, interesting readings for students at the sophomore level, in their first disciplinary course, is challenging. While there are excellent texts, such as *Cross-Talk in Comp Theory*, that provide a variety of theoretical articles, incoming students likely lack the context and experience as college-level writers to engage meaningfully with such wide-ranging collections, particularly in the module structure of the course. Many collections are also geared to master's-level students who are learning about the discipline while simultaneously teaching first-year writing. Further, most of the pieces assume that readers are coming from English or literary studies and are at least passingly familiar with the disciplinary differences. We faced the task of choosing how much of the backstory to share with students and how much we felt was reasonable—and meaningful—for them to process and retain. By including a range of perspectives—from writing scholars, published writers, and students—we aim to show students that writing is a discipline with principled (if various and diverging) methods of inquiry and reflection.

Issues in Writing introduces students to prominent ideas and concepts that shape contemporary understandings of writing.[4] The module is divided into four units: the writing process, social construction and the rhetorical situation, genre, and academic integrity. To begin, we discuss the writing process. While many students are familiar with portfolios from a high school or first-year writing course, most have not considered the rationale behind the required revision process. With readings that represent a writing teacher, a creative writer, and a student, students are able to see multiple perspectives on the drafting process, revision, creativity, and intellectual engagement. We discuss our own writing processes, and how motivation, circumstances, and external expectations shape the drafting process; students are then encouraged to experiment with different strategies—incorporating, for example, more discussions with fellow writers, or allotting

---

4. One of the other first courses students in the major take is Communication Theory, described in the catalog as "acquaint[ing] students with current theories as they apply to a variety of communication environments" (Rowan 2009, 322). While this course introduces students to communication theory generally, it does not offer writing-specific treatments of communication.

additional drafting time and reflecting on any changes in the quality of the finished piece.

After discussing the intellectual and creative challenges inherent in writing, we shift gears and focus on writing as an inherently social activity. Since many students are familiar with writer's workshops and peer review sessions, we begin with those practices, considering how readers, reviewers, teachers, and other writers impact the creation and evolution of a text. In defining terms like "intertextuality," "rhetorical situation" and "collaboration," the unit provides students with a shared vocabulary for discussing writing contexts and practices. It also provides a foundation with which students can approach collaborative writing tasks in other courses and with a framework for participating in group writing activities, such as feedback workshops. It also underscores the importance of understanding the writing context when interpreting or evaluating a text's effectiveness.

Since understanding context fully requires an appreciation of genre, we discuss the meaning of, and flexibility of, the term. Many of our students enter the classroom with only a vague sense of genre; for example, they very often confuse novels with any kind of book, fiction or nonfiction. Essays are recognizable, but non-academic genres are relatively unfamiliar. In this module we physically show and encourage students to explore examples of non-academic writing to introduce them to the range of writing they may choose to do for their personal pleasure or as a profession. Ranging from shopping lists, lab reports, and "Dear John letters" to microfiction, book reviews, accident reports, literary analyses, and slash fiction, in-class examples are meant to illustrate and enliven the often abstract discussion of genre. In an effort to improve students' information literacy, critical to our major, certainly, but also fundamental to the ability to act effectively in an information-saturated culture, students learn to distinguish between and identify textual features of academic and non-academic writing.

In the final week of the Issues module, students read about intellectual property and theories of plagiarism, including Rebecca Moore Howard's notion of "patchwriting," which illustrates for students that textual borrowing is a complex and controversial topic, even for writing experts. Tying together and practically applying many of the module's concepts, students analyze multiple texts side by side, learning how to acknowledge the ideas and language of other writers. Using a problem-solving approach, students identify correct, incorrect, and ethically ambiguous uses of texts. In so doing, we aim to improve students' ability to use research effectively, to refine their understandings of intertexuality, to acknowledge the "traces" that inform their own writing, and to think like writers when they work with other writers' texts.

TECHNOLOGIES AND THE FUTURE OF WRITING

In preparing this module we were confronted with the realization that in order to successfully prepare students for the courses they would be taking in the major we would first have to address students' and others' preconceptions about the relationship among various technologies and writing. And, in doing so, we also needed to address how one defines "technology" and "writing." This realization stemmed from observations and discussions with students in the Writing, Research, and Technology courses and our colleagues in other departments. For example, after a meeting of the College of Communication technology committee a colleague from journalism asked Bill, "Why is someone from writing arts so interested in technology?" This question, addressed without sarcasm and with genuine curiosity, suggested to us there might be an unintentional lack of awareness about the role of technologies in the processes of writing in different media and genres.

Experiences with students suggest that one reason for this disconnect might be found in how "technology" and "writing" have been defined by users. Two comments on student evaluations from Bill's Writing, Research, and Technology course reflect this: "More writing, less computer!!!" and "The 'technology' aspect is nonexistent save for two classes in the beginning of the semester." The former student requests less time with technology; the other suggests that there was little use of technology in the course. And, yet, the varying impressions of technology in the classroom stem, then, not merely from the amount of technology used in the classroom but from students' impressions of what is considered to be a "technology." Furthermore, when the topic of text messaging emerged from discussions on Jay David Bolter's *Writing Space: Computers, Hypertext, and the Remediation of Print*, students were surprised (and somewhat chagrined) at the realization that in the process of text messaging they were, actually, writing and reading—perhaps more than they had been at any time in their life.

Complicating the apparent need for discussions of theoretical issues relating to technology and writing was that one of the primary goals of this module was to provide students with hands-on experience working with technologies and writing spaces they have access to as Rowan students and will use in classes within the major and without. These include: learning how to access personal areas on Rowan servers; building blogs; contributing to wikis; composing podcasts; using an electronic portfolio. The questions then became: how do we balance the need for theoretical discussions of technology and writing with the very real need for hands-on experiences with various technologies—all within a four-week time span?; which theories and technologies will provide students with a level of critical awareness and use to serve as a foundation for the remainder of their careers as writing majors?

To answer these questions, we decided to approach this module in terms of one of the important skills that students will need to learn over the course of the major: storing and organizing vast amounts of information found in multiple online resources. In effect, to tackle the same concerns that Vannevar Bush addressed in his classic 1945 *Atlantic Monthly* piece, "As We May Think." Only recently—with the pervasiveness of social bookmarking software (such as Delicious and Diigo) and the ubiquity of RSS feed readers (such as Google Reader and Netvibes)—have technologies been available for all Internet users to compose their own dynamic storage spaces in multiple interconnected online locations.

Whereas Bush suggested the creation of the Memex, we decided to ask students to design their own online information ecology, which Nardi and O'Day define as "a system of people, practices, values, and technologies in a particular local environment. In information ecologies, the spotlight is not on technology, but on human activities that are served by technology" (1999, 49). Students' personal online information ecologies are comprised of four interrelated, symbiotic spaces: personal accounts on the Rowan server system, an evolving Netvibes ecosystem, an evolving Del.icio.us or Diigo social bookmarking space, and a collaborative professional blog using Wordpress.com. Discussions and hands-on in-class use of each of these technologies will complement readings in four one-week units:

- *Writing Spaces.* Readings ask students to consider how new media technologies are changing the way people write, compose, and think about both; students begin designing their collaborative blogs;

- *Origins.* Readings challenge students to rethink their perceptions of technology and the relationship between technology and literacy; students learn how to connect to and organize their Rowan server space;

- *Ownership and Identities*: Readings ask students to think about how identities are constructed in electronic spaces and how electronic spaces are forcing us to rethink questions of ownership; students will begin constructing their own knowledge ecology using the RSS reader, Netvibes;

- *The Future of Writing*: Readings ask students to become critical users of social bookmarking applications, to consider the implications of tagging, YouTube, and Facebook, as well as to become introduced to visual rhetoric; students will begin to populate their own social bookmarking account on Del.icio.us or Diigo.

Ultimately, we hope this module will help students understand that the idea of "text" and "writing" and what constitutes both is more robust and convoluted than previously thought, that evolving technologies require us to continually reassess text, writing, and the spaces in which they are produced.

CONCLUSION

Alison Schneider says of black studies, "The discipline's strengths (its eclectic, expansive, experimental curricula) and its weaknesses (its eclectic, expansive, experimental curricula) are on full display in the one course intended to provide a unified view of disunity" (2000, A20). So, too, do we see Introduction to Writing Arts as unifying the disunity: of the curriculum; of the major; of the past, present, and future of writing and writing studies.

We have argued for an introductory course that establishes a sense of disciplinarity for our writing arts students and that posits a model reflecting what we view as key values for writing studies more widely. Because the course is delivered in a module-based format, students hear about aspects of the discipline from three different voices—voices that have discussed, developed, and converged, reflecting the overlap among the modules themselves.

Perhaps most obviously the History and Materiality of Writing and the Technologies and the Future of Writing modules complement one another. The transitional stage of writing we now find ourselves in because of contemporary writing technologies and the ongoing shifts they have created show the ephemerality of the current writing moment. This affords us the opportunity to see how quickly this period has developed and how quickly it might change. But the Issues in Writing module plays an equally important role in overlaying these other two modules. The concerns of Issues in Writing—the writing process, social construction and the rhetorical situation, genre, and academic integrity—play out in an environment mediated, remediated, and, perhaps, overwhelmed by technologies.

Ultimately Introduction to Writing Arts finds its justification not in any one of the modules but in the interplay of the three and the additional framework at the beginning and end of the semester. Albertine Gaur argues, "The story of writing is a tale of adventure that spans some twenty thousand years and touches all aspects of human life" (1992, 7). To share that story with our writing majors helps them to see that they too are participants in, affected by, and creators of this adventure that is the writing life.

REFERENCES

Bolter, Jay David. *Writing space: Computers, hypertext, and the remediation of print.* Second Edition. Mahwah: Lawrence Erlbaum Associates, 2001.

Bush, Vannevar. "As We May Think." 176.1 (July 1945) http://www.theatlantic.com/doc/194507/bush (accessed October 13, 2009).

"Writing majors at a glance." Committee on the Major in Rhetoric and Composition. NCTE. 9 January 2009. http://www.ncte.org/library/NCTEFiles/Groups/CCCC/Committees/Writing_Majors_Final.pdf (accessed October 13, 2009).

Connors, Robert. 2002. "Advanced composition" and advanced writing. In Shamoon et al. 2002.

Crowley, Sharon. 1998. *Composition in the university: Historical and polemical essays.* Pittsburgh, PA: University of Pittsburgh Press.

Delli Carpini, Dominic. 2007. Re-writing the humanities: The writing major's effect upon undergraduate studies in English departments. *Composition Studies* 35:15–36.

Gaur, Albertine. 1992. *A history of writing.* New York: Cross River Press.

Jamieson, Sandra. Theories of composing. In Shamoon, Howard, Jamieson, and Schwegler 2002.

Lauer, Janice M. 1984. Composition studies: Dappled disciplines. *Rhetoric Review* 3:20–29.

Lunsford, Andrea. Histories of writing and contemporary authorship. In Shamoon, Howard, Jamieson, and Schwegler 2002

McClure, Randall. 2007. Projecting the shape of the writing major. *Composition Studies* 35:39–40.

Nardi, Bonnie A., and Vicki L. O'Day. 1999. *Information ecologies: Using technology with heart.* Cambridge, MA: MIT Press.

O'Neill, Peggy, Angela Crow, and Larry W. Burton, eds. 2002. *A field of dreams: Independent writing programs and the future of composition studies.* Logan: Utah State University Press.

Rowan University. 2005. *Rowan university undergraduate catalog, 2009–2010.* http://www.rowan.edu/catalogs/pdf/2009_ugrad_catalog.pdf (accessed October 13, 2009).

Royer, Daniel, and Roger Gilles. 2002. The origins of the department of a department of academic, creative and professional writing. In O'Neill, Crow, and Burton 2002.

Schneider, Alison. 2000. Black studies 101: Introductory courses reflect a field still defining itself. *Chronicle of Higher Education* 46:A20. http://chronicle.com/article/Black-
Studies-101-Introduc/27824/ (accessed October 13, 2009).

Shamoon, Linda K., Rebecca Moore Howard, Sandra Jamieson, and Robert A. Schwegler,
eds. 2002. *Coming of age: The advanced writing curriculum.* Portsmouth: Boynton/Cook.

Sharlet, Jeff. 2000. Taking black studies back to the streets. *Chronicle of Higher Education*
46:A18. http://chronicle.com/article/Taking-Black-Studies-Back-to/5956 (accessed
October 13, 2009).

Yancey, Kathleen Blake. 2004. Made not only in words: composition in a new key. *College
Composition and Communication* 56:297–328.

Yood, Jessica. 2002. "Revising the dream: Graduate students, independent writing programs, and the future of English studies." In O'Neill, Crow, and Burton 2002.

15

TOWARD A DESCRIPTION OF UNDERGRADUATE WRITING MAJORS

Lee Campbell
Debra Jacobs

Nearly fifteen years after the institution of a graduate program in rhetoric and composition at Purdue University, Janice Lauer, who helped to create the program and served as its director for over two decades, provided an account of its initiation and its ongoing development and maintenance. Her account, an essay titled "Constructing a Doctoral Program in Rhetoric and Composition," was included in the well-known spring 1994 special issue of *Rhetoric Review*, an issue widely commended for providing detailed information on doctoral programs in rhetoric and composition across the country obtained from an in-depth survey conducted by Stuart Brown, Theresa Enos, and Paul Meyer. Offering an optimistic and insightful forecast of the future of rhetoric and composition as a graduate discipline, Lauer cites the (then) relatively new ability for those interested in graduate program development in rhetoric and composition "to discuss mutual concerns, to share and disseminate information to prospective students and other interested parties, to foster regional exchange among programs, and to lobby for common needs" (396–97). Specifically, Lauer was referring to a recently formed forty-five-member Conference in College Composition and Communication (CCCC) graduate program consortium. Her point, however, was that the creation of forums and venues for sharing ideas and for collaboration among colleagues at other institutions would prove vital to offering "a stronger argument for the importance of academic space for serious scholarship and research on written discourse" (397). To conclude her essay, Lauer states, "As we get clearer profiles of [graduate programs in rhetoric and composition], the complex paralogy of Rhetoric and Composition Studies will speak to its central position in a postmodern academy" (397).

Given that the development of undergraduate writing majors has been made possible largely by the work of those who completed their graduate degrees at many of the graduate programs of rhetoric and composition described in the 1994 special issue of *Rhetoric Review*—including at Purdue, where the present authors completed their degrees—the existence of this present volume of essays further attests to the extent to which rhetoric and composition studies has become successfully ensconced in graduate programs as a scholarly discipline. Needless to say, its disciplinary status did not depend on the kind of rigid standardization that concerned John Schilb in 1994. While understanding that a certain degree of homogeneity may be necessary and perhaps desirable for disciplinarity, Schilb expresses a worry in his *Rhetoric Review* essay that the field's efforts to discipline itself could lead it to "sacrifice a vital heterogeneity" (404). Schilb states, "I suppose I'll always want composition and rhetoric to be a dynamic, multidimensional enterprise—the sort of field that will always be too restless and expansive to be completely mapped" (404–5). To the degree that undergraduate writing majors reflect the diversity of graduate programs in rhetoric and composition—and we suggest that there is a great degree of similarity in this particular regard—we celebrate along with Schilb that the field has not suffered a forfeiture of its crucial multidimensionality.

Nevertheless, some effort toward mapping undergraduate writing majors may be of service to colleagues embarking on creating a writing major or on reviewing, revising, or maintaining one that has already been created. We offer in this essay one way of "mapping" undergraduate writing majors, of "picturing" them as an abstraction that may offer ideas or a sense of direction to those involved in the difficult work of program design. Thus, we wish to point out the heuristic potential of our map. Although this effort represents the converse of the kind of monumental work done by Brown, Enos, and Meyer in surveying graduate programs and providing detailed descriptions of their findings—and by no means do we suggest that our brief analysis here compares to their in-depth study—we would claim that an abstraction offers one alternative way to work toward providing a description that may facilitate thinking about designing a writing major. Indeed, we anticipate that others will take on the project of cataloging undergraduate writing majors in perhaps much the same way that Brown, Enos, and Meyer produced their work, and we believe that such a project would be of great value. Further, we hasten to add that we characterize our work as an effort *toward* providing *a* description not only because we wish to acknowledge that it is preliminary and therefore incomplete; any abstraction, any "map," is incontrovertibly incomplete.

COURSE TRAJECTORIES: APPROXIMATING DESCRIPTIONS

One task that may be undertaken by faculty members involved in designing an undergraduate writing major is to research how such a major has been configured at similar and dissimilar institutions. Such research can be useful for determining how to position the major with respect to its given "market," and it can be invaluable for determining possible courses to include in the major based on the institution's mission, the mission of the major, faculty strengths, perceived student needs and interests, facilities, and so on. One compilation of writing majors and minors we find to be especially helpful has been prepared by Gina L. Genova of the writing program at the University of California, Santa Barbara.[1] We found from our review of the forty-three programs Genova includes, along with several other programs not included in Genova's document, that there is a tremendous array of individual course titles and individual course descriptions, and often courses with the same or similar titles had very different course descriptions. We do not intend our observation to be a criticism. However, the great variety of courses among majors and even within majors points to the difficulty of making general claims about *the* writing major as a singular entity. Instead, we think it is more appropriate, at least at this moment in time in the development of writing majors, to understand a writing major as offering the possibility for different kinds of *trajectories*, which underscores the experiential elements of time and motion. Although the notion of a trajectory admittedly suggests a more or less "plottable" *forward* motion in time, we find this idea to be consonant with the from-to order of course sequencing apparent in the writing majors we reviewed.

The trajectory of courses of a given writing major—the from-to direction of movement—provides a way to characterize the kinds of majors offered among the majors we reviewed. The main trajectories we have identified occur along two continua, one from general to specific and the other from liberal to technical.

---

1. The compilation is based on a Web site maintained by Sandra Jamieson, who acknowledges Doug Downs for having provided the "basic list," which she has updated and revised.

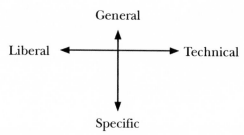

These familiar continua may serve well to describe the two kinds of differences in courses that reviews of writing programs find. In fact, we acknowledge in retrospect that the two continua may seem so readily apparent that we might have been able to predict them from the outset of our inquiry. We did not, however, begin with an *awareness* of any such preconceptions, although we admit that we can never be fully aware of our own predispositions. Thus, we do not present the continua as representing the fundamental differences or similarities among writing courses. We readily acknowledge that readers might disagree with our way of making sense of the wide array of writing courses that are offered or that could potentially be offered in the various programs that have instituted or that may institute a writing major. Nevertheless, we do hope that readers might find some heuristic value from the continua we have identified. As a heuristic, the two continua can, we believe, be useful for aiding in the development of a writing major and for critically examining a writing major.

TOWARD DESCRIBING TYPES OF WRITING COURSES

We have placed along the continua of general-specific and liberal-technical a selection of courses from all kinds of institutions around the United States offered in different departments with various prefixes. Surveys find courses such as Theories of Rhetoric, Argumentation, Research Writing, Travel Writing, Writing about Film, and Newspaper Practicum; as well as Writing as a Profession, Business Writing, Proposal Writing, and Independent Professional Writing Project. One way to consider the relationship of courses such as these *within* each of the two lists is with regard to their relative degrees of generality-specificity, from the broad spectrum of rhetorical theories or the range of careers in writing to specific subject matters of writing, contexts for writing, or particular writing projects. Distinctions along the continuum of general to specific are not always easy to make, but we have tried to provide for six gradations:

1. courses that could *conceivably* require little or no writing but rather study of theories of rhetoric, communication, language, grammar, criticism, and so on

2. broad, introductory courses featuring writing practice that classify writing by aims, modes, or professional domains

3. more advanced, focused courses on component skills or applications of the writing introduced in (2)

4. writing courses focusing on broad genres of writing as determined by elements of the discourse context, such as purpose, audience, subject, and medium

5. courses on the various species of the genres of writing identified in (4)

6. document-specific courses that involve the writing of individual projects or writing in internships

We have attempted to show the gradations from general to specific within each of the columns of our matrix. First-year writing courses have not been included because, in terms of writing programs, they are usually conceived of as part of the preparatory general education core, the first forty or sixty hours as opposed to the second eighty or sixty hours of college courses. However, we note that a recent proposal by Douglas Downs and Elizabeth Wardle (2007) to transform first-year composition into Introduction to Writing Studies would put courses like Composition I and Composition II on the map at the most general level. The distance between first-year composition and writing majors or minors is practically erased by their proposal.

The gradations across the rows suggest the relative degrees to which the courses focus on or presuppose specialized knowledge and skills. These gradations may thus be captured by the ancient distinction between knowledge and skills useful or applicable to any literate person as opposed to studies much narrower in scope, those applied to particular fields with peculiar knowledge and skill sets. Applied to the two lists of courses discussed above, the liberal-technical continuum provides a way to understand the relationship from one list to the next (i.e., across columns). The relationship between Theories of Rhetoric and Writing as a Profession, Research Writing, Proposal Writing, and so on might be understood according to the principle of degree. In fact, representing liberal-technical as points along a continuum presupposes this principle and therefore may be seen as an advance over the ancient classification scheme of "general" versus "special."

We identify four gradations along the continuum of liberality:

1. courses that are grounded in no particular fields or technologies beyond word processing but instead present writing as primarily a literary act of an individual addressing a broad audience interested in the literary aim

2. courses in which non-literary aims of writing (informative and persuasive) dominate, in which writing is presented primarily as a kind of civic discourse, including journalism

3. courses in which writing is definitely situated as a professional rather than a civic activity applicable to broad areas such as "business," the "professions," and "technical" fields and to written genres like reports, proposals, or procedures

4. courses in which writing is studied in specific fields or studied in terms of the demands of specific technology or media, such as the computer and Internet

In terms of identifying writing courses according to their generality and liberality, we see no principled reason to exclude creative nonfiction courses, which foreground the literary aim. For different reasons, Celest Martin argues elsewhere in this volume against the bifurcation of writing courses into creative and non-creative. In fact, creative writing courses in fiction, poetry, and drama could readily be placed in a column to the left of the nonfiction courses; at different times and in different cultures the acquisition of creative writing abilities has certainly been considered part of what it means to be literate and liberally educated. As Martin points out, creative and non-creative writing share many skills, a fact that is evidenced when poets also teach or engage in business or technical writing, as they do in our departments. Fiction, poetry, and drama writing courses are also taken as electives in many writing majors.

With respect to writing technologies, our continua presume a baseline knowledge in undergraduates of only script, print, and electronic word processing; courses in typing or keyboarding, for example, do not appear. (It may seem laughable to mention script here, but we have noted news reports of the decline in the teaching of cursive scripts, meaning that many undergraduates have access to only block scripts.)

The continua, then, provide for different cells for general courses on the computer and its applications and on the field of information technology, desktop or computer-aided publication, and publishing on the Web. Because of the minimal amount of technological expertise we assume, courses on subjects such as these are placed at the technical end of the liberal-technical continuum. Courses could well be placed differently if more technological expertise was assumed. Also, the placement of technology courses at the right of the matrix and creative nonfiction courses at the left does not imply, of course, that the skills of these two areas do not or should not complement one another, often in the same individual. The writer of creative nonfiction, for example, sometimes engages in the technical demands of designing, publishing, managing, and advertising on a Web site.

The courses we have placed along our continua are actual courses. We have invented no titles. The two most general and liberal courses we include were not found to exist in any writing program, but they are offered by departments of philosophy. These courses, Theories of Introspection and Theories of Creativity, have been included due to their potential relevance to any given writing major.

NEGOTIATING SITUATIONAL CONSTRAINTS AND ISSUES OF DESIGN

Almost all the titles of courses we have placed along the continua of general-specific and liberal-technical have been taken from Genova's list of courses or from our own searches on the Internet. We have not referenced which courses belong to what programs because such identification is not relevant here; we are not interested in typing existing programs. But we suggest that programs might be examined using the continua we have provided. Besides providing a way to picture different types of writing programs, this typological matrix suggests three principal issues of design (besides sequencing of courses) in writing majors: balance, emphasis, and generality. Identifying issues of design can serve a heuristic function, eliciting questions to guide faculty deliberations about the particular writing major they wish to develop. As Lauer notes in her narrative about Purdue's graduate program in rhetoric and composition, any program is necessarily "shaped to some extent by existing resources—faculty departmental ideologies, financial resources, and its particular historical moment." But it is equally the case that program development ought to entail principled thinking—that a program should be "shaped by both deliberate design and its specific context" (1994, 392). Without any wish to propose any sort of blueprint for writing majors, we suggest that the issues of balance, emphasis, and generality can help guide faculty in their deliberations about the design of a writing major.

The map suggests that writing programs might be designed to provide balanced coverage of the four broad kinds of writing courses: general and liberal, specific and liberal, general and technical, and specific and technical. But would a program with such a balance have any coherence? Or is such balance exactly what might best prepare undergraduates for multifarious careers in writing?

The map suggests that programs might require or provide the option of emphasis, concentration, along the continuum of liberality. Typically, a particular emphasis would be realized by a student taking a number of courses from the same column—running down a column from general to specific. Broadly speaking, the map shows four emphases: creative nonfiction, rhetoric and journalism, professional writing, and technical writing. Which of these is an institution or department's faculty capable of providing? Which fits an institution or department's mission?

The third issue concerns the degree to which a writing program gets specific. Some writing programs, perhaps by design, are top-heavy: they offer, and often require as part of a core group, a great many courses from the top half of the map. Sometimes a program offers courses only from the top half and then, skipping to the bottom, a capstone or internship experience. How many opportunities should undergraduates have to write in courses the specific kinds of documents—such as reviews, grants, or usability studies—that they might be expected to write in internships or in their careers?

The questions we raise here are meant to offer an illustrative sketch of the way the continua of our "map," and the issues of design they suggest, may assist faculty as they think about designing, developing, or revising a major. As we have indicated, we have included on our map courses from all kinds of institutions and different departments across the country. Mapping any one program's courses on our grid provides a partial picture of the kind of program the courses create. As a heuristic that may aid in the thinking about writing courses and programs, the map can be used to retrospectively rationalize or review writing majors or minors already instituted, inform the design of new writing programs, or suggest options for course development in a given program. Important to note is that we intend to present the map and the courses typed by it in an impartial way: the map does not favor any type of course or any particular configuration of courses. The success of a certain configuration of courses depends on elements we have already mentioned, as well as many more. One type of writing program will not be workable or desirable at every institution. We take this relativity to be axiomatic. Last, we again acknowledge that readers may have different ideas about how to map or otherwise devise an abstraction of writing majors, and we encourage them to revise our mapping or devise new mapping systems. Heuristics are designed to encourage thinking on a problem, not to become ends in themselves.

REFERENCES

Brown, Stuart C., Theresa Enos, and Paul R. Meyer. 1994. Doctoral programs in rhetoric and composition: A catalog of the profession. *Rhetoric Review* 12 (Spring):240–51.

Downs, Douglas, and Elizabeth Wardle. 2007. Teaching about writing, righting misconceptions: (Re)envisioning "First-year composition" as "Introduction to writing studies." *College Composition and Communication* 58:552–84.

Genova, Gina L. 2006.Writing majors at a glance. University of California, Santa Barbara. http://www.writing.ucsb.edu/faculty/mcleod/ documents/Writing_Majors_Final.doc (accessed July 2, 2007).

Jamieson, Sandra. 2006. Writing majors, minors, tracks, and concentrations. Drew University. http://depts.drew.edu/composition/ majors.html (accessed March 12, 2006).

Lauer, Janice M. 1994. Constructing a doctoral program in rhetoric and composition. *Rhetoric Review* 12 (Spring):392–97.

Schilb, John. 1994. Getting disciplined? *Rhetoric Review* 12 (Spring):398–405.

Map of Writing Courses
(Adv=Advanced, W=Writing, PW=Professional Writing)

GENERAL				
Theories of Introspection Theories of Creativity	Theories of Rhetoric Communication Theory Visual Communication Theories of Composing Theories of Literacy Critical Literacy Modern Engl. Grammar Linguistics Stylistics Journalism	W as a Profession Public Relations Mass Media	Information Technology Hardware and Software Microcomputer Applications	
Creative Nonfiction	Exposition Argumentation Persuasion Adv Composition Speechwriting	Business W Professional W Technical W Science W	W for Computer Industry Legal W Engineering W Medical W Public Relations W Advertising W Professional Presentations	
Adv Creative Nonfiction	Revising and Editing W with Style Adv Topics in Argumentation Research W Freelance W	Adv PW Technical Editing Technical Style Research in PW Document Design Graphics/Visuals Special Topics in PW	Adv Legal W Adv Engineering W Adv Medical W Computer-Aided Publication Web Publishing User-Centered Design Hypermedia Theory and Application	
Memoir and Autobiography Biography W Personal Essay	News W Article W Critical W Review W Outdoor/Nature W Travel W Sports W Science Reporting	Manual W Grant W Report W Proposal W Procedures W Newsletter W	W Computer Documentation Marketing Communication Design Web Advertising	
W about Sexuality W about Class	Magazine Article W Feature W Book Reviewing W about Film	Community/ Service W W Grants for Arts and Humanities Feature W for Business	Usability Studies for Technical Communication Graphic Design for Corporate Indentity W for Specialized Audiences Specialized Documents	
Creative Nonfiction Portfolio W Seminar	Newspaper Practicum W Seminar	Electronic Portfolio Independent PW Project PW Capstone Project	Internship in PW	
SPECIFIC				

The leftmost vertical label reads: LIBERAL. The rightmost vertical label reads: TECHNICAL.

AFTERWORD

Susan H. McLeod, University of California, Santa Barbara

This collection of essays marks an important moment in the development of rhetoric and composition as a discipline. It has been clear for awhile that the undergraduate major in writing is growing at a remarkable rate, in terms of both the number of institutions that have such a major and the number of students enrolling in it. When the Conference on College Composition and Communication Committee on the Major in Rhetoric and Composition (which I chaired at the time) did our first survey of the major in 2005–06, we found 45 institutions that had such a major. Just three years later (2009), we found 72 majors and tracks at 68 institutions. Several essays in this book testify to the popularity of our new major: witness the astonishing increase at Rowan University, from 30 students in 1999 to 350 students in 2007. The numbers will no doubt have a ripple effect; as Brooks, Zhao, and Braniger state in their essay, the growth of the undergraduate major means that we will begin to see more prepared students in our graduate programs, which will allow us to begin those programs at a higher level. With the publication of this book, we can now say that the undergraduate major is not just a good idea: it has arrived, and it is big. We have cause to celebrate.

We also have cause for concern. Although most of the essays here are upbeat, several are cautionary tales. Developing a new major always brings up issues of turf and power in academe, and when the major is in a field that some of our colleagues view as low status (associated as it is with first-year students and with an area where faculty from many disciplines fancy themselves expert), the task is made more difficult. As Lowe and Macauley lament in their essay, how can one design a first-class major in a department where composition is considered to be a second-class subject? (It is no wonder that we are seeing an increase in the number of separate writing departments and programs.) Even when one's departmental colleagues are not skeptical of our field as worthy of a major, the "literature-centric" view of English studies (as Langstraat,

Palmquist, and Kiefer call it) can result in a writing major that actually contains more literature than writing. Writing departments outside of English departments are not immune from the issues of turf and power, as the essay by Anderson demonstrates. At the same time that the numbers in our major are increasing, the literature major in English is decreasing (Laurence 2007), a fact that makes some of our literature colleagues feel threatened. These and other constraints documented in these essays can take their toll. Although there are a great many exemplary majors in our field, Andrea Lunsford (2008) has pointed out that a large proportion of them are still unfocused—as Gertrude Stein said of Oakland, California, "There is no there there." As just one indicator, a glance at the 2009 list of majors shows that there is little agreement on what the major should be called: although we generally refer to graduate programs in rhetoric and composition, there are few undergraduate majors with that title.

I see the present book, then, as a splendid stimulus for what I hope will be a discipline-wide discussion about the major in writing studies, not only because it raises important questions but also because it describes model programs. Although I agree with David Beard that the question before us in such a discussion is not what the ideal major in our field should look like, I do think that we can come to consensus about a few issues. A number of institutions across the country have developed learning outcomes for their majors (see, for example, the essays here by Baker and Henning, and by Courtney, Martin, and Penrod). Here is a good starting point for a national conversation about shared outcomes, a conversation that might result in a document not unlike the Council of Writing Program Administrators' Outcomes Statement for First-Year Composition. Starting with outcomes will then help us answer some of the curricular questions raised in this book: what is the place of civic rhetoric, of creative nonfiction, or of new media in the major? Once we have begun to discuss outcomes, we can then discuss what the gateway course to the major should be (Tweedie, Courtney, and Wolff give an excellent example), and what the capstone course or experience should be. These and many other issues are ones we should start discussing among ourselves, on listservs and at national meetings. I look forward to the conversation.

REFERENCES

Committee on the Major in Rhetoric and Composition. 2009. Writing majors at a glance. Conference on College Composition and Communication. http://www.ncte.org/cccc/committees/majorrhetcomp (accessed June 1, 2009).

Laurence, David. 2007. Trends in Bachelor's Degree Awards, 1989-90 to 2005-06. *ADE Bulletin* 143:3-7.

Lunsford, Andrea A. 2008. The future of writing programs—and WPAs. Plenary address at the Conference of the Council of Writing Program Administrators, Denver.

ABOUT THE CONTRIBUTORS

GREG A. GIBERSON is assistant professor of writing and rhetoric at Oakland University in Rochester Michigan. He coauthored a proposal that established an undergraduate degree in writing and rhetoric at OU and is the chief advisor for undergraduate majors in the Department of Writing and Rhetoric. He has presented and published on various aspects of the development and implementation of undergraduate degrees in writing, most recently in *Composition Forum*. He is also coeditor of the collection, *The Knowledge Economy Academic and the Commodification of Higher Education* from Hampton Press.

THOMAS A. MORIARTY is associate professor of English and director of the writing across the curriculum program at Salisbury University. He is the author of *Finding the Words: A Rhetorical History of South Africa's Transition from Apartheid to Democracy* (Praeger/Greenwood, 2003) and is currently writing a book on downtown revitalization in small-town America.

~~~

WALLIS MAY ANDERSEN has been has chaired the Department of Rhetoric, Commu-nication and Journalism at Oakland University, has served as associate dean and associate provost, and chaired the general education and assessment committees. Most recently, she chaired a university ad hoc committee on first-year seminars and developed a funded proposal to integrate first-year seminar principles into the FYC program at Oakland. Her teaching, service, and research interests include technology, general education, and assessment.

LORI B. BAKER is professor of English at Southwest Minnesota State University, where she oversees the writing center and served as department chair for five years. She earned her Ph.D. in rhetoric and composition from Purdue University. She has most recently published in *Praxis* and serves as a peer reviewer for the *Writing Lab Newsletter*.

DAVID BEARD is assistant professor in the department of writing studies at the University of Minnesota–Duluth. He is co-editor (with Richard Enos) of *Advances in the History of Rhetoric* (Parlor Press 2008), former editor of the *International Journal of Listening*, and author/co-author of several articles in the history and historiography of rhetoric.

CARMELLA BRANIGER is associate professor of English at Millikin University. After coordinating the first-year writing program for five years, she currently serves as the writing major director. Her book of poetry *No One May Follow* was released by Pudding House Publications in May 2009. She served as the chair of the pedagogy forum for the 2009–2010 Associated Writers and Writing

Programs' Conference. Her teaching and research interests are in creative and contemplative pedagogies and practices.

RANDY M. BROOKS is dean of the college of arts and sciences and professor of English at Millikin University. His areas of academic research include professional writing curriculum, web publishing, book publishing, and Japanese poetry. From 1990 until 2008, he was the director of the English writing major. He is a proponent of active learning and was a founding member the student book publishing company, Bronze Man Books.

LEE CAMPBELL, Ph.D. in English (rhetoric and linguistics) from Purdue University, teaches courses in writing, linguistics, and rhetoric at Valdosta State University. He has published and presented on argumentation, the history of rhetoric, and applied linguistics. He and Debra Jacobs co-authored "'Sinks, snakes, caves w/water': Floridian Imagery in the Poetry of Jim Morrison" in *Florida Studies* (Florida College English Association 2009).

JENNIFER COURTNEY is associate professor of writing arts at Rowan University, where she teaches courses in the undergraduate major and graduate program and serves as the graduate program adviser. Her research interests include curriculum development, writing program administration, and popular culture. She has published articles and book chapters in venues such as *Composition Forum, Rhetoric Review,* and *Teaching Academic Writing.*

DOMINIC DELLICARPINI, associate professor of English, is the writing program administrator at York College of Pennsylvania, where he directs the first-year writing program and professional writing major. He has served as executive board member of the Council of Writing Program Administrators. His books include *Composing a Life's Work, Conversations* (with Jack Selzer) and a forthcoming interdisciplinary reader, *Issues in the Disciplines.*

REBECCA DE WIND MATTINGLY lectures in the program for writing and rhetoric at the University of Colorado at Boulder. Her primary professional interests lie in rhetorical theory, especially as it touches on the pedagogy of argumentation, the practical applications of speechmaking and the contextualization of grammatical systems for students. She has written about grammar issues in online, writing-center-style tutoring sessions and has coauthored an instructor's manual for Pearson Education.

RODNEY F. DICK is assistant professor of English and director of the writing center at Mount Union College in Alliance, Ohio, where he teaches professional writing. His recent essay, "Does Interface Matter?" (*Business Communication Quarterly* June 2006), argues for a more critically reflective pedagogy when teachers incorporate non-traditional web-based composing in their writing classes. He is interested in a return to the centrality of rhetoric in business and professional writing courses for undergraduate non-writing majors.

PATRICIA HARKIN is professor of English and communication at the University of Illinois at Chicago. She is author of *Acts of Reading: An Introduction to Literary and Cultural Studies* and co-editor of *Configuring History: Teaching the Harlem Renaissance through Virtual Cityscapes* and of *Contending with Words: Composition and Rhetoric in a Postmodern Age*. Her work on history and theory of rhetoric appears in *College English, CCC, Rhetoric Review,* and *JAC*.

TERESA HENNING is assistant professor of English and director of the professional writing and communication major at Southwest Minnesota State University. She teaches first-year and advanced composition, practicum for tutoring writing, copyediting, and business and technical writing. She has published in *Writing Lab Newsletter, English Journal, English Leadership Quarterly, Teaching English at the Two-Year College, Journal of Effective Teaching,* NCTE's lesson plan website, *ReadWriteThink,* and has a chapter in *Writing and the iGeneration: Composition in the Computer-Mediated Classroom*.

DEBRA JACOBS is associate professor at the University of South Florida, Tampa. She teaches in the graduate program in rhetoric and composition and in the undergraduate writing program, and she directs the graduate certificate in teaching composition. She has published and presented on rhetorical theory, composition pedagogy, writing program administration, and cultural studies. She and Lee Campbell co-authored "The Standards Movement and the Commodity of American Standardized English," in the forthcoming *Knowledge Economy*.

KATE KIEFER is professor of English at Colorado State University. She co-founded the journal *Computers and Composition,* of which she is emeritus editor. Her most recent work focuses on the ways in which reading, writing, and thinking can be considered complex adaptive systems. She has recently contributed pieces to *Computers and Composition; Brave New Classrooms: Educational Democracy and the Internet; Effective Learning and Teaching of Writing;* and *Technological Ecologies and Sustainability*.

LISA LANGSTRAAT is associate professor at Colorado State University, where she has directed the graduate program in rhetoric and composition, the CSU WAC program, and the CSU writing center. She is currently researching the rhetoric of emotion in contemporary culture, particularly in light of legal discourse and community literacies. She has published recent articles in *JAC,* as well as in the volumes *Culture Shock* (Hampton, 2006) and *Rhetorical Agendas* (Lawrence Erlbaum, 2005).

JANICE M. LAUER is professor of English emerita at Purdue University. She has received the CCCC's Exemplar Award and RSA's Distinguished Service Award, a Distinguished Professorship at Purdue, and an Honorary Doctorate at St. Edward's University. She has also coordinated the Consortium of Doctoral Programs in Rhetoric and Composition, offered thirteen two-week international rhetoric seminars, and founded/directed the rhetoric/composition doctoral program at Purdue. Her latest publications include *Rhetorical Invention in Rhetoric and Composition* as well as essays in collections.

KELLY LOWE was the writing program director at Mount Union College until 2006, when he took the position of associate professor of English and academic director of the First-Year Experience at the University of Wyoming. He died suddenly in the summer of 2007, just as he was preparing to become the next English department chair at Emporia State University. He is sorely missed by his colleagues at MUC, Wyoming, and across the U.S.

DEB MARTIN is associate professor in the department of writing arts at Rowan University, Glassboro, NJ. She directs the Rowan writing institute, which houses the university writing center as well as other campus and community writing initiatives. Her academic interests focus primarily on issues related to reading and writing literacy and pedagogy. Deb's publications have appeared in a wide range of journals including *Disability Studies Quarterly, Assessing Writing, Middle School Journal,* and *The American Journal of Recreation Therapy.*

BILL MACAULEY is the director of writing at the College of Wooster, where he directs both the program in writing and the writing center. His research has focused on studios, writing centers, working-class studies, assessment, and most recently is focused on creativity, critical thinking, and critical revision.

SUSAN McLEOD is research professor of writing and the former director of the writing program at the University of California, Santa Barbara. Her publications include *Strengthening Programs for Writing across the Curriculum; Writing Across the Curriculum: A Guide to Developing Programs; Writing about the World* (a multi-cultural textbook); *Notes on the Heart: Affective Issues in the Writing Classroom; WAC for the New Millennium; Composing a Community: A History of Writing Program Administration,* and *A Reference Guide to Writing Program Administration,* as well as numerous articles on writing across the curriculum and writing program administration.

JODDY MURRAY is associate professor of rhetoric and new media at Texas Christian University in Fort Worth, Texas. His book, *Non-Discursive Rhetoric: Image and Affect in Multimodal Composition* (SUNY P, 2009), theorizes how image and the affective domain accommodate simultaneity and layers of dynamic meaning in the texts we author in multimedia environments.

MIKE PALMQUIST is professor of English, associate vice-provost for learning and teaching, and university distinguished teaching scholar at Colorado State University, where he directs the university's institute for learning and teaching. His published work includes articles, chapters, and books, including *Transitions: Teaching Writing in Computer-Supported and Traditional Classrooms,* with Kate Keifer, Jake Hartvigsen, and Barb Godlew. With Jill Salahub and a host of WAC colleagues, he coordinates the development of Writing@CSU and the WAC Clearinghouse.

DIANE PENROD is professor of English and director of the university writing program at East Carolina University. She is the author of several books, book chapters, and articles focusing on various topics connected to writing pedagogy. Her current research centers on how trust functions in the first-year writing class. She is currently at work on a book discussing the influence of social media on writing instruction and a history of the cultural influence of the 1970s on composition studies.

SANFORD TWEEDIE coordinates the undergraduate major at Rowan University in Glassboro, New Jersey, where he teaches in the first-year writing and graduate programs. His work has appeared in *College Composition and Communication, English Journal, Journal of College Reading and Learning,* and *Composition Forum,* among others. He has recently completed a book of essays entitled *GDRtifacts: In the Shadows of a Fallen Wall* based on his experiences living in the former East Germany.

WILLIAM I. WOLFF is assistant professor of writing arts at Rowan University. Most recently, his work has appeared in *Technical Communication Quarterly* and the online journal *Currents in Electronic Literacy*. His current research investigates how Web 2.0 applications are transforming literacy in the new media age. He teaches courses in new media, web design, information architecture, and technical writing.

MICHAEL J. ZERBE is associate professor of English at York College of Pennsylvania, where he teaches first-year writing and upper-level courses in prose style, editing, and rhetoric in the professional writing major. He published *Composition and the Rhetoric of Science* (SIUP 2007) and "From the Frontiers of IMRAD: Nontraditional Medical Research in Two Cancer Journals" in *Rhetoric of Healthcare: Essays Toward a New Disciplinary Inquiry* (Hampton Press 2008). He was awarded a Fulbright to teach in Bulgaria in 2009.

DR. PEILING ZHAO teaches applying writing theory, feminist rhetoric, and first-year writing courses as an assistant professor of English at Millikin University. She is also the director of first-year writing at Millikin. Her book *Reconstructing Writer, Student, Teacher, and Gender Identities* appeared in 2008. While having diverse interests in feminist rhetoric, intercultural rhetoric, writing pedagogy, and ESL writing, she is currently doing research on emotion in relation to rhetoric, pedagogy, and intercultural rhetoric.

DATE DUE